THE LAW STUDENTS' GUIDE TO EFFECTIVE LEGAL WRITING

THE LAW STUDENTS' GUIDE TO EFFECTIVE LEGAL WRITING

Edward H. Telfeyan
McGEORGE SCHOOL OF LAW

Carolina Academic Press
Durham, North Carolina

Library of Congress Cataloging-in-Publication Data
Names: Telfeyan, Edward H., author.
Title: The law students' guide to effective legal writing / Edward H. Telfeyan.
Other titles: Guide to effective legal writing
Description: Durham, North Carolina : Carolina Academic Press, 2024. | Includes bibliographical references and index.
Identifiers: LCCN 2024021069 | ISBN 9781531031084 (paperback) | ISBN 9781531031091 (ebook)
Subjects: LCSH: Legal composition. | LCGFT: Textbooks.
Classification: LCC KF250 .T44 2024 | DDC 808.06/634--dc23/eng/20240511
LC record available at https://lccn.loc.gov/2024021069

Carolina Academic Press
700 Kent Street
Durham, North Carolina 27701
(919) 489-7486
www.cap-press.com

Printed in the United States of America

To Richard Neumann and in memory of Ralph Brill:
Legends, Mentors, Friends.

Contents

Preface xiii

Acknowledgments xv

Chapter One **The White-Glove Inspection in Legal Writing** **3**

A. Introduction 3
B. Preparing the Error-Free Document 5
C. The Piles on the Reader's Desk 7
D. The White-Glove Inspection in Boot Camp 9
E. Making Sense of Proofreading 10
F. The Legal Writer's White-Glove Inspection 12
Chapter Summary 14

Chapter Two **Organization of a Legal Document** **17**

A. Introduction 17
B. The Jigsaw Puzzle of the Law—Sorting Out the Rules 19
C. The Hierarchy of Courts 26
D. Finding the Rules in Cases—The Case Brief 31
E. Organizing the Elements of a Legal Document 40
1. Issues 41
2. Facts 43
3. Analysis or Argument 44
Chapter Summary 45

Chapter Three **Effective Use of Paragraphs in a Legal Document** **47**
A. Introduction 47
B. Paragraph Length 49
C. CREAC and C-RAC—The Predictive and Persuasive Paradigms 51
1. CREAC 52
a. The CREAC Rules 52
b. Rule Explanation: The RA Paragraph 54
c. Rule Application: The RA Paragraph 59
d. The Methods of Legal Reasoning 64
e. The CREAC Conclusions 73
2. C-RAC 74
Chapter Summary 79

Chapter Four **Avoiding Structural and Organizational Confusion in a Legal Document** **83**
A. Introduction 83
B. Headings 84
C. Umbrella Paragraphs 95
D. Organizational Devices 97
1. Parentheticals 97
2. Signals 101
3. Transitions 103
E. Organizational Impediments 106
1. Non Sequiturs 106
2. Irrelevancies 108
3. Redundancies 109
Chapter Summary 110

Chapter Five **The Perfectly Constructed Sentence in a Legal Document** **113**
A. Introduction 113
B. The Elements of a Sentence 115
C. The Basic Structure of a Sentence 118
D. Compound and Complex Sentences 120

1. Compound Sentences	121
2. Complex Sentences	122
E. Barriers to Good Sentence Structure	124
1. Passive Constructions	124
2. Mixed Constructions	126
3. Nominalizations	129
4. Misplaced Modifiers	130
5. The Nowhere "There" and the No Thing "It"	132
6. Misuse of "This" and "That"	132
7. Double Negatives	133
8. Double Possessives	134
9. Contractions	134
F. False Alarms—Alleged Barriers that Aren't	135
1. Split Infinitives	135
2. Ending Sentences with Prepositions	135
3. Beginning Sentences with Conjunctions	136
G. Specific Parts of Legal Documents that Require Special Attention to Sentence Construction	136
1. Rule Statements	136
2. Headings	138
3. Conclusions	141
4. Lists	142
Chapter Summary	145
Chapter Six **Correct Grammar and Punctuation in a Legal Document**	**149**
A. Introduction	149
B. The Punctuation Marks	151
1. The Period	151
2. The Comma	152
3. The Semi-Colon	153
4. The Exclamation Point	155
5. The Question Mark	156
6. The Colon	156
7. The Dash	157
8. The Hyphen	158

9. Parentheses 158
10. Brackets 159
11. The Apostrophe 160
12. Quotation Marks 161
13. Ellipses 162
C. Putting Them All Together—Colon, Semi-Colon, or Comma 163
D. Results of Incorrect Usage 165
1. Run-On Sentences 166
2. Comma Splices 167
3. Fragments/Non-Sentences 167
E. Parts of Sentences 167
1. Clauses 168
2. Phrases 169
F. Potential Pitfalls 171
1. Length 171
2. Tails 172
3. Parentheticals and Parentheses 172
4. Quotations 173
5. Citations 173
6. Footnotes 174
G. Complex vs. Complicated 174
Chapter Summary 176

Chapter Seven **Proper Citation to Authority in a Legal Document** **177**
A. Introduction 177
B. The History of Citations 178
C. A Guide to Research 180
D. The Research Outline 182
E. The Citation Triggers 185
F. Signals 186
G. Citation Manuals 186
1. Cases 188
2. Constitutions 190
3. Statutes 190
4. Regulations 191

5. Rules 192
6. Secondary Sources 193
Chapter Summary 194

Chapter Eight **The Ten Steps of the White-Glove Inspection 195**
A. Introduction 195
B. Step One—Logical Consistency and Organizational Flow 196
1. The Format and the Delineation of Substantive Points 196
2. Headings and Umbrellas 197
3. Logical Flow and Leading with Your Best 199
C. Step Two—Paragraph Structure and Paragraph Length 200
D. Step Three—Logical Sentence Flow and Cohesiveness 203
E. Step Four—Sentence Accuracy, Simplicity, and Brevity 206
F. Step Five—Grammar and Punctuation 211
1. The Requisites of a Complete Sentence 211
2. Commas, Comma Splices, and Run-On Sentences 213
3. Colons and Semi-Colons 216
4. Parallelism in Series 219
5. Quotation Marks and Parentheses 220
6. Apostrophes 222
7. Misplaced Modifiers 223
8. Pronouns 224
G. Step Six—Case and Party Names and Citations 226
H. Step Seven—Typos 227
I. Step Eight—Spell and Grammar Check 229
J. Step Nine—The Pleasure Read and One-Voicing 230
K. Step Ten—The Printed Version 230
1. Pagination 231
2. Widows and Orphans 231
3. Skipped or Blank Lines 232
4. Italics and Underlines 232
5. Margins 232
6. Hard Copy for Mailing 233
L. A Final Point—The Value of Cleaning as You Go 233
Chapter Summary 234

Index 237

Preface

This textbook is the result of over two decades of teaching legal writing to students at the University of the Pacific's McGeorge School of Law. It draws heavily from the "white-glove inspection," which I developed a few years after beginning my work at McGeorge in 2000.

The writing and research topics I cover in the book are those that my colleagues and I teach in our Global Lawyering Skills classes at McGeorge. Over the years, however, I have added some of my own concepts to the material, which is largely why I chose to author this textbook. The book is intended to supplement the material presented by my colleagues in our "Legal Writing and Global Lawyering Skills" textbook, now in its third edition (West Publishing), and in any other of the fine basic legal writing textbooks that are currently in use. To the extent that what I offer in this textbook differs from anything presented in those publications, I only intend to provide other ways to consider and understand the basic principles of effective legal writing and analytic reasoning.

The book is structured in line with the ten steps of the white-glove inspection. Thus, after introducing the specific steps of the inspection in Chapter One, I explain the ways to organize legal documents in Chapter Two. In Chapter Three, I discuss the way paragraphs need to be crafted and how they can be understood within the basic paradigms for objective and persuasive legal writing.

In Chapter Four, I explain the purpose and value of headings and umbrella paragraphs in legal documents. In that chapter, I also describe the organizational devices that lawyers use in legal documents and how organizational impediments can appear in legal documents. In Chapter

Five, I explain the importance of well-written sentences in legal documents. In that chapter, I also review the ways in which sentences can be effectively constructed, the barriers to effective construction, and the value of perfectly constructed rule statements and headings.

In Chapter Six, I review all of the basic rules of grammar and punctuation that students need to know to avoid the kinds of errors in legal documents that can badly influence a reader's impression of a document's potential impact. In Chapter Seven, I provide a guide to effective legal research and explain the general citation methods that must be part of a completed legal document.

And, finally, in Chapter Eight, I explain how each of the ten steps of the white-glove inspection should be conducted, what possible errors can be found by conducting each step, and the value of "cleaning as you go" in drafting any legal document.

Throughout the book, I stress the importance of precision, clarity and brevity in all legal documents. My goal is to impress on students the dedication to professionalism that should be evident in all of their written communications as attorneys. That professionalism will then be evidenced by their reader-friendly, error-free legal documents.

Edward H. Telfeyan
McGeorge School of Law
Sacramento, California

Acknowledgments

I have been blessed in the two dozen years that I have taught legal writing at McGeorge to have worked with and learned from the many other colleagues in our Legal Writing department. I am especially indebted to Hether Macfarlane for her guidance and instruction as I moved from the practice of law to the classroom and to Mary-Beth Moylan and Stephanie Thompson for providing the inspiration for this book by envisioning the Global Lawyering Skills textbook that incorporates all of the communicative skills for today's lawyers.

Others at McGeorge who have guided, taught and supported me are Claude Rohwer, John Sprankling, Brian and Dorothy Landsberg, Jay Mootz, Mike Vitiello and Michael Hunter Schwartz. And for much of the nuanced understanding of how lawyers think and reason, I am grateful for the years of friendship I had with Don Prinz, who, beginning from my days as a law student, taught me the value of critical thinking.

At Carolina Academic Press, I have been greatly assisted by Carol McGeehan, who saw the value of what I have tried to provide in this book. Also at CAP, Ryland Bowman and Steve Oliva steered me through the editing process and made valuable suggestions. And for introducing me and my book to Carol, I am eternally indebted to Richard Neumann at Hofstra Law School. Richard helped me to realize that my book could be appreciated by students everywhere and educated me on the business of academic publishing.

In addition to my excellent research assistant, Sharon Witkin, I am indebted to many of my past students who helped me conceptualize this project. In particular, I thank Joshua Bailey (JD, McGeorge 2020) for his invaluable assistance on the drafts of several chapters. And for last edits and final white-gloving, Dan Croxall and Jeri Paik were as diligent as I hope I was in putting it all together. Any remaining white-glove glitches are wholly mine and serve as proof that perfect error-free writing is always worth another inspection.

THE LAW STUDENTS' GUIDE TO EFFECTIVE LEGAL WRITING

Chapter One

The White-Glove Inspection in Legal Writing

A. Introduction
B. Preparing the Error-Free Document
C. The Piles on the Reader's Desk
D. The White-Glove Inspection in Boot Camp
E. Making Sense of Proofreading
F. The Legal Writer's White-Glove Inspection

A. Introduction

Do you remember the first essay you wrote way back in maybe the third or fourth grade? Your teacher probably asked you to write about what you did on your summer vacation, or maybe the assignment was to describe your favorite game, or it could have been to explain your relationship with your family's pet.

Whatever it was, the essay required you to think about a topic and then figure out how to write about it in a way that would be interesting and informative to your reader. The purpose of the assignment, of course, was to force you to think about how you would organize your thoughts and how you would then communicate those thoughts using the rules of writing you had learned to that point in your formal education. And so, you may have put together a little outline and then started writing. Hopefully, you used some basic grammar so that you composed complete sentences. Maybe you thought about breaking up your thoughts into paragraphs. You might even have started with an introductory paragraph and ended with a concluding paragraph.

In the end, you had a two- or three-page paper that was likely your first serious written document. You may have even felt a little proud of it, since you had succeeded in doing something you'd never done before. You probably also received some criticism from your teacher when the essay was returned to you. Maybe there were some red marks on it where you had misspelled some words or where you had an incomplete sentence. Maybe your teacher had written a comment at the end that included the suggestion that you "proofread" your final draft before you hand it in.[1]

Fast-forward a dozen or more years, and you will have a similar experience when your first-year law professor provides you with your first legal-writing assignment. You probably won't get to choose your topic. Your professor will instead give you a fact pattern that includes a legal issue that you must analyze. But the process you use to compose it will be much the same as you may have used in that first essay assignment. You'll develop an outline and think about how you want to organize the points you want to make. Then you'll draft the document into paragraphs that, when taken together, present your analysis of the issue you have been assigned from the fact pattern.

When your professor returns it to you, you will almost certainly see some more of those red marks in the comments your professor provides by way of feedback. Those comments might also suggest that you figure out a way to "proofread" your final draft before you hand it in.

Ah, proofreading: that nasty final step that forces us to read through our draft to catch any typos or other nit-picky errors that will cause the professor to use that dreaded red pen (or its equivalent). Proofreading

---

1. Proofreading is a generic term. It can be defined in a number of ways: To proofread means to "read and correct mistakes" in either a written or printed piece of writing. Merriam-Webster, *available at* http://www.merriam-webster.com/dictionary/proofread. Proofreading is the process by which writers read their written or printed work to mark mistakes in order to correct them. Macmillan Dictionary, *available at* http://www.macmillandictionary.com/us/dictionary/british/proofread. Proofreading is the process by which a writer carefully examines the text of a written work in order to "find and correct typographical errors, mistakes in grammar, style, and spelling." *Available at* http://writing.wisc.edu/Handbook/Proofreading.html.

is the bane of most writers' work. It is just plain bothersome, partly because finding those irritating mistakes is so difficult. Many seasoned lawyers are just as perplexed and bedeviled by the task of proofreading as first-year law students. And all of them, just like you, wish there was a better way.

In fact, there is. It's called the White-Glove Inspection.

B. Preparing the Error-Free Document

Any serious writer will agree that the purpose of a thoroughly proofread final draft is to make it error-free. All good legal writers would also agree that the goal of an error-free written product has added significance because legal documents can produce rules, and rules must always be precisely stated.

Lawyers need their writing to be understood, but even before that result is achieved, they need their writing to be read by the writer's intended reader. Thus, an error-free legal document must not include anything that inaccurately states the writer's intended thought or that would cause the reader to lose, even for a moment, the thought that the writer seeks to convey. In other words, an error-free legal document is one that a reader can read from start to finish without ever having to wonder about any technical aspect of the writing. (We distinguish here the substantive from the technical. Readers may well pause to consider a substantive point in a document, but they shouldn't have to pause to consider a technical glitch or apparent mistake.)

The challenge with language is that it can be unclear. The goal of effective legal writing is to eliminate ambiguity and make documents as clear as possible. However, the best legal writers also know how to use ambiguity to their advantage. Thus, "error-free" does not necessarily mean that the document is free of ambiguity. Many rules, for example, can be deliberately ambiguous, as is true of much of the U.S. Constitution, where the drafters purposefully used ambiguous and vague language.[2] "Error-free" means that the document is substantively accu-

2. Rakove, J. (1997). *Original Meanings: Politics and Ideas in the Making of the Constitution*. New York: Vintage Books. Rakove explores one of the greatest debates

rate and technically free of errors. However, it also means that the document is clear to the reader and ambiguous only where the writer intends it to be.

Consider the following paragraph:

> This case establish that victim who dies in the commission of a robbery. The court used the felony-murder to satisfy the malice requirement. In the case: defendant drives the get-away car and didn't otherwise participating in the crime.

How many times did you have to stop to process what the writer was trying to communicate in that short paragraph? You probably stopped momentarily after the third word (questioning "establish" instead of "establishes" or "established") and again before the fifth word (wondering why the article "a" or "the" was omitted before "victim") and then yet again at the end of what looks like the first sentence (which is actually not a complete sentence). And in the second sentence, you had to stop again to realize that the word "rule" was missing after "felony-murder." The last sentence caused you to pause—first to wonder why the colon was included, and then to ponder the sudden tense change ("drives" and "didn't"), and finally to mentally auto-correct "participating" to "participate."

Now, it's true that most serious readers would auto-correct many of the kinds of errors that are contained in that short paragraph. Those auto-corrections, however, can cause the reader to lose the train of thought the writer intended, especially when the reader is constantly required to make them while working on what is already a tough read just because of its substantive content. And if a reader is forced to endure too many of those errors, the reader may just give up on reading the document, deciding that it is not worth the trouble.

Not having an intended reader understand your legal document can be a disaster, especially if the document represents countless hours of work on your part and has the potential to swing the case in your cli-

---

in constitutional law: What did the framers mean when they wrote it? Of course, the answer to this question is complex and nuanced. Rakove details the events and players surrounding the formulation, authoring, and ratification of the Constitution and the very different meanings it has taken on throughout its very consequential history.

ent's favor. But even if the document is less significant or would potentially have less impact, not having it read by the intended reader is never an acceptable result.

C. The Piles on the Reader's Desk

Legal documents are normally intended to be read by lawyers or other professionals in the legal profession. And if those individuals are as busy as most active legal professionals typically are, then one fact is almost always true: They usually have far more material to read than they have time for. They are constantly bombarded with a vast array of "stuff" that comes to them either in hard copy or electronically, and, to a greater or lesser extent, they must pay some attention to all of it.

As a result of this constant deluge of material on their desks (or on their computer), most intended readers in the legal profession, either deliberately or intuitively, prioritize the necessity of reading each document. In the pre-computer/email days (when some of your professors were starting their legal careers), they would put those documents in one of three piles. Which pile a document ended up in largely determined whether the document would be read and studied fully, skimmed and regarded more casually, or ignored (or even discarded outright).

Today, most written material arrives in an attorney's workspace via email. Thus, the piles of pre-Internet days have been replaced with clicks on the computer (either to "open," "save," or "junk"). But the decision the recipient of the document must make is much the same, so let's stick with the piles metaphor to appreciate the importance of that initial decision by the intended reader.

The first pile will consist of material that, for one reason or another, the intended reader will want—or need—to read immediately (or as soon as possible, and certainly before the end of the workday). This pile is the "read-now" pile. That's the pile that gets read before the intended reader closes up for the day (or that goes home with the reader in the reader's laptop).

The second pile is made up of material that the intended reader immediately recognizes is not worthy of the reader's time (or is just of no interest). Some of this material is immediately identified as junk mail. Some of it is misdirected or is an unnecessary courtesy copy. This material is quickly set aside or deposited in the trash can under the reader's desk (or in the computer "junk" equivalent). These documents have been placed, euphemistically, in the "read-never" pile.

And then there's that third pile: the "read-later" pile. This pile is where everything goes that the intended reader would really like to read (or may even need to read) at some later time. A law review article might go there, or a letter from a colleague, or a lengthy newsletter from the county bar association. Your document might end up there for any number of reasons, two of which are completely within your control.

If your document does end up in that read-later pile, the great likelihood is that it will never be read. The reason is very simple. Documents in the read-later pile ultimately get moved to the read-never pile. Why? Because too much other "stuff" keeps getting added to the read-now pile, as more material (day by day) keeps getting put on top of it (or as it gets buried on the computer). And no one wants an overly heavy briefcase or an overly cluttered computer with read-later material in or on it. So legal professionals invariably move reading material from their read-later piles to their read-never piles. Such is the sad fate of all documents that, for whatever reason, don't make it into the coveted read-now pile.

So what are those two reasons that are completely within your control that gets your document—the one you put your heart and soul into—placed in that dreaded read-later pile? One reason might be that your intended reader started to read it and quickly determined that it was going to be a "hard" read (*i.e.*, one that is replete with errors, like those in the example above). Another reason could be that the intended reader has struggled with prior documents you have written and has come to know that they are more trouble than they are worth (in terms of the time and effort required to get through them). Either way, your reader is probably not going to fully appreciate the product of your hard work.

Of course, if your document is a court document (*e.g.*, a brief or a motion) that you have sent to opposing counsel, that attorney will have to read it. But even those documents can receive similar amounts of attention or be given similar levels of respect as those in the piles metaphor. So even if the document you have sent will be read, it might not be fully absorbed, largely discounted, or completely disdained in the same way that non-essential material can be placed in one of those three "piles" of written material that attorneys have on their computers.

The ultimate impact of the quality of your writing will be the reputation you get within your legal community. Attorneys are certainly judged by how they think and by how knowledgeable they are. But their reputation is largely based on the way they communicate those thoughts and that knowledge. And most of that communication takes place in the form of written documents. So while attorneys no longer have piles that represent the priority they give to correspondence they receive, they do have attitudes or perceptions regarding the writers of that correspondence. And attorneys should never want to be considered as a "read-later" writer. That kind of negative reputation will quickly spread to all of the attorney's work.

D. The White-Glove Inspection in Boot Camp[3]

The white-glove inspection is an old military term, referring to the kind of inspections to which new recruits used to be subjected in their initial training period that was commonly referred to as boot camp. In boot camp, all of the new recruits were housed in a single structure (called the barracks), where they and their living space would be regularly inspected by the commanding officer of the unit (or someone in a position of authority). Traditionally, that inspecting officer would wear a white glove, which the officer would swipe over any surfaces (countertops, dressers, windowsills) in the barracks. If any dust or dirt or grime then appeared on the glove, the entire unit would be penalized (usually with a loss of a weekend pass or maybe extra latrine duty).

---

3. The white-glove inspection is actually used extensively in the military. It is even part of the regular ceremony of the changing-of-the-guard at the Arlington National Cemetery. See http://www.arlingtoncemetery.mil/Explore/Changing-of-the-Guard.

Military veterans will tell you that they have vivid memories of the humiliation they felt and of the punishment that was inflicted for a failed white-glove inspection. They will also tell you that after their unit failed the first such inspection, they all wised up and figured out that the best way to avoid failing a subsequent inspection was to conduct their own white-glove inspection before the inspecting officer arrived for the next official one. The logic is that if you can pass your own white-glove inspection, you are more likely to pass the inspector's.

Most of those vets will also tell you that they recall learning that the best way to make the barracks ready for an unannounced inspection (another nasty trick that was seemingly intended to make boot camp even more miserable) was to employ a "clean-as-you-go" rule. Thus, to the extent possible, they would discipline themselves to keep their space clean at all times so that their barracks were always prepared to pass a white-glove inspection (the commanding officer's or their own).

E. Making Sense of Proofreading

Many kinds of errors can exist in every legal document. Here's a partial list of common errors:

1. The separate points that the document presents may not be well organized. They may not develop and explain the overall thesis or message intended by the writer in the most easily followed logical development or in the most effectively persuasive presentation.
2. Paragraphs may be overly burdensome for the reader, either because they address more than one topic (a substantive error) or because they appear to be overly long (a presentation error).
3. The flow of the document, from sentence to sentence, may appear illogical to the reader, with too many seemingly unconnected jumps from one idea to the next.
4. Individual sentences may not be crafted as carefully as they need to be so as to impart exactly the meaning intended by the writer.

5. Grammatical and punctuation errors may exist.
6. Case names and party names may be misspelled and citations to legal authorities may be inaccurately indicated or improperly noted.
7. Typographical errors may (and almost assuredly will) exist throughout the document.
8. Words may be misspelled throughout the document, some even to the point of indicating an entirely different word (*e.g.*, "not" for "now," "form" for "from," "statue" for "statute") that might change the meaning of the sentence.
9. The tone of the document may be inappropriate for the intended reader (too stilted or too casual, too aggressive or too passive, too opinionated or too neutral).
10. The printed version of the document may not have the final appearance the writer intended or expected.

With so many different kinds of errors and so many ways that errors can appear in a legal document, a standard single pass at proofreading a final draft is almost certainly doomed to miss many of those errors. At best, most of the typos might get corrected, but even some of those will slip past the proofreader's glance in the process of also trying to catch the many other possible mistakes in the document. Or, as is often the case with proofreading, the errors will be missed because the writer is not fully engaged in the task of finding them. (Maybe the writer is "multi-tasking" or just not as focused as necessary. Most writers, after all, consider proofreading to be tedious at best compared to the hard work that is involved in the drafting of the document.)

And yet, the value of all that hard work can be lost if the document is never read or doesn't receive the attention it deserves. (Remember the reader's read-later and read-never piles.) So how can the writer of a legal document make it error-free? One way is to have a colleague do the proofreading, but that option is fraught with risk. Even assuming the colleague will give the task the attention the writer wants it to receive, will that "volunteer" know what errors might exist? A colleague might catch the obvious ones (typos, misspellings, incorrect punctuation), but other errors won't necessarily be evident (incorrect cites or an improper characterization of a case, for example.)

Proofreading really has to be the writer's responsibility. No one else can know what the writer wanted to convey in every instance, and no one else can be expected to have the investment (both in terms of personal energy expended and with respect to the interests of a particular client the writer is representing). But how can the writer ensure that all those possible errors are caught? How can the final draft that the intended reader gets be made absolutely error-free?

We need a system, one that establishes a step-by-step process that catches each of the different types of errors that can appear in a legal document. The white-glove inspection is that system.

F. The Legal Writer's White-Glove Inspection

The white-glove inspection consists of ten steps, each of which is intended to identify a specific type of error that can appear in a legal document. The steps are meant to be conducted in order, so that the final draft that is being inspected is reviewed from the broadest perspective to the most minute. (Another way to think of the order of the steps is that they proceed from the macro to the micro.)

And the steps are intended to be conducted separately so that each constitutes a separate "session" with the draft. In other words, at the conclusion of each step, the writer should take a break and do something else. What that something else is doesn't matter, so long as it doesn't involve working on the document. The point of this requirement is to have the writer approach each step with a clear head and view the document from the exact perspective that the specific step of the inspection process requires. Each step is demanding and difficult, and meaningful breaks between each one will help to avoid the kind of mental fatigue that can result from tedious repetition.

Obviously, perfection can be elusive and is rarely found in the deadline-driven environment of the law. The legal culture is one that includes many absolute deadlines. As a result, lawyers often write and prepare pleadings or briefs with little time left to do any kind of proofreading. But by establishing goals that provide a sense of what needs to be done and when, we can modify the culture and produce clean legal documents that have been carefully reviewed.

A complete white-glove inspection of a complex legal document will take time, perhaps as long as a full workday or even several workdays. But the result, if each step is undertaken conscientiously and meticulously, will be a nearly error-free document that is most definitely not going to end up in a read-later pile (at least not because it is strewn with errors that make reading it more trouble than it is worth).

Here are the ten steps:

1. Review the document's organization. Make sure that the points presented flow logically from one to the next.
2. Consider the length and content of each paragraph. No paragraph should contain more than one basic point. No paragraph should be overly long or so long as to lose its eye-appeal for the reader.
3. Review the flow of the sentences within each paragraph. Beware of non sequiturs or abrupt shifts of perspective or seemingly unrelated points that are made.
4. Read each sentence to confirm that it says exactly what you wanted it to say and that it does so in the minimum number of words necessary.
5. Check every sentence for grammatical accuracy and for correct punctuation.
6. Review all cites and references to cases and parties. Ensure that all cites are correctly positioned and that all case names and party names are correctly spelled.
7. Correct all typos.
8. Check and verify the correct spelling and grammar and usage of all red, green, and blue underlined words and phrases or sentences. Don't assume the computer is wrong. Prove to yourself that you are correct and that the computer is incorrect.

9. Read the entire draft one last time. Consider whether the tone expressed is appropriate. Ensure that whatever "voice" the reader will hear is the same throughout the document. Note any remaining errors that may not have been previously corrected.
10. Carefully inspect a printed copy of the final document to ensure correct pagination, margins, and print quality.

Those ten steps, when taken in order and completed conscientiously and in separate sessions, will produce as close to an error-free document as is humanly possible. But the white-glove inspection can be made easier to complete if the second boot camp lesson is observed: Clean as you go. And using that idea provides the basis for the way a legal document can be drafted in the first place.

Chapter Summary

Any legal document should be free of errors before it is given to its intended reader. An error in a legal document is anything that inaccurately states what the writer intends or that might cause the reader to lose the train of thought intended by the writer. Proofreading is the traditional way to catch such errors, but the kinds of errors that need to be caught are too numerous for a simple last read-through of a document to suffice.

Readers of legal documents always have too much material to read. Documents that contain errors tend to get placed in an intended reader's "read-later" pile, which is where documents are placed that end up never being read. A legal document should never end up unread (or regarded disrespectfully), especially if the reason is that it is too heavily strewn with errors that should have been corrected.

The white-glove inspection provides a systematized process for finding and correcting the many different kinds of errors that can appear in a legal document. Properly utilized, it makes sense of proofreading. And, as the rest of this text will demonstrate, the steps of the inspection can be extended to provide a complete process for the drafting of competently written legal documents. The chapters that follow will provide detailed approaches to the first six steps of the white-glove inspection. The last four steps are covered briefly in the closing chapter, which is a full review of the entire process.

The purpose of this textbook is to provide a process for effective legal writing through a system that has benefited thousands of law students for almost a quarter of a century. That system is called the White-Glove Inspection. A white-gloved legal document is error-free and reader-friendly. It communicates precisely what the writer intends in a way that ensures the reader's understanding.

The goal is error-free, reader-friendly legal documents. This textbook will assist in getting to that goal.

Chapter Two

Organization of a Legal Document

A. Introduction

B. The Jigsaw Puzzle of the Law—Sorting Out the Rules

C. The Hierarchy of Courts

D. Finding the Rules in Cases—The Case Brief

E. Organizing the Elements of a Legal Document

A. Introduction

Step One of the White-Glove Inspection entails reviewing the organization of the legal document. In that review, we must evaluate each of our arguments to ensure that every point flows logically from one to the next. Therefore, the focus of this chapter will be on the construction of legal analyses and arguments and how to most effectively organize them.

Lawyers analyze issues and construct arguments to resolve issues by one basic method: by applying law to facts. And rules are the form of the law that is applied to facts. The facts are those that lead to or result in a controversy or dispute that causes a client to seek the assistance of a lawyer in the first place.[1]

1. Facts can be obtained in a variety of ways, including those provided by the client, those determined by an investigator, and those ascertained from interviews with witnesses. Attorneys usually consider the facts carefully because every fact matters in the legal argument.

That approach—applying law to facts—constitutes the basic organizational paradigm for the drafting of any legal document[2] that is either predictive or persuasive. It is the way attorneys organize their thoughts and the way they communicate those thoughts. It is also the first concept a new law student must grasp and understand to write effectively.

So, how does applying law to facts work? And what does it mean to use that approach in dealing with a legal issue?

The issues in a case can be either legal or factual, but for purposes of legal writing and the work of drafting a legal document, they will be legal. And a legal issue is identified as such because, to resolve it, we must identify a rule (law) that is not innate in science or human experience.

Consider, for example, this hypothetical case: V is dead; either D or T shot him with a gun. Which of the two suspects, D or T, killed V is a factual issue. Analyzing evidence (witness reports, perhaps ballistics analysis) may resolve this issue without any need for a legal principle, doctrine, or concept. In other words, we don't need anything other than basic human experience and, perhaps, some scientific knowledge to resolve that issue.

But whether D or T murdered V (assuming in our hypo that one of them did) is a legal issue. It can only be resolved by applying a legal principle, doctrine, or concept (which we call a rule) to the facts of our hypo.[3] For our hypo, we would need to know a couple of rules. Murder is an act done with malice that takes the life of another. (Note: That sentence constitutes a rule that we would not know just from human experience or scientific knowledge.) And what is malice? Is it some-

---

2. "Legal document," as used in this text, refers to any legal memorandum or legal brief that can take the form of either a predictive (objective) memorandum or a persuasive brief. Law clerks and associate attorneys typically write legal memoranda, while trial and appellate lawyers generally file legal briefs with the court. Other legal documents include what courts and lawyers refer to as "pleadings," which are formal legal documents in a lawsuit that set forth or respond to one party's legal claims or allegations.

3. In the practice of law, many words have a second, more esoteric meaning. For instance, in the legal context, "hypo" and "issue" take on a much more particular meaning than in common speech. A "hypo" (hypothetical) is a set of facts used to facilitate the analysis of the application of a rule to those facts. An "issue" is a legal question created by such a set of facts.

thing we can know from human experience or scientific knowledge? No. We can only know what malice is from a specific rule that defines and identifies that word. Thus, whether V was murdered presents a legal issue.

And if we were drafting a legal document that analyzed whether V had been murdered (the legal issue), we would seek a definition of malice to apply to the facts of our hypo. That legal document would begin by identifying the legal issue and the facts that gave rise to it. It would then identify the law (the rules) that might resolve that legal issue and would show how that law (those rules) would most probably resolve the legal issue. The factual issue, whether D or T killed V, would be resolved without the use of rules; the legal issue (whether either D or T murdered V) could only be resolved through the use of rules.

That simple hypo illustrates the basic organization of all legal documents: We apply law (rules) to facts that arise from a client's case to resolve a legal issue that the facts present.

B. The Jigsaw Puzzle of the Law—Sorting Out the Rules

Imagine that for every conceivable case or controversy for which a client might seek the assistance of an attorney there is a rule that would resolve the legal issue at the heart of the case or controversy. What would the composite of all those rules look like? One conceptualization that lawyers use is a jigsaw puzzle, where every rule is a piece of that puzzle and all the rules put together constitute the picture of how The Law[4] can potentially resolve every case or controversy.

Lawyers thus speak of "pieces of the puzzle" when they are trying to identify particular rules that are relevant to a specific case or controversy (or, put another way, rules that would resolve the legal issue in that case or controversy). So we say that an attorney first needs to

---

4. The Law is a term of art that encompasses the entire body of rules that exists in our jurisprudential system, including statutes, court decisions, and principles of public policy. *See, e.g.*, Alexander Lincoln, *The Relation of Judicial Decisions to the Law*, 21 Harv. L. Rev. 120, 122 (1907).

identify the correct piece of the jigsaw puzzle (the rule) that resolves the client's case or controversy.[5] Then, once the attorney finds that puzzle piece, all the attorney needs to do is draft a legal document that shows how that piece (rule) does indeed resolve the legal issue in the client's case.

So, what are these rules, where do they come from, and how do we find them?

The answer to the first of those questions is that **a rule is any legal principle, doctrine, or concept that can resolve a legal issue**.

The easiest way to understand what we mean by a rule is to consider a typical jury trial (as, for example, where the jury must determine whether a crime has occurred). The jury is fully capable of deciding the facts of the case (believing certain witnesses while disbelieving others, for example). But to determine whether the actual crime has been committed, the jury must be told what the rule is for that crime. Here is an example of such a rule: Malice exists in any action that is committed in reckless disregard of the likely death of an individual. That rule (a definition of malice) would resolve our hypothetical murder case in the previous example since applying it to the specific facts of the case would allow a decision to be reached on whether V was murdered.

Lawyers find rules in sources that they refer to as **authority**. To make sense of that last sentence, consider the way our constitutional system works. The Constitution establishes three branches of government: the judicial, legislative, and executive branches. In elementary school, we learn that only legislatures can pass laws, but lawyers recognize that rules can come from all three branches of government.

The judiciary can create rules from the opinions the courts deliver to resolve specific cases. In deciding a particular case, a court will identify and articulate a rule that resolves the issue presented by the case.

---

5. The issues clients bring to attorneys are not always capable of being resolved through the method envisioned here. Not infrequently, a client will seek a legal resolution that is not available or is impractical. For example, a client may be the victim of a tort by someone who has gone bankrupt. In that instance, even though the attorney can establish duty, breach of the standard of care, causation, and damages, the client still may not get a satisfactory resolution (may not recover anything) because the defendant is insolvent.

The court then publishes those opinions. Lawyers read the opinions and identify the rules the courts have stated (or implied) in those opinions. Thus, court opinions are a source of rules, and when they are published, they become authority. In those court opinions, the courts interpret statutes and give them meaning. Court opinions, for example, provide the test for establishing a claim for discrimination under a government statute that prohibits discrimination "because of race, religion, or national origin."[6] Without a court opinion that determines the test for what type of causation the phrase "because of" requires, the statute has far less meaning and clarity.

The legislative branch can create rules by passing laws in the form of statutes or codes (as some states refer to them). A statute identifies conduct that is either proscribed or excused. It can dictate certain requirements for actions by individuals or groups of individuals. It can establish when certain activities are lawful and when they are not. All of these enactments by a legislative body create rules, and when published, they become authority.

The executive branch can also create rules. It can do so through the issuance of regulations that provide the means to enforce statutes. Many statutes direct the executive branch to promulgate methods of enforcement. These regulations are rules, and when published by the agencies that draft them, they become authority.[7]

So those are three places (cases from courts, statutes from legislatures, and regulations from government agencies) where rules can come from. However, rules can also be identified from sources that are totally unrelated to any of the three branches of government. These

6. Civil Rights Act of 1964, PL 88-352, July 2, 1964, 78 Stat. 241; *U. of Texas S.W. Med. Ctr. v. Nassar*, 570 U.S. 338, 350 (2013) (explaining that the ordinary meaning of "because of" is "by reason of" or "on account of"; thus the "requirement that an employer took adverse action 'because of' [race, religion, or national origin] [means] that [race, religion, or national origin] was the 'reason' that the employer decided to act," or, in other words, that "[race, religion, or national origin] was the 'but-for' cause of the employer's adverse decision").

7. Informal rules and agency memoranda published by administrative agencies can also become legal authority if adopted in agency decisions. Thus, administrative law judges can create rules through their opinions and decisions. For example, an adjudication before the Equal Employment Opportunity Commission can also provide rules through the opinions the administrative law judges issue.

"rules"[8] are not derived from constitutional authority as are those promulgated by a jurisdiction's legislative, judicial, or executive bodies. Instead, they can be asserted (or proposed) by individuals outside of government who comment on the law, who study and write about the law, or who contemplate what the law should be: people such as your very own law professors. Those individuals have not been elected or appointed through our constitutional system, but they still have the ability to formulate (or at least suggest) rules. Law reviews and legal periodicals publish these commentaries, and when they do, the rules contained in them can become authority (albeit they will never be mandatory authority that a court or agency must recognize unless they are adopted by a court).

When lawyers and judges use those commentaries from non-constitutional sources, the lawyers are using them to suggest or state rules (either as asserted by attorneys in legal briefs or as cited by courts in judicial opinions).[9] Persuasive authority is not as compelling as mandatory authority (since any rules from non-constitutional sources are really only "proposed rules"), and distinguishing between the two kinds of authority is often critical in presenting or making a legal argument. At the least, rules from persuasive authority can add weight to an argument or analysis that was initially made with mandatory authority. But in some instances, persuasive authority can be the sole source of a new rule a court might create in attempting to define a provision in a statute or in expanding the understanding of a constitutional right.

For example, one of the most famous law review articles, co-authored by Justice Louis Brandeis, entitled *The Right to Privacy*,[10] has been cited over 3,900 times. Although the article was published in 1890, Justice Brandeis and attorney Samuel D. Warren explored such fundamental principles of the concept of personal privacy that the article is still relevant today in the debate over the proper relationship

8. When referring to authority from a non-constitutional source, a "rule" is really a proposed rule. No court is bound by this kind of rule; such references would only qualify as persuasive authority.

9. See previous footnote clarifying this kind of rule as a proposed rule, which is how all persuasive authority must be viewed.

10. Samuel D. Warren & Louis D. Brandeis, *The Right to Privacy*, 4 Harv. L. Rev. 193 (1890).

between technology and privacy. The Supreme Court notably cited the article in two free speech cases that were delivered years after the article's initial publication.[11] Thus, the ideas in a law review article can influence lawmakers or the court and then become authority when the article is cited. In that sense, the law review article has provided a rule.

And there are other private sources of rules, such as businesses or private individuals. Every time any of them devise a means by which they will interact or conduct their business or personal affairs, they are creating rules. A perfect example would be an employment contract. When a worker and a business agree to the terms of employment, that contract becomes a rule, and when published/memorialized, it becomes authority for any disputes between the signatories. Similarly, when an individual dies, that individual's last will and testament will become a potential rule that can be recognized as authority.[12]

Here is one last source of possible rules: the editorial or op-ed page of your daily newspaper. Yes, once published in any citable document, even the opinions of a single writer can become a "rule" (in the form of a proposed rule) and be cited as persuasive authority.[13] In essence, lawyers can find and use potential rules in any written document that can be cited (by reference to the printed or online publication where it can be found).

As we have implied, the rules that come from the constitutional branches of government have more weight as authority. Lawyers distinguish rules that come from one of the three branches of government from all the other sources of rules by the terms **primary authority** and **secondary authority**. Primary authority consists of all rules that come from any of the three branches of government. So, if it's a statute, a court opinion, or an agency regulation, it's primary authority.

Everything else is secondary authority. All of those law review articles your professors write, the intriguing op-ed column by the former

---

11. *See Bartnicki v. Vopper*, 532 U.S. 514, 534 (2001), and *The Florida Star v. B.J.F.*, 491 U.S. 524, 551 (1989).

12. The "rules" discussed in this paragraph are limited to the disputes between the parties who created them (in contract litigation), or the potential beneficiaries who are affected by them (in estate litigation).

13. At most, the use of editorials and op-eds could only constitute persuasive authority. But these sources may also provide context for the cited proposition. *See* Michael J. Gerhardt, *Non-Judicial Precedent*, 61 VAND. L. REV. 713, 774 (2008).

chairperson of the Federal Reserve Board, or the summaries of law in any of the Restatements, are secondary authority. And, as you have probably already guessed, primary authority is accorded significantly more weight in a legal analysis or argument than secondary authority.

The relative weight given to a particular rule is also determined by the geographic location (the jurisdiction)[14] of the primary authority with regard to the specific case and the specific issue in that case.[15] Thus, primary authority can be either mandatory or persuasive, depending on whether the setting of the branch of government is in the same or a separate jurisdiction[16] as the client's case.

Consider, for example, a statute from California that makes certain conduct a crime. Assume that the action that would constitute that crime takes place in Nevada, which has no comparable statute. The prosecutor in Nevada may assert the authority of the California statute and would correctly identify the statute as primary authority, but the attorney would then have to acknowledge that, since it comes from a "sister state" and not from Nevada, it is only persuasive authority, not mandatory authority. If, on the other hand, the conduct occurred in California, where the defendant was facing trial, that same statute could now be asserted as mandatory authority. Thus, where the facts of a case occurred and where it will be litigated factor significantly in determining the weight of primary authority (*i.e.*, whether it will be mandatory or persuasive authority).

The same calculus would exist for a rule from a California Supreme Court case or from a state agency in California: mandatory authority if

---

14. Geographic jurisdiction changes as a case progresses through the system or depending upon the subject matter of the controversy. For instance, a misdemeanor criminal case's geographic jurisdiction may be the superior court of that particular county, but a case on appeal with a federal question may be in the geographic jurisdiction of the federal court.

15. Depending upon the court where a case is being litigated, primary authority sources can be either mandatory or persuasive. For example, a rule from a Ninth Circuit case will be mandatory in any federal district court within the circuit, but it will be only persuasive when arguing in front of the Supreme Court.

16. Here, jurisdiction refers to the geographic area within which a court is empowered to exercise its authority.

the case is being litigated in a California state court, but only persuasive authority if the case is being litigated in Nevada.

So, we distinguish the types of authority as primary or secondary based on whether they come from one of the branches of government or from a non-constitutional entity or individual. And we further distinguish primary authority as mandatory or persuasive based on whether it comes from the same jurisdiction as the conduct in question or from a different jurisdiction (one that doesn't have direct/constitutional control over the conduct in question).

While we distinguish primary authority as either mandatory or persuasive, we don't do the same for secondary authority. Secondary authority is always persuasive, never mandatory. If you are following the logic of these designations, the reason should be obvious: Nothing in the constitutional system of government gives the author of secondary authority the ability to create binding rules.

To summarize, rules can come from anywhere, so long as they are published in some form (so as to be citable in a legal document[17]). They will be given relative weight depending on whether they are created by one of the three branches of government with geographic jurisdiction (primary mandatory or primary persuasive) or are suggested by private individuals or entities without any constitutional ability to create law (secondary authority).

One last point on primary authority: It can exist at the federal, state, or local level. Thus, a county ordinance will be primary authority just as a federal statute will be. And that county ordinance might be mandatory, while the federal statute might only be persuasive, depending on the jurisdiction of each body with regard to the conduct in question.

And one last point on secondary authority bears mention: Some secondary authority is more persuasive, and some is less persuasive. A law review article by a recognized expert in antitrust law, for example, would presumably be accorded more weight than an op-ed column by a journalist on the same issue. In fact, that journalist might cite to the antitrust expert's statements to make the journalist's column more persuasive.

17. Citations are explained in Chapter Seven.

C. The Hierarchy of Courts

Any understanding of the significance of court opinions as primary authority must include the level of court that delivers a particular opinion. Simply stated, all courts are not created equal, and they do not all have the same responsibility.

Within the judicial branch of any jurisdiction, a hierarchy of courts exists, with one level in the hierarchy set aside for trying cases. Trial courts, as they are called, are where disputes between litigants are initially resolved. At the trial level, the court is responsible for deciding which rules (law) apply (*e.g.*, the definition of malice the jury will be told to use in a murder case) and what happened factually. Trial courts are where juries sit, and the jury's responsibility is to decide which of the facts presented in evidence are correct and, based on the relevant rules (as instructed by the trial judge), which side should prevail in the litigation. Thus, at the trial court level, a jury resolves the factual issues in the case after the judge makes a preliminary decision as to which rules should be applied to those facts to reach a verdict.[18]

After the trial court renders a verdict or final decision, the losing party may seek an appeal at the next level of court in the jurisdiction's hierarchy. In the federal system, these courts are the Circuit Courts of Appeals. (The trial level courts in the federal system are the District Courts.) There are thirteen circuit courts in the United States. Eleven are distributed geographically across the country. The other two are in Washington, DC. One of those (the Federal Circuit) has jurisdiction over particular kinds of cases that are primarily, if not exclusively, federal (*e.g.*, patent cases brought under federal patent law). The other

---

18. The federal Constitution guarantees the right to a trial by jury in criminal cases. U.S. Const., 6th Amendment. Article I, § 16 of the California Constitution also guarantees people a right to a jury trial where the jury is composed of a cross-section of the community. In a trial by jury, the members of the jury decide factual issues and determine the credibility of witnesses, whereas the judge's role is limited to determining what evidence is admissible and other legal questions. Trials can also be conducted without a jury. In these "bench trials," the judge weighs the evidence, makes a determination on the credibility of witnesses, and decides all questions of fact and law.

GEOGRAPHIC BOUNDARIES OF U.S. COURTS OF APPEALS AND U.S. DISTRICT COURTS

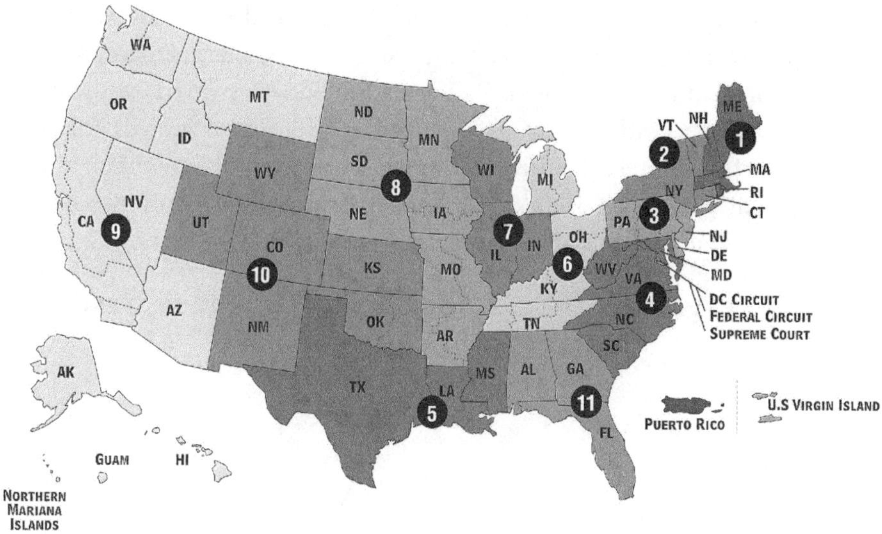

circuit court in DC (the DC Circuit) handles appeals from cases that arise out of federal litigation brought by or against any of the many federal agencies that reside in the District of Columbia.

The map above depicts the geographic location of the eleven federal circuit courts, plus the DC Circuit Court and Federal Circuit Court.[19]

The U.S. Supreme Court is above the thirteen federal circuit courts in the federal hierarchy. It is responsible for all appeals it chooses to accept[20] from the lower federal courts or from the highest state courts

19. Image available from http://www.uscourts.gov/about-federal-courts/court-role-and-structure.

20. In most instances, SCOTUS (Supreme Court of the United States) will look at "Petitions for Certiorari" drafted by the party seeking review of a lower court decision. These petitions will be reviewed by the Justices' law clerks, rated, and (if you are lucky) subsequently discussed in conference. Petitions are usually either granted, denied, rescheduled, relisted, or "GVR'ed" (Granted, Vacated, Remanded), among other more obscure responses.

(assuming a federal question or constitutional issue exists to give the Court jurisdiction).[21]

Many state courts have a similar three-tiered hierarchy, with the lowest tier housing the trial courts, and with the intermediate and supreme courts above them. California has Superior Courts at the trial court level, with the six separate (geographically separated) District Courts of Appeal and the Supreme Court above them. Other states (smaller ones like Rhode Island and Vermont) have only two court levels: one for trials and the other for appeals from those trials.

LEVELS OF THE CALIFORNIA STATE COURT SYSTEM

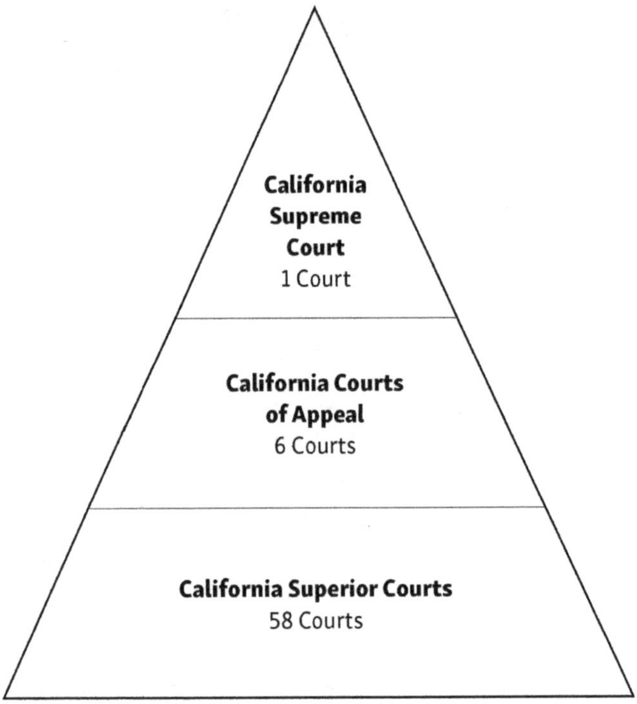

21. Even the Supreme Court has limited jurisdiction; it cannot hear certain cases on appeal. The Supreme Court generally has absolute power to review decisions from federal courts and issues of federal questions in state court. However, SCOTUS has no jurisdiction over cases that only involve questions of state law. For example, the Supreme Court would never review a state breach of contract case if the only issue presented in the case was whether the contract was breached under state law.

LEVELS OF THE FEDERAL COURT SYSTEM[22]

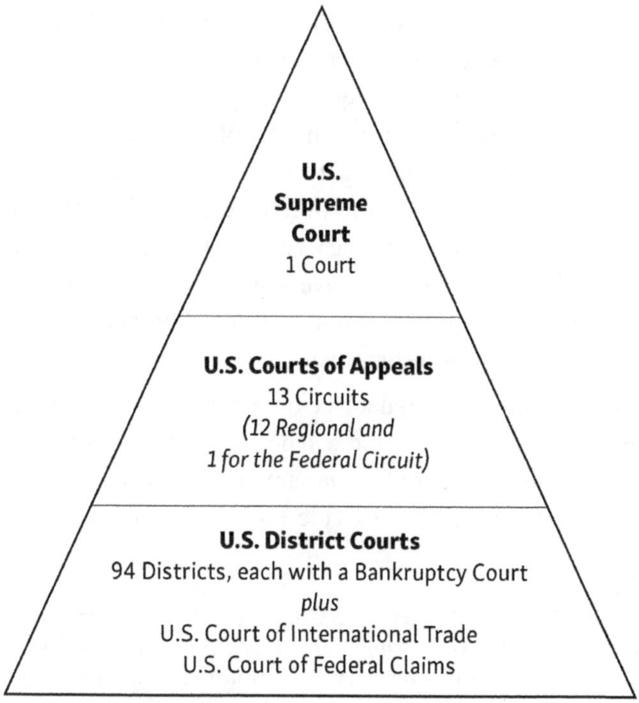

The differentiation between levels of courts in a judicial hierarchy matters when, in conjunction with mandatory authority, we overlay the concepts of **precedence** and **stare decisis**. These terms are similar in effect but are not the same thing.

We speak of a court's opinion in a case having precedence (or precedential impact) when that court is higher in the judicial hierarchy of a jurisdiction than the court where a legal issue is being considered. Thus, a trial court must always recognize the precedence in a court opinion from an appellate court above it in the judicial hierarchy. Similarly, an intermediate court must recognize the precedence of a court opinion from that jurisdiction's highest court. (And, of course, all courts must recognize the precedential impact of a U.S. Supreme Court

22. Image available from http://judiciallearningcenter.org/levels-of-the-federal-courts/.

ruling that interprets the Constitution because the Supreme Court is the ultimate rule-making body on matters of constitutional law.)

When a court abides by stare decisis (Latin for "to stand by things decided" or "let the decision stand"), it will not change the rule on a particular issue that it has already provided in a prior case. For example, the U.S. Supreme Court, when it applied stare decisis, did not change the rule on a woman's right to abortion[23] (until it determined stare decisis was inapplicable and overruled the earlier decision[24]), or the applicability of the exclusionary rule for Fourth Amendment violations,[25] or the requirement to give specific warnings to a criminal defendant in custodial interrogation settings (*Miranda* warnings[26]) in subsequent cases that came before it.[27]

If a higher court has stated a rule on a particular issue, its decision will stand under stare decisis and will be controlling on lower courts in its jurisdiction as precedent for the same issue. Thus, a federal circuit court of appeals cannot issue a rule re-instating a woman's right to

---

23. *Planned Parenthood v. Casey*, 505 U.S. 833 (1992). In this landmark opinion, the constitutionality of several Pennsylvania abortion statutes was challenged. Although the court expounded on the situations in which a state is permitted to regulate abortion, the core holding of *Roe v. Wade*, 410 U.S. 113 (1973), that a woman has a right to choose and to be free from unreasonable burdens on that right, was preserved.

24. *Dobbs v. Jackson Women's Health Org.*, 142 S.Ct. 2228 (2022).

25. *Ker v. State of Cal.*, 374 U.S. 23 (1963). In this case (the first after *Mapp v. Ohio*, 367. U.S. 643 (1961), to reach the Supreme Court) involving the seizure of marijuana found incident to arrest for sales of marijuana, the Court danced around the decision in *Mapp*, careful not to conflict with its precedence. The Court distinguished *Ker* from *Mapp* but made clear that the principles in *Mapp* still applied as law. Often, the Court will need to engage in this kind of "clarification" to fully flesh out a body of law, but it is extremely rare to find Court decisions directly overturning prior precedent due to the Court's respectful adherence to stare decisis.

26. *Missouri v. Seibert*, 542 U.S. 600 (2004). In this case, a defendant charged with murder was given *Miranda* warnings mid-confession, but the Court ruled that such an ineffective warning violated *Miranda* principles, and even when the confessions were repeated after the warnings were given they were deemed inadmissible at trial.

27. Stare decisis is of "fundamental importance to the rule of law." *Payne v. Tennessee*, 501 U.S. 808, 842 (1991), quoting *Welch v. Texas Dept. of Highways and Public Transportation*, 483 U.S. 468, 494 (1987). However, stare decisis is not an "inexorable command," and the Supreme Court has consistently declined to apply the doctrine rigidly in constitutional cases. *Burnet v. Coronado Oil & Gas Co.*, 285 U.S. 393, 405 (1932).

abortion or in violation of the exclusionary rule or in abrogation of the requirement to give *Miranda* warnings even if its panel of judges would interpret the Constitution differently if it had the power to do so. It is bound by the U.S. Supreme Court's rule on those issues. But a federal circuit court can issue a rule that would be binding on the district courts in its jurisdiction, and that rule would be binding until the U.S. Supreme Court issued a contrary rule.

Similarly, a state trial court judge cannot deviate from prior appellate court rulings in its jurisdiction (hierarchy) in a trial dealing with any of those issues to which the prior rulings apply for the same reasons.

From these concepts (mandatory and persuasive authority, precedence, and stare decisis), the significance of **the Rule of Law**[28] can be understood. In essence, the Rule of Law represents our system of jurisprudence, wherein every issue in every case is capable of being resolved by identifying and applying successfully the correct piece of the jigsaw puzzle, or, put another way, by successfully applying the correct law (rule) to the facts.

D. Finding the Rules in Cases— The Case Brief

Much of the work in law school (and in the practice of law as well) consists of reading and understanding cases. Indeed, much of the dreaded Socratic Method[29] is based on how well a particular case or series of cases is understood. Every good legal writer is skilled at reading a court opinion and identifying from that opinion the relevant rule

---

28. The "Rule of Law" refers to a legal system that consists of laws that are enacted through a constitutional process, which is honored in the courts and respected by the people. In our system, the courts "were designed to be an intermediate body between the people and their legislature" to ensure the people's representatives acted only within the authority given to Congress under the Constitution. Alexander Hamilton, *Federalist* No. 28, in THE FEDERALIST: A COLLECTION OF ESSAYS WRITTEN IN FAVOUR OF THE NEW CONSTITUTION, AS AGREED UPON BY THE FEDERAL CONVENTION SEPTEMBER 17, 1787 (1788).

29. The purpose of the Socratic Method is to assist students in understanding a case, rule, or other concept under discussion. It works, when properly employed by the professor, when a question is posed that forces the student to reason out an an-

for a particular issue. And the case brief is the way lawyers and law students deconstruct a court's opinion. The standard case brief consists of sections that identify the various parts of a court's opinion. In its entirety, a case brief serves as a summary of the court's consideration and resolution of an issue or series of issues.

To begin, let's review why a court is writing an opinion in the first place, which can be summarized easily: A case has presented an issue that must be resolved to allow the case to proceed to a conclusion of the litigation.[30] In other words, courts write opinions to resolve issues that are presented by the facts of a particular case. Implicit in that last sentence is a basic truism that cannot be overemphasized: **Facts give rise to issues.**

So, in reading a case, the first thing to make note of (after identifying the court issuing the opinion, the date of the case, and the jurisdiction of the court) is the factual information with which the court concerns itself. We call this part of our case brief the **Facts of the Case** or **The Facts.** But we aren't talking about all of the facts that the court may include in its opinion. Some facts may be background or may be otherwise unrelated to the issue in the case. The facts we want to include in our brief are the facts that give rise to the issue the court is seeking to resolve.

Some courts mention many more facts in their opinions than need to be included in a brief of the case. Most courts (as is true of most people) find the factual setting of a case interesting (*e.g.*, who are the people involved? what prior history did they have? what else was happening on that particular day?), but many of the details provided in a court's opinion won't need to be included in the case brief because they don't give rise to the issue the court is addressing.[31]

---

swer by using what the student already knows. Ideally, the Method helps students to understand what they don't yet know by relying on what they do know. Some professors use the Socratic Method in a more prosaic manner (*e.g.*, just to pull out the facts of a case, which are presumably already known by the student).

30. Most published cases are issued by an appellate court that is reviewing a lower court's decision. Thus, most cases you will read in law school are appellate and Supreme Court cases resolving issues from the trial court level or lower appellate courts.

31. Some of your professors will be interested in the additional details in a court's opinion and may want you to include them in a description of the facts in class. Note

Now, here's a corollary to that first truism: **The facts that give rise to an issue are the same ones that are used to resolve that issue.** Think about that one for a few seconds. Does it make sense? It should. Because if we apply rules (law) to facts to resolve issues, then shouldn't the facts that give rise to an issue be the same facts to which the rules are applied to resolve the issue? It really is as simple as it sounds.

After the court has provided the facts of the case, it will, in one way or another, indicate the issue that it is going to address and resolve. Unfortunately, trying to identify the issue in reading a court's opinion can get tricky because appellate court judges/justices have a nasty habit of misidentifying or not identifying at all the issue they are actually addressing. You may, for example, find this kind of statement in a court's opinion—"This case presents for our review the issue of whether the defendant was negligently driving her vehicle when she hit the plaintiff as he walked across the street"—only to find as you read the full case that the court's actual focus is on whether the plaintiff's recovery will be reduced because he was illegally crossing a busy intersection when he was struck by the defendant. Thus, the real issue the court is addressing is whether the conduct of the plaintiff constituted comparative fault. (In that case, the plaintiff's complaint claimed negligence by the defendant, but the issue the court sought to resolve was comparative negligence.)

So, because issues aren't always definitively stated by courts in their opinions, you will often have to glean the actual issue from a full reading of the case, aided, of course, by the corollary truism above (that the facts that give rise to issues are the same ones used to resolve those issues).

And remember to distinguish the legal issue from the factual issue. Since almost all of the cases that get reported are appellate court cases, a court's opinion will almost always address a legal issue as opposed to a factual one. Factual issues are resolved at the trial court level; they are almost never in dispute (or in need of resolution) at the appellate level. For example, referring to the earlier murder hypo, once a trial judge has instructed a jury on the meaning of malice, the jury will then determine the factual issue of whether the defendant acted with malice in

---

that the model case brief discussed in this section only includes the pertinent facts that give rise to the issue the court is seeking to resolve.

shooting the victim. The appellate court would then address the legal issue of whether the trial judge gave the jury the proper definition of malice. (Malice is the legal issue; whether the defendant acted with malice is the factual issue. A jury would need to be instructed as to what malice is; it would then have to decide, factually, if the defendant exhibited malice in the action taken.)

Another common mistake for new law students is to state a procedural issue in a substantive case. Many cases are appealed to reverse a trial court decision that flows from a procedural ruling (*e.g.*, whether a motion to dismiss or for summary judgment was properly granted). While the appellate court must ultimately decide whether that particular ruling was correct—hence, it is an issue—in a torts class the underlying substantive torts issue is what your professor will want you to note (*e.g.*, was the defendant negligent?). (Bottom line: Find the substantive issue in the case that relates to your course.)

In the case brief, we identify the issue in a separate section (called **The Issue**, for want of a better word). The preferable way to state the issue (once you have figured out what it is) is to frame it as a question that can be answered yes or no. Yes or no questions are more likely to provide definitive answers, which is what you will want when you get to the holding of the case. Moreover, in memo- and brief-writing, issues that are phrased as yes or no questions will be easier to tie to the prediction or assertion you will be making in the document. (By comparison, issues that begin with "whether …" tend to be less precise and definitive and often suggest less precise and definitive answers, which is usually not a desirable way to convey a prediction or an assertion.)

And the issue should be stated with specificity to the facts that give rise to it. Remember: **Facts give rise to issues.**

Compare these two issues:

> Was the defendant negligent?
>
> Was the defendant negligent when he left a banana peel on the floor of the grocery store?

The first correctly identifies the substantive question the court must answer, but it gives no indication why it is the issue. The second makes clear why negligence is an issue in the case. So, always give the factual context of the issue the court is addressing in your case brief. Doing so will make the rest of the work in understanding the case much easier.

But also pinpoint the legal aspect of the issue. Negligence is a basis for a cause of action, but it consists of various elements (requirements to prove the case), one of which is duty. If, in our hypothetical banana peel case, the more finite legal question is whether the defendant breached a duty, we should specify that point in our statement of the issue. Thus, the more precise and more helpful issue in that case brief would be as follows: Did the defendant have a duty that he breached when he left a banana peel on the floor of the grocery store?

We can verify that we have accurately identified the issue in the case if the court's negligence analysis focuses on whether the defendant had a duty to pick up the banana peel. And we will know that the proper facts have been identified in our issue when the court applies a rule on duty to the very facts we have included in our issue.

Once you get past the facts and have an issue identified, you will be into the meat of the court's opinion, which is where the court provides an analysis that ultimately resolves the issue it is addressing. Reading through a court's analysis can be a laborious task, especially if you don't know what you are reading or why and how it is important. But it isn't all that complicated if you recognize that the judges who write these opinions are using the same basic approach that all lawyers use, to wit: They are applying law (rules) to facts.

Thus, in a typical appellate court opinion, once the court has provided the facts of the case and given some hint of what issue it will be addressing, the judge who writes the opinion will present a rule or a series of rules that the writer will then apply to the facts of the case. This approach will reflect the court's **analysis** and will result in a **holding**. The court's analysis is composed of the identification of relevant rules and the application of those rules to the facts of the case. The court's holding is the answer to the issue the court has addressed. A competent case brief will identify both of these elements of the opinion, and these elements will be what most professors will want you to clearly identify and explain when engaging in a Socratic dialogue in class.

So what you are reading in this part of the court's opinion is either the identification of the rule that will resolve the case or an application of that rule to the facts of the case. But in many opinions, either of these parts of the analysis can be extensive. For example, you may read an opinion in which the court discusses any number of earlier cases, relating, perhaps in great detail, the facts of those cases, the issues raised in those cases, and the results in them. When a court engages in this kind of extensive review of a series of cases on a particular subject, it is just trying to identify the correct rule to apply to the facts of the current case. (Appellate court judges would say that they are educating their readers on the correct rule to apply; in fact, they are doing both: identifying the rule and educating their readers.)

But, of course, most opinions won't say why the extensive review is being presented. Instead, they will review all of those old cases, distinguishing some, clarifying others, and maybe accepting still others as being on point. (In large part, the court here is responding to the opposing attorneys' briefs on the case where these historical cases are used in arguments.) In the process, the court will be identifying the actual rule that best fits the facts of the case. It can then proceed with its application of that rule to the facts of the current case.

A simple way to understand this part of the opinion is to consider it as the court's identification of the **inherited rule** to be applied to the facts. That rule is "inherited" because it comes from prior cases (or, in some instances, from statutes or other sources of authority). The identification of the inherited rule is a major task in reading some cases, and it can require careful attention to the court's consideration of each case in the potentially long list of cases the court will review in its opinion.[32]

But the inherited rule will usually not be the rule that results from the court's opinion. In many instances, a new rule will be produced in the court's opinion. That rule will be drawn from the **holding** in the case, and it can be referred to as the **resulting** or **formulated rule**. So let's understand what those highlighted terms mean and how we can identify them.

The **holding** of the case is the single statement that represents the court's answer to the issue in the case. Again, most often this statement

32. In more extended or complicated court opinions, an inherited rule may be the court's synthesis of a number of prior rules, which the court first explains separately in the opinion.

will not be expressly stated by the court. Instead, it will be implied in the way the court resolves the case.

For example, in a murder case where malice is the issue, the holding of the case might be that malice was exhibited when the defendant shot his gun at the victim, intending only to wound him. (Assume that the inherited rule the court used was that malice exists in an intent to kill.) That holding would be the answer to a malice issue that might have been phrased thusly: Did the defendant exhibit malice in firing his gun at the victim when he only intended to wound the victim?

Stop here for a moment and compare the holding to the issue. Note how the holding answers the question in the issue by referring directly to the facts in the case. And that is what the holding is—the answer to the issue that incorporates the facts that were included in the issue. (Again, the point to remember here is that facts give rise to issues and those same facts are used to resolve the issue.)

So, the facts of the case gave rise to the issue, which was resolved through the application of inherited rules. That resolution was the holding of the case. Now, how do we get the **resulting** or **formulated rule**? We get it by generalizing the holding, that is, by wording the holding without specific reference to the facts. In our example, the resulting rule might be worded as follows: Malice for murder exists in an act that is only intended to wound a victim where death results from that act.

But how did the court reach that resolution of the issue? That part of the opinion is contained in the analysis the court makes of the inherited rule's application to the facts of the instant case (the case the court is reviewing to resolve the issue before it). And it is in the court's analysis that the formulated rule can be created. Here's how that process works:

In applying the formulated rule to the facts of the instant case, the court will consider how closely that rule fits to the facts. If the fit is perfect, the analysis is done and no new rule will be created. (Note that those instances are relatively rare, since most appellate cases that are reported (published) go beyond merely affirming an existing rule.) But often, the court will indicate how the inherited rule should be interpreted in light of the new set of facts provided by the instant case. And that interpretation is where a new rule (the resulting or formulated rule) is developed.

If we go back to our murder example where the defendant only intended to wound (not kill) the victim who still died, the court's analysis might read something like this:

> *In this case, while the intent to kill is not met by the stipulated facts, malice can still be found from the use of potentially deadly force where death did indeed result. Hence, we hold that the defendant did exhibit malice when firing his gun at the victim, only intending to wound him.*

What has the court done in that short analysis? It has considered how the inherited rule (existing law) can be made to "fit" the facts of the case before it. And in a very subtle, but definitive, modification of that rule, it has created a new one. So, in our hypothetical, where malice had previously required an intent to kill, it can now be found in an intent to cause serious bodily injury (the gunshot wound) with death resulting.

To summarize the foregoing, consider the progression from **facts** to **issue** to **inherited rule** to **analysis** to **holding** to **formulated rule**:

> **Facts**—D shot V intending to wound him; V died from the wound.
>
> **Issue**—Did D murder V when D shot V intending only to wound him?
>
> **Inherited rule**—Malice exists in an intent to kill.
>
> **Analysis**—Inherited rule applied to facts with rule slightly modified in court's calculus.
>
> **Holding**—D murdered V when D shot V, intending only to wound him.
>
> **Formulated rule**—Malice exists in an act committed with intent to inflict serious injury that causes the death of the victim.

Note what we have done in that example. We have identified an **issue** from **facts**; we have understood in the court's **analysis** its identification of an **inherited rule** that it then applied to the facts of the case to resolve the issue; we have stated the court's resolution of the issue as a **holding** that answers the issue; and we have generalized the holding into the **resulting** or **formulated rule** from the case. Our brief might then consist of these sections:

Facts

Issue

Inherited Rule

Analysis

Holding

Resulting Rule

We might also split the Analysis section into **Inherited Rule—Identification** and **Inherited Rule—Application** to differentiate between the two fundamental parts of the court's analysis.[33] Under **Inherited Rule—Identification**, we would summarize how the court identified the rule (*e.g.*, what cases it reviewed, what earlier rules it considered). Under **Inherited Rule—Application**, we would explain how the court applied the rule to the facts of the case. In fact, we can devise any method of organizing our case briefs as we wish because they are only a way to systematize our notes on a case. No one else ever needs to see them.[34]

While most appellate cases will yield a formulated or resulting rule, as we noted previously, sometimes a court's opinion will only serve to re-state an existing rule. These cases are usually not published by courts because they don't advance the law or provide any greater understanding of existing law. In those instances, the inherited and resulting rules gleaned from the court's opinion will be one and the same. This circumstance will commonly occur when the issue can be easily resolved by the direct application of a well-settled rule, as in this fictional example:

---

33. Depending on the breadth of litigation that has gone into clarifying a particular rule, the court may spend most of the opinion simply explaining what the rule is and where that rule came from. In these cases, a separate section devoted to the "evolution" of the rule may be desirable.

34. A written case brief is vastly preferable to a book brief. Book briefing through annotating the casebook (underlining sentences and writing notes in the margin) is a shortcut to typing or writing out a case brief. It does not provide a meaningful way to recall a case for in-class discussions or to recall the case when using it in a legal document.

> A decedent had a will prepared and signed it before two witnesses, but only one witness signed the will. The case was appealed when the trial judge ruled that the will was only valid when both witnesses signed the will. The appellate court, on appeal, identified the well-established rule that a will, to be valid, had to be witnessed by two people, only one of whom must have signed the will. It applied that rule and reversed the trial court's judgment.

In that example, the formulated/resulting rule and the inherited rule would have been the same rule. The rule was simple and well-established, and the court just had to identify it and apply it to the facts. But if the court had applied this existing rule—"A will, to be valid, must be witnessed by two people" (and if the rule was silent on who needs to sign the will)—then the resulting rule would have been different (since it would add the point that only one of the two witnesses needed to sign the will).

The difference between an inherited rule and a resulting or formulated rule can have significance far beyond the resolution of the particular issue in a specific case. In many instances, an issue before an appellate court is novel enough that the formulated or resulting rule, being different from the inherited rule, adds another piece to the jigsaw puzzle of The Law. (Think about that point, and then read the next paragraph.)

The law is always becoming. It is always evolving, and one of the ways that it evolves is through the appellate process we have just described.

E. Organizing the Elements of a Legal Document

So far in this chapter, we have discussed how lawyers think and reason, how rules can be found from cases, and how to properly craft and organize a case brief. Step One of the White-Glove Inspection requires a review of the organization of the entire document to ensure that each point flows logically into the next. The organization of a legal document is a key to helping the reader understand the analysis, which is why Step One is so important.

As we will now see, there are many similarities between a case brief and a formal legal document. And both have parallels to a typical court opinion. Each involves the facts of a case that give rise to an issue. And all of them identify rules that are then applied to those facts to predict or assert a resolution of the issue. Thus, there is merit in studying and understanding the structure of basic court opinions because they are written with the same organizational design as the typical legal document.

1. Issues

Most legal documents (both predictive memos and persuasive briefs) begin with an identification of the issue (or issues) that the document addresses. And, as with court opinions, that issue will be identified with specific reference to the facts that give rise to it. Issues can be presented in a variety of ways. The most common is a simple yes or no question indicating the facts that give rise to the substantive issue.

Here is an example of a single issue (sometimes called **Issue Statement** or **Issue Question** or **Question Presented**) from a predictive memo:

> Did the defendant store employee have a duty when he failed to pick up a banana peel that he observed on the floor of the grocery store?

Note that the question, as written, elicits a yes or no answer and that it includes the facts that occurred in the case that make duty the issue. Are there enough facts? Consider this alternative:

> Did the defendant store employee have a duty when, moments before the store opened, he noticed, but failed to pick up, a banana peel on the floor of the grocery store where he worked?

What about this one?

> Did the defendant store employee breach a duty when, moments before the store opened and knowing that many customers would be in the vicinity, he noticed a banana peel on the floor but failed to pick it up because he was not responsible for that part of the store?

Obviously, at some point the question can become overly laden with facts, especially when we try to put everything in one question. Here's another alternative:

> Defendant failed to pick up a banana peel he saw on the floor in the grocery store where he worked. The store was about to open, and Defendant knew that many customers would soon be in the vicinity of the banana peel. Defendant was not normally responsible for that part of the store. Did the defendant breach a duty by failing to pick up the banana peel?

Some memo formats provide for that kind of extensive factual description to set up the actual question that presents the legal issue.[35] Some go even further and include the relevant law for the issue. In that instance, the full issue might read like this:

> Defendant failed to pick up a banana peel he saw on the floor in the grocery store where he worked. The store was about to open, and Defendant knew that many customers would soon be in the vicinity of the banana peel. Defendant was not normally responsible for that part of the store. Employees, in the normal scope of their employment, have a duty to keep the premises where they work free from safety hazards. Did the defendant breach a duty by failing to pick up the banana peel?

35. The specific format of briefs and memoranda differ from court to court and law office to law office. The format presented in this chapter is a generic alternative for purposes of instruction. In practice, you should identify the format that your supervising attorney prefers, and also identify any federal, state, or local rules that dictate the content and form of briefs filed with the court.

In this last example, the facts giving rise to the issue have been provided in sizeable detail, and the legal principle (rule) that will resolve the issue has been included. Most legal documents, however, will have a separate section for the presentation of the facts of the case.

2. Facts

We have indicated the importance of identifying the facts of the case that give rise to the issue in the case, and we certainly need to include those facts in the section of the legal document that is expressly entitled "Facts" or (as it is often called) "Statement of the Facts." But this section of the legal document is where the full story should be told. However, as is often true in legal writing, some judgment calls must be made.

Our goal in this section of the legal document is to give the reader a clear understanding of what happened. Think about these five W's: Where and When did Who do What to Whom? (The sixth W—Why—may not always be clear in the facts, but if it is, we want to include it as well.) And we want to give that understanding in a way that makes the reader interested in the story. (If your readers aren't interested in the facts of the case, they are going to have a hard time getting interested in the potentially dense legal analysis you will be providing later.)

Constructing an interesting statement of the facts is a challenge. Some approaches are readily apparent and work well in most instances. The most obvious is the basic chronological flow of the events, as in "Once upon a time ..., (here's where the details come in) ... and they all lived happily ever after (or, more probably, ended up hating each other, if it's a case that needs a lawyer's involvement)."

The best factual summaries will present the facts accurately but in a way that supports the analysis or argument that will follow. In other words, the facts should suggest the analysis or argument without making that analysis or argument. Drafting the facts, as you can see, can be tricky stuff. One way to know you are going too far is if you find yourself using loaded modifiers to describe the events, as in this sentence: "Defendant clearly saw the banana peel on the floor and yet deliberately decided not to pick it up, thereby creating a terrible condition that led to Plaintiff's tragic injuries." Leave out the adverbs ("clearly" and "deliberately") and adjectives ("terrible" and "tragic") to create a straightforward recitation of the facts. In other words, let the facts speak for themselves.[36]

This section of the legal document is best written as a work in progress. Start with an initial summary of the facts as you first understand them. Then, after you have lived with the case for a while, add or delete information that you have come to realize is more important or not really important at all. Revisiting this section of your document repeatedly will ensure that you are telling the relevant story for your analysis. It will keep you on target as you develop your arguments. Much as the entire document is a work in progress, so, too, this section should be constantly subject to revision.

In whatever manner you approach the drafting of the facts section of your document, the key is to include all the facts you use in your analysis or argument in this section. That point is sacrosanct. **Never refer to a fact in your analysis of the issue that you haven't included in the "facts" section of the document.**

3. Analysis or Argument

The heart of the document is the section where you show your actual lawyering skill—where you explain your analysis or make your arguments regarding the issue you are addressing. And you will make that presentation by using a basic structural paradigm that is built around the identification of the relevant rules for your issue. To be specific, you will identify the relevant rules, explain them, and apply them to the facts of your case. And the degree to which you will explain and apply each rule will depend on the type of document you are drafting and the complexity of the analyses (or arguments) you are making. (The difference between a predictive and persuasive document largely controls how much rule explanation is provided.)

---

36. Ethical considerations may also restrict the "coloring" of facts in a brief.

The predictive and persuasive paradigms (CREAC and C-RAC, respectively) are addressed fully in the next chapter. As we will see, they are not really all that different, as both rely on the proper identification of relevant rules and on the application of those rules to the facts of your case.

For now, however, here is a basic point that will be inviolate in the use of either paradigm for any specific document: **The rule that you identify and state must be the same rule that you apply.**[37] How you identify that rule will vary from document to document and how you apply it will vary from issue to issue and from analysis to analysis. But the rule identified must be the rule applied in order for the presentation of an analysis or argument to read as if it has been prepared by a lawyer. As should be obvious from that last sentence, precision in stating the rule is critical. In other words, the way the rule is stated must match precisely the way the rule is being applied to the facts of the case. Lack of precision in rule statements will almost always result in an analysis or argument that lacks clarity.

Chapter Summary

All legal writing revolves around the identification of issues that must be analyzed by the application of law to facts. This basic paradigm defines how lawyers think. It is, in essence, what separates lawyers from lay people, which, for our purposes, is the rest of humanity.[38]

So, as lawyers, we consider carefully the facts of our case as the way to identify the legal issues presented by those facts. And we distinguish legal issues from factual issues by considering whether the question presented can be answered by scientific knowledge or basic human understanding. If it can be, the issue is factual, not legal.

Legal issues can only be resolved by the application of specific rules, which are part of the jigsaw puzzle that represents The Law. Every piece

37. A rule is applied to a client's case by considering whether the rule "fits" the client's facts and provides a potential resolution to the issue presented by those facts.

38. Many lay people may occasionally think and reason like lawyers, but lawyers do not (at least in the legal documents they write) think or reason like lay people.

of that giant puzzle is a rule that provides a potential answer to a specific legal issue. The lawyer's job in a legal document is to show how a particular rule resolves the specific legal issue presented by the client's unique set of facts.

The rules that comprise that giant puzzle come from a variety of possible authorities. Those that come from the constitutional system (either from the judicial, legislative, or executive branches of government) are primary authority. Those that come from all other sources are secondary authority. Primary authority can be either mandatory or persuasive, depending on the jurisdiction of the rule-making entity. Secondary authority is always persuasive, never mandatory. Thus, rules from secondary authority are really only "proposed rules."

The judicial branch of government consists of a hierarchy of courts. Each jurisdiction (the fifty separate states and the federal system) has its own hierarchical structure for its courts. At the bottom of the hierarchy are the trial courts, which are responsible for resolving factual issues after deciding what rules are applicable to the case. The appellate courts in the jurisdiction are responsible for determining whether legal issues have been properly resolved by the lower courts. Appellate courts do not try cases and do not make factual findings.

Appellate courts write opinions that reflect how a legal issue has been resolved. Lawyers (and law students) gain an understanding of the rules the court has developed by studying those opinions. A case brief represents an attorney's organization of the attorney's notes on a case. It identifies the facts that gave rise to the issue the court resolved. It identifies the inherited rule the court determined should be applied to the facts of the case and the manner in which the court applied that inherited rule. It identifies the holding of the court, which is the court's answer to the issue in the case, and the resulting or formulated rule from the case, which is a generalized statement of the holding of the case.

Legal documents use the same basic organization that a court uses in delivering an opinion and that an attorney uses in a case brief. They identify issues that flow from facts and rules that are applied to facts to produce an analysis or argument. The basic organizational paradigm thus applies law (rules) to facts. It is the way lawyers think and reason, and it is what separates them from lay people.

Chapter Three

Effective Use of Paragraphs in a Legal Document

A. Introduction

B. Paragraph Length

C. CREAC and C-RAC—The Predictive and Persuasive Paradigms

A. Introduction

Have you ever heard public speakers who, without a written script, sound as if they are speaking in paragraphs? It is a supreme compliment to praise a person who appears to be speaking fluently without a prepared script. Most of us put our spoken thoughts together sentence by sentence, or perhaps phrase by phrase, or maybe even word by word. Rarely can we think in paragraphs, let alone speak in them. And as listeners, we understand that most speakers will only rarely be speaking in paragraphs. We expect public speakers to put their thoughts together in sentences, and then our job, as active listeners, is to try to discern the over-riding point or thesis of those sentences, thereby creating the paragraph our speaker ultimately might have wanted us to hear.

Writing differs from speaking on this point. Good writers write in paragraphs. They create a series of sentences that make a singular point or address a particular thesis, and the paragraph is the way they present that particular point or thesis. And as the readers of the paragraph, we understand implicitly that the writer wants us to grasp the point or thesis by the way the sentences flow from sub-point to sub-point.

In a legal document, paragraphs are the linchpin for organizing and presenting the thoughts the writer wants to convey. They are the tools by which the writer hopes to make the document more readily understood. The effective use of paragraphs in a legal document conforms to the way lawyers analyze an issue and compose an argument. The flow of the paragraphs should thus represent the paradigms that lawyers use in legal writing (the acronyms for which are CREAC and C-RAC).

Good legal writers think about the appropriate paradigm for the document they are writing and then construct paragraphs that represent the distinct parts of the paradigm for that document. In a legal memorandum that presents an objective analysis of an issue, the writer will construct paragraphs that explain rules (rule explanation, or RE, paragraphs) and paragraphs that apply rules (rule application, or RA, paragraphs). In a legal brief that presents an argument on an issue, the writer will construct rule application (RA) paragraphs. Both types of documents can also include umbrella paragraphs (discussed in Chapter Four). Even in less formal documents, the writer will still construct paragraphs that address particular aspects of the writer's reasoning.

But in addition to being organizational tools, paragraphs also serve to make the document readable. Just as the public speaker who speaks in paragraphs is more pleasing to listen to than the speaker who struggles to construct sentences (or even to find the "right" words), so, too, should the legal writer construct paragraphs that are pleasing to read. Thus, the well-crafted paragraph in a legal document will not be overly long, will not contain more than one thesis, and will not include extraneous material unrelated to that thesis.

To serve these two purposes—organization and readability—paragraphs in a legal document must be structured with care. Sometimes a single argument must be separated into sub-arguments so that a single long paragraph can become a series of shorter paragraphs. Sometimes, thoughts that are valuable for the overall purpose of the document but that don't really further the particular thesis in a paragraph must be removed from one paragraph and placed in a different, newly constructed, paragraph. Sometimes, paragraphs that seem to represent one thesis will be found, on closer inspection, to contain two or more theses and thus will need to be split into separate, smaller paragraphs.

Sometimes, a series of shorter paragraphs may constitute a single substantive point, thus requiring them to be joined in a single paragraph. In each instance, the care given to the construction of each paragraph is a critical part of drafting a well-written legal document.

B. Paragraph Length

At some point in your pre-college education, you may have been taught what were then the requirements of a well-constructed paragraph. Those requirements included starting with a thesis sentence, following that opening sentence with at least three explanatory or expository sentences, and ending it all with a concluding or summative sentence. Your teachers may have told you that all paragraphs had to have those elements but, most importantly, that if you didn't have a thesis or topic sentence, you couldn't construct a proper paragraph.

Many lawyers and judges have, regrettably, locked themselves into those requirements in the legal documents they have written. The result has been a lot of unduly ponderous reading that could have been made a lot less so by jettisoning those burdensome requisites.

Paragraphs are to reading what breathing is to exercise. When we exercise heavily, we need to breathe often. When we are reading, paragraph breaks signal to our brain to take a breath. And, continuing with the exercise analogy, the heavier the reading, the more often it is desirable to "take a breath" at the end of a paragraph.

The preceding paragraph suggests some hostility to long paragraphs, and it is meant to. Do a little survey with yourself: How often have you seen a long paragraph and felt energized to read it? At best, you'll say that you do not mind an occasional long paragraph, but if you had your preference, you would be happier if any given paragraph didn't exceed a certain length. What constitutes that "tolerable" length will depend on a variety of factors, of course, but one factor that would certainly rank highly would be the complexity of the document. The more complex it is, the more you'd prefer that the paragraphs be shorter.

Liking short paragraphs does not mean that you don't like to read, any more than liking to breathe often while exercising means that you don't like to exercise. But shorter paragraphs make the heavy lifting in reading the document less burdensome. It reduces the amount of brain sweat, if you will.

So, if we accept the preceding proposition, a goal should be to keep our paragraphs short enough that their very length doesn't make the actual reading of the document we are preparing any more ponderous than it already might be. (Remember, as noted in Chapter One, legal documents normally do not constitute light reading. They are work for the reader, even if they are beautifully written and are about the most intriguing and scintillating of topics.)

Here, then, are some new rules for paragraph construction in a legal document:

1. Don't obsess about thesis/topic sentences. Not every paragraph needs to have one.
2. Don't obsess about the three expository-sentence requirement. If one sentence suffices on the point you are addressing, that sentence will suffice for your paragraph.
3. Don't add a summative sentence unless the paragraph is complicated enough to warrant one.
4. Use rule statements as topic sentences wherever appropriate.
5. When you use more than one case to explain (or apply) a rule, construct one paragraph for each case instead of squeezing all the cases into one paragraph.
6. If you use a case to set up the application of a rule and then apply the rule to the facts of your case, use two paragraphs to do so: one to identify and explain the case, and the second to apply the rule (and the case) to your facts.
7. Always look for convenient and appropriate spots in longer paragraphs to break them into shorter paragraphs. Such spots often begin with transitional phrases like "In this regard," "With respect to," "In considering," "Therefore," and "Even if."
8. If a single sentence makes a separate and distinct point, make it a single-sentence paragraph in your document.

9. Use headings in lieu of thesis/topic sentences where appropriate; avoid repeating the substance of a heading as a thesis/topic sentence for a paragraph.
10. When nothing else seems to allow breaking up a long paragraph, think of sub-theses or sub-topics within the primary thesis or topic that the paragraph covers.

These new rules will require some work if you are locked into the outmoded rules for paragraph construction. Happily, these new rules comport well with the use of the predictive and persuasive paradigms, where rules are often the thrust of a paragraph in any event.

C. CREAC and C-RAC[1]—The Predictive and Persuasive Paradigms

Lawyers use one of two basic organizational paradigms for the legal documents they write.[2] The two have specific purposes, one being to present a predictive analysis of a legal issue, the other being to present a persuasive argument about a legal issue. They are identified by respective acronyms: CREAC for the predictive documents and C-RAC for the persuasive documents.[3] The Cs in both acronyms stand for Conclusion, which thereby indicates that in legal documents we tell our reader what our conclusion is both before and after providing our reasoning.

The heart of both of these paradigms is contained between the Cs. There, the lawyer presents the analysis of the issue that supports the prediction or argument the lawyer is making. It is in those paragraphs that rules are identified, explained, and applied, and it is in those paragraphs that the writer's ability to think and reason "like a lawyer" must be evident. The CREAC paradigm comprises the **Discussion** section of

1. C-RAC and CRAC identify the same paradigm. Some professors prefer to pronounce it C-RAC (pronounced "See Rack") rather than CRAC (pronounced "Crack").

2. Lawyers who are engaged in the practice of law utilize the same legal writing paradigms that are taught in law school.

3. Predictive documents are referred to generically as memoranda (or "memos") and persuasive documents are referred to as briefs.

a formal predictive memorandum, while the C-RAC paradigm constitutes the **Argument** section of a brief or other persuasive document filed with a court or adjudicative body.[4] The paradigms are different, but, as we will see, they are really not very different.

1. CREAC

The R-E-A part of CREAC stands for Rule-Explanation-Application, wherein the rule is identified, explained, and applied to the facts of the case under consideration. One way to organize a document with this paradigm would be to set out the rule in one sentence, to explain it in another, and to apply it to the facts of your client's case in a third. And when considering the most simple of issues with correspondingly simple rules, that approach would probably work just fine.

But most legal issues are not so easily resolved. Instead, most will require identification of a rule that either has various parts or components or that has been interpreted in a variety of different ways by the courts. In either event, the R-E-A of CREAC is going to be more complicated than the three straightforward sentences suggested by the acronym.

A better way to look at the predictive paradigm is to think of it as consisting of two parts, one being RE (Rule Explanation) and the other being RA (Rule Application). You might, thus, think of the acronym as really being CRERAC, with the heart of the analysis contained in the separate but parallel RE (Rule Explanation) and RA (Rule Application) sections. The RE will then consist of either a number of sub-rules that are part of a larger **composite rule** or a number of interpretations of a rule that, considered in the aggregate, can be stated as a **synthesized rule**. Composite rules and synthesized rules are similar in appearance, but they are technically different, and the way they are developed and explained can vary as well.

a. The CREAC Rules

A **composite rule** is a rule that consists of multiple requirements (elements) or considerations (factors). The definition of burglary is a

4. Administrative hearings and alternative dispute resolution (ADR) proceedings can also require the filing of written briefs.

good example of a composite rule. Burglary, as it is generally defined, is the breaking and entering the dwelling house of another with the intent to commit a felony therein. We would identify this rule as a composite rule because it consists of five separate elements. And in a predictive memo dealing with whether a burglary has been committed by a defendant, we would need to explain the separate elements with separate RE paragraphs.

Thus, in our predictive memo where burglary is the issue, we might have one RE paragraph to explain the breaking and entering elements, a second RE paragraph to explain the dwelling-house-of-another element, and yet a third RE paragraph to explain the intent element. In sum, the RE part of our memo would consist of separate explanations of the parts (elements) of the rule, which, taken together, would then give us our composite rule. (See Table 1 on page 55.)

A **synthesized rule** is a rule that can be envisioned (or that develops) from a series of case interpretations of a concept or principle. Synthesized rules are not as easy to identify and define as composite rules because they only exist when an attorney has analyzed several cases dealing with the same issue and has found, as a result, that a single rule represents the amalgam (or synthesis) of all of the cases.

The rule for probable cause might be a synthesized rule. Probable cause is required by the Fourth Amendment of the Constitution for the issuance of search warrants.[5] But defining probable cause (developing a rule on what constitutes probable cause) requires distilling a series of cases. Thus, the definition of probable cause would be a synthesized rule, because it would be developed from the consideration of a number of court opinions that dealt with the issue. And, therefore, in a predictive memo where probable cause was the issue, we would have separate RE paragraphs, with each showing how a particular court opinion identified the presence or absence of probable cause from a set of facts. We would then synthesize those cases into a rule on probable cause that would result from a consideration of all of the cases.

---

5. The Fourth Amendment has two clauses. The first clause guarantees people the right "to be secure in their persons, houses, papers, and effects, against unreasonable searches and seizures." The second clause guarantees that "no Warrants shall issue, but upon probable cause, supported by Oath or affirmation, and particularly describing the place to be searched, and the persons or things to be seized."

b. Rule Explanation: The RE Paragraph

Whether we are dealing with a composite rule, a synthesized rule, or a simple rule that needs nothing more than a single sentence to explain it, the ultimate analysis of the issue in our memo will turn on how the rule is explained. Therefore, each RE paragraph must be tightly constructed with case illustrations precisely crafted to explain or illustrate the rule (or portion of the rule) that the writer has identified.

As the sample RE sections in Table 1 (below) of a predictive memo reflect, any number of paragraphs can be necessary in the RE portion of a predictive memo on a single issue before the entire rule has been explained. Thus, we need to anticipate how those separate paragraphs will effectively communicate the complete rule to be applied in the RA part of the memo.

That last thought suggests the key point about rule statements in RE paragraphs: They must state exactly and precisely the rule that will then be explained in the rest of the paragraph. We talk a lot about precision in legal writing and, when we do, this particular requirement is emblematic of what we mean. The rule we state must be exactly the same as (or equal to) the rule we explain. And since the essence of the rule explanation paragraph is the rule itself, the best way to start that paragraph is with the rule statement. The statement of the rule thus becomes the thesis sentence of the RE paragraph.

Stating rules precisely can take a lot of work. The slightest amount of imprecision can open an analysis or argument to attack (by showing, for example, that the rule as stated is not the rule that is being applied, or, even more troubling, that the rule is not an accurate statement of what can be derived from the particular case that is cited for the rule). Imprecisely stated rules are rules that will, invariably, be explained poorly (lacking clarity). And the result of a poorly explained rule will most often be an uncertain and unreliable analysis. Simply stated, a case can be lost solely because a rule has been stated imprecisely.

A second point regarding rule statements in legal writing flows from this first requirement: That same rule statement must be consistent with the rule we are going to apply to the client's facts in the RA part of the memo. In other words, the rules we state must be the rules we explain, and the rules we explain must be the rules we apply; therefore, the rules we apply must be the rules we state.

Table 1—RE Paragraph Examples

Composite Rule: The elements of burglary are the entering of an inhabited dwelling house with the intent to commit a felony.
Composite Rule Explanation: "Entry" occurs when a person who is outside a residence goes inside. *Magness v. Superior Court*, 54 Cal.4th 270, 275 (2012) (holding the defendant's opening of a garage door with a remote control did not constitute entry because defendant did not physically enter the house). A dwelling is inhabited if someone lives there, even though the person is absent at the time of the burglary, so long as the homeowner intends to return to the home. *People v. Meredith*, 174 Cal.App.4th 1257, 1266 (2009) (finding that a home was inhabited where the owner had temporarily entered a skilled nursing facility but intended to return to his home, and no evidence showed that owner had moved out). A jury can infer from the circumstances of a case and the conduct of the accused that a defendant's purpose in entering the house was to commit a theft. *People v. Stewart*, 113 Cal.App.2d 687, 690 (1952) (holding the defendant's forced entry with felonious intent to commit burglary was sufficient to show the defendant committed burglary, even though the defendant abandoned his unlawful purpose after entry).
Synthesized Rule: Probable cause to search requires a reasonable belief that evidence of crime will be found in a certain place at a certain time.
Synthesized Rule Explanation: A search warrant must be justified by the existence of probable cause. U.S. Const. amend IV. A search warrant must establish the basis for the belief that evidence exists in a specific location. *Illinois v. Gates*, 462 U.S. 213 (1983) (holding anonymous letter included sufficient verifiable information to justify issuance of search warrant). A search warrant must be executed within the time when evidence is reasonably believed to be present at the location to be searched. *U.S. v. Bedford* 519 F.2d (1975) (holding execution of warrant eight days after issuance was reasonable because informant's tip indicated evidence would be present at time of search).

Two conceptualizations reflect this requirement. The first is that A must equal B, which must equal C, where A is the rule statement, B is the explanation of the rule, and C is the application of the rule. And, of course, taking that equation (A=B=C) one step further, A, the rule that is stated, must equal C, the rule that is applied. (A second way to conceptualize this requirement is in what we refer to as **the mirror-image approach**, which will become more evident when we discuss the RA paragraphs later in this chapter.)

> A: Statement of the legal rule that relates to the issue
>
> B: Explanation of that same rule through the illustration of the rule from the case that gave rise to it
>
> C: Application of the exact same rule to the facts in your case that have given rise to the issue using the exact explanation of the rule already provided

Using simple algebraic concepts, if A equals B and B equals C, then A must equal C. So in legal writing the rule stated must be explained exactly as it is stated and the application of the rule must be based on exactly how it was explained. Adherence to that approach must then result in the rule as originally stated being applied to the client's facts.

As we have already indicated, the most common and readily available way to explain a rule is by illustrating its use in a case, and often that case will be the case that gave rise to the rule in the first place. And so, we use in-text illustrations of rules as the RE part of the paradigm whenever possible. But here we must distinguish between providing a full brief of the case and using the case to illustrate the rule.

The full brief of a case is for your case briefs (the systematized note-taking you do when you want to recall how a court's opinion resolves an issue in a case you've read). (See Chapter Two for a full description of a case brief.) The in-text illustration of a case that explains a rule needs to be limited to those details from the case (and no more) that actually illustrate and, thereby, explain the rule, as in the examples in Table 1.

Another way to understand this requirement is to recall the work involved in constructing the elaborate gadget that comes with any number of separate parts and a long list of instructions on how to put all of those parts together. If, after following all of the instructions, you end up with an extra part, you will probably feel confused, if not frustrated, or even angry, because something is wrong. Either you missed something in the instructions, or the list of parts gave you the incorrect number of gizmos, or your gadget isn't properly constructed. That spare/unused part is the problem. It doesn't fit; it doesn't seem to belong; it's just there.

If the explanation you provide of your rule includes an unused part (maybe a stray fact from the case you are using to explain your rule), your reader is going to be confused, if not frustrated, and maybe even angry if that pattern is repeated throughout your memo. So we say, "no spare parts; no missing parts," so that A (the rule statement) will always precisely match B (the rule explanation). And then, when we get to RA (the rule application), we'll want the same result: no spare parts, no missing parts. Thus, if we state the rule precisely and explain exactly what we have stated and then apply exactly what we have explained, we will always have an analysis that clearly applies the rule we have stated to our client's facts.

For example, if the rule we state is that a burglary requires breaking into and entering a building or structure, and the case we are using includes facts relating to other elements of the crime of burglary (dwelling house of another, with intent to commit a felony), we would not include those facts or the court's reasoning about them in the RE paragraph that explains "breaking and entering a building." Rather, we would only provide the facts and the concomitant reasoning regarding the breaking and entering elements of the crime in our in-text illustration of the rule. The paragraph might read like this (*Smith v. State* is not a real case):

> Burglary requires the breaking and actual entering of a building or structure. *Smith v. State*, 23 Utopia 587 (1946). In *Smith*, the defendant pushed open an unlatched side door of his neighbor's residence and reached his hand into the structure. The court held that by pushing open the door and sticking his hand into the residence, the defendant had satisfied the breaking and entering elements of the crime.

That paragraph would be sufficient as written without including other aspects of the case or other facts (such as evidence of what might have been the defendant's intent) regarding the burglary allegedly committed by the defendant in the case. The rule stated at the outset of the paragraph only identified the breaking and entering elements of a burglary, and to explain that limited rule, only the relevant portions of *Smith* had to be provided in the RE paragraph. To have included more would have created two potential problems. First, it would have created possible confusion for the reader as to exactly what is meant by "breaking and entering," and second, it would have given the reader more to read than the rule required. And in legal documents, as noted in Chapter One, we never want to burden our reader with any more text than is necessary to make our point. The following RE paragraph, again using the fictional case of *Smith v. State*, is an example of how too much detail from a case can be included in the RE paragraph:

> Burglary requires the breaking and actual entering of a building or structure. *Smith v. State*, 23 Utopia 587 (1946). In *Smith*, the defendant pushed open an unlatched side door of his neighbor's residence and reached his hand into the structure. **The defendant was looking for something to eat because he had not eaten in two days.** The court held that by pushing open the door and sticking his hand into the residence, the defendant had satisfied the breaking and entering elements of the crime.

The writer of this paragraph has included facts (in the **added sentence**) from *Smith* that do not relate to the "breaking and entering" rule the writer has stated in the first sentence. In doing so, the writer has violated the A=B part of the equation that RE paragraphs require. A reader of the paragraph would wonder why those added facts were included (how they are supposed to relate to the stated rule) and may be even more confused when they aren't mentioned in a corresponding RA paragraph on the same rule.

Before we leave the preferred *Smith* RE paragraph, look at its structure. It is a model to use for all in-text illustrations that explain a rule from a case. Note that it starts with a single sentence that states the rule.

That sentence is immediately followed by the name and citation of the case that will be used to explain the rule. The very next sentence refers back to the case in shorthand form ("In *Smith*,") and then goes on to provide the key facts from the case and the court's holding that substantiates the rule. That specific structure/format should be used for all RE paragraphs that use a case to explain a rule. Study and learn its structure, which, again, is as follows: rule statement—case name and citation—shorthand title of case—facts and reasoning of court in support of rule. (As noted in the next paragraph, if the explanation/illustration of the rule from the case is sufficiently complex, a summary sentence, restating the rule, can be added at the end of the paragraph.)

While the single RE paragraph to explain a rule (as in the *Smith v. State* example) is common, some in-text illustrations to explain a rule might require multiple paragraphs. For example, you might need one paragraph to provide the relevant facts of the case and a second to provide the court's reasoning in showing how those facts support the rule from the case. On the other hand, some illustrations of the rule can be contained in a parenthetical. (Parentheticals are explained in Chapter Four.) In such instances, the rule and the parenthetical explaining it can be contained in a single sentence or two. And where the explanation of the rule is lengthy or unduly complicated, a concluding sentence at the end of the paragraph can re-state the rule. But again, that re-statement must be of the same rule. If a different rule is stated at the end of the RE paragraph, the explanation is probably imprecise.

Once all of the necessary RE paragraphs have been provided for the reader, the writer can summarize the composite or synthesized rule that results from the separate explanations. That rule should be stated in a separate paragraph. It can begin as follows: "From these cases, the rule is ..." The balance of the sentence (or sentences) will be the composite rule or the synthesized rule, the parts of which have been explained in the separate RE paragraphs.

c. Rule Application: The RA Paragraph

Having completed the RE portion of the predictive paradigm, the memo would then need to provide the actual analysis of the issue, which is what happens in the RA paragraphs. A good way to start this portion of the memo is by stating, clearly and succinctly, the prediction/conclusion you will provide in the analysis to follow. This one-sentence paragraph can start with this wording: "Based on this rule, . . ." followed by the answer to the issue you stated earlier in the memo.[6]

The most important requirement in constructing the RA paragraphs is that the material in them must match what is in the corresponding RE paragraphs. This requirement is met with the **mirror-image approach**, so named because it reflects how the two sections of the memo should look when you subject them to a side-by-side comparison. Consistent use of the mirror-image approach will be of great benefit in crafting the overall analysis in a predictive memo because the approach effectively eliminates extraneous information (spare/unused parts) and tightens the analysis to the exact substantive points that support the prediction you are making. This approach can be easily understood after a little practice with it.

The basic point behind mirror image is that we only explain in our RE paragraphs what we will apply in our RA paragraphs, and we never apply anything in our RA paragraphs that we haven't first explained in our RE paragraphs. Read that last sentence several times. Think about it. Understanding it will make the relationship between RE paragraphs and RA paragraphs much more meaningful.

Now let's see how the mirror-image approach works in constructing the memo, and, specifically, how it directs the crafting of each RA paragraph in the predictive paradigm.

Each RA paragraph should show how the rule from a corresponding RE paragraph applies to the facts of the case you are analyzing. Remember, we apply rules (law) to facts; thus, we are applying the individual rules we explained (paragraph by paragraph) in the RE part of the memo to the facts of our case (paragraph by paragraph) in the RA section. And what the mirror-image approach requires is that every

---

6. Placing another C between the RE and the RA is a technical deviation from the CREAC (or CRERAC) paradigm. Thus, some law offices and professors may not recommend (or want) it as a transitional tool.

detail we included in the RE paragraph of a rule must be referred to in the RA paragraph of the rule.[7]

Therefore, a perfectly appropriate (though not essential[8]) way to start a paragraph that applies a previously explained rule is to restate the rule. As in the RE paragraph, the rule serves as the thesis sentence in the RA paragraph. The rest of the paragraph then shows how the case that explained the rule would be applied to the case at hand (the client's case).

For example, using our little RE paragraph on breaking and entering, in our RA paragraph on that rule, we would need to refer to the specific facts from the *Smith* case that we included in our RE paragraph in setting up the analysis of our facts. So, presumably, we would be showing how the defendant's act of pushing open the side door and sticking his hand into the residence compared favorably or unfavorably to whatever the defendant did in our case. In doing so, we would be creating an analogy or counter-analogy (discussed below). Thus, our application of the rule on breaking and entering would mirror the explanation of the rule we provided from the *Smith* case.

But note the second half of the mirror-image approach: We never apply anything in RA paragraphs that we haven't first explained in corresponding RE paragraphs. Thus, in the RA paragraph on breaking and entering, we would not introduce or refer to a new point from *Smith* (or, even worse, bring in a separate case not included in the explanation of the rule on breaking and entering). In other words, the RA paragraph reflects solely what we indicated about the particular rule in the RE paragraph. If we want to include something else in that RA para-

---

7. Table 2 presents the correct order for each RE and RA paragraph in the CREAC format for predictive memos. Note that all RE paragraphs precede the corresponding RA paragraphs. The separate RA paragraphs state and explain the component parts of the synthesized or composite rule that are then applied in the RA paragraphs. This pattern is not used the C-RAC format for persuasive documents. There, separate parts of a rule are immediately applied in a series of mini-arguments.

8. The RA paragraph can inferentially refer to the rule that was stated in the RE paragraph (as in Table 2). Many attorneys use that approach effectively, but the "safer" approach for beginning law students can be to just re-state the rule.

graph (maybe another point from the *Smith* case or a comparison to another case), we need to go back and include it in the RE paragraph.

The "mirrored" RA paragraph from our previous RE paragraph on *Smith* might then be written in this way:

> Burglary requires the breaking and actual entering of a building or structure. *Smith v. State*, 23 Utopia 587 (1946). In *Smith*, the court held that the defendant, by pushing open an unlatched door and reaching inside, had satisfied the breaking and entering elements. Similarly, in our case, the defendant broke and entered the building when he smashed the window and stuck his hand inside.

Table 2—CREAC Structure Example

<table>
<tr><td colspan="2">(Situation: A Hawaiian counselor defrauded a client for thousands of dollars, and the counselor's employer is sued for negligent hiring. The employer wants to assert privilege over its attorney's advice about the hiring.)</td></tr>
<tr><td>C</td><td>The employer was given "business advice" regarding the hiring of the counselor, and that advice is likely not eligible for privilege because it was not "legal advice."</td></tr>
<tr><td>RE</td><td>The privilege is recognized in the receipt of legal advice, but not in the receipt of business advice. Metzler Contracting Co. LLC v. Stephens, 642 F. Supp. 2d 1192, 1202 (D. Haw. 2009). In Metzler, the defendant asserted privilege over material in business reports. The court concluded that, even if the defendant had been directed by her attorneys to create the reports, they would still not be protected by privilege because they were the result of business advice not involved in the litigation. Id. at 1204.</td></tr>
<tr><td>RE</td><td>A three-factor test is used to determine whether a communication is legal or business advice. Upjohn Co. v. U.S., 449 U.S. 383, 403 (1981). In Upjohn, the court held that the attorney must be advising whether an employee's conduct can bind the employer, must be assessing the legal consequences of specific conduct, or must be formulating legal responses to current or impending litigation.

Based on these rules, the advice given to the employer in our case was not legal advice and is, therefore, not eligible for privilege.</td></tr>
</table>

RA	In *Metzler*, the court did not recognize the privilege where the attorney provided business advice. Similarly, in our case, the privilege will not be recognized where the advice given to the counselor's employee involved the routine business of the employer. Though the employer may have acted at the direction of the attorney in hiring the counselor, the employer was relying on business, not legal, advice.
RA	The three-factor test from *Upjohn* is applicable in our case. The employer claims not to have known in advance about the fraudulent conduct of the counselor. Thus, the attorney could not have been advising whether fraudulent conduct would bind the employer. Further, the employer admitted that the attorney gave hiring advice regarding all potential employees. Thus, the employer was even more likely not assessing the consequences of the specific employee's unknown conduct. Finally, the employer had no idea it would be involved in litigation at the time of the hiring, given the two aforementioned assertions. Therefore, the employer could not have been preparing for litigation.
C	The employer's standard consultation regarding the hiring of an employee whose bad conduct was not known to the employer was likely business advice and, thus, not eligible for privilege.

Note in Table 2 how the RA paragraphs "mirror" the information contained in the corresponding RE paragraphs. The rule has now been stated ("A") exactly as it was explained ("B") and had been applied ("C") exactly as it was explained. Thus, we have applied (C) precisely the rule that we stated ("A").

The mirror-image approach ensures that the RE and RA paragraphs refer directly and precisely to each other. It eliminates extra information that can leave a reader wondering one of two things: Why was I told this point about the rule (referring to material in the RE paragraph that isn't used in the RA paragraph)? Or, where did this point come from (concerning references in the RA paragraph that weren't introduced/covered in the RE paragraph)?

The other benefit of the mirror-image approach is that it tightens the analysis, and it does so in two ways. First, it makes the identification and explanation of the rule much more precise than it would otherwise be. We have already seen that if a rule is not stated precisely, it will be difficult to explain it clearly, but if that precisely stated rule isn't explained with precision, it won't be meaningful when it is applied to the facts in the RA component of the paradigm. And second, the mirror-image approach makes the application of the rule that much more compelling than it would otherwise be because the reader can clearly track the rule's application from its prior explanation (in the RE paragraph).

The actual structure of the RA paragraphs also warrants considerable attention. Just as the structure of the typical RE paragraph follows a set pattern (rule statement—case and citation—description of rule, with case illustration where appropriate), so will the RA paragraph have a basic structure, albeit one that is less rigid. When in doubt, start with the rule statement that identifies the rule you are going to be applying. Then follow it with the citation for the rule. Thereafter, summarize the case illustration provided in the corresponding RE paragraph (again, using the mirror-image approach). But what will make this paragraph an RA paragraph will be your application of whatever you indicate about the rule to the facts of your case. Remember, in all you do analytically, you are applying law (rules) to facts. A concluding sentence may then be helpful, especially if you have shown an analogy or counter-analogy or have made a policy argument.

And remember that a single RA paragraph may be better presented as multiple paragraphs in which you show how the application of a rule supports your prediction. (Review the ten rules for paragraph construction at the beginning of this chapter.)

d. The Methods of Legal Reasoning

With this understanding of the basic approach in constructing the RA paragraphs, several different methods of reasoning can be employed. Each makes use of the authority for the rule in a variety of ways. Four principal methods of legal reasoning exist.

Inductive reasoning by analogy (or *counter-analogy*) is probably the most commonly used method of legal reasoning. It works by directly comparing (or contrasting) the facts of a case that provides a rule that would resolve the issue if it were applicable.[9] If the facts are sufficiently

9. In this sense, "applicable" and "applied" are two distinct concepts. "Applicable" indicates that a particular rule controls the resolution of the specific issue being ad-

similar, then by inductive reasoning, the result should be the same. Simply stated, analogies work by this logic: If the facts from a prior case dealing with the same issue can be shown to be similar to facts in the case you are analyzing, then the rule from that prior case should resolve your issue.

Analogical reasoning flows from the holy grail of all legal research (discussed more fully in Chapter Seven), which is to find the perfect case, the one that is exactly the same as your case and thereby fully resolves your issue. Of course, as most lawyers will tell you, that perfect case doesn't exist (or if it does, you won't be asked to draft a legal memo on the issue, because the answer is obvious). So, instead, we try to show that the case is "sufficiently similar," and we do so by creating an analogy.

Analogical reasoning is an effective form of reasoning in legal documents because our legal system is built around the Rule of Law (discussed more fully in Chapter Two) and relies heavily on precedent (which often exists in the form of prior cases). So it is only natural for lawyers to argue that a prior case controls the issue in their case by showing the similarity of the cases, in essence saying, "if the court held this way when the facts were so similar to ours, precedent requires that it hold that way now."

Good analogical reasoning works very well with the mirror-image approach. In the RE paragraph, we'd identify the exact facts that are similar to those in our case. Then, in the RA paragraph, we'd compare those facts to the facts of our case, thereby showing the analogy. Thus, the two paragraphs would mirror each other, with each fact mentioned in the RE paragraph referred to by comparison in the RA paragraph.

Of course, there is more in analogical reasoning than just comparing the facts favorably. Often, a potentially favorable case will have a

---

dressed. "Applied" refers to the process of determining whether a particular rule is controlling on the specific issue being addressed. Thus, we "apply" a rule to determine if it is "applicable." The process of "applying" a rule can include noting an analogy or counter-analogy that will show that the rule is or is not "applicable." In analogical and counter-analogical reasoning, the writer is comparing the current facts to that of a previous case in which the rule was actually applied in order to point out similarities and differences. These similarities and differences will, in turn, affect whether the rule is "applicable."

fact that is not a fit for your case. That fact can't be ignored because to do so makes the analogy suspect. So, instead, the facts that don't compare favorably must be shown to be insignificant or irrelevant with regard to the rule. Dealing with such a fact in the RA paragraph will, of course, require that it be covered in the RE paragraph as well. (Always think mirror-image.) But the result will still be a tightly crafted memo because all the information provided in the RE paragraph will be useful in the RA paragraph.

Once the factual comparisons have been made, and the non-analogous facts have been shown to be irrelevant, the analogy must be closed (completed). To do so, the writer might want to indicate the basis for the rule that is being applied (it would also be noted in the RE paragraph) and then conclude with a sentence that reads something like this: "Because of the similarity in the facts from the *Smith* case and because *Smith* dealt with the same issue we face here, the rule from *Smith* should be applicable to resolve the issue in our case."

Analogies are great when they work in your favor (as when they provide the result your client needs or support the prediction you are making on your issue). But frequently the case you find that appears similar on its facts may work contrary to your client's needs or to the prediction you are making on the issue. In those instances, counter-analogical reasoning will be your friend. In counter-analogical reasoning, we distinguish key facts from a prior case and show that those different facts justify concluding that the rule from the prior case is inapplicable (or that the similar looking facts are less significant than the dissimilar facts). In other words, counter-analogical reasoning uses the same basic technique (comparing the facts) but with a different goal in mind.

Lawyers will often speak of finding ways to distinguish a case, which is another way of saying they are counter-analogizing to the case to avoid its applicability on the issue they are arguing.[10] When a case can

---

10. Counter-analogical reasoning is one of the tools that lawyers employ every day. When confronted with a precedential case that is averse to a client, a lawyer "can argue that while the precedent case does stand for the legal proposition for which it has been cited, the case at bar is different; that is, the cases are factually distinguishable." Paul M. Perell, *Stare decisis and techniques of legal reasoning and legal argument*,

be distinguished, the court is not required to use the rule from it. This kind of reasoning is not absolutely controlling (inductive reasoning never is), but it may be the best reasoning available to avoid the rule from a case that otherwise deals with the same issue.

Deductive reasoning in the direct application of a rule is the most common form of reasoning when a rule is clearly relevant to the facts of the case you are assigned. Lawyers refer to this type of reasoning as "rule-based reasoning," because we apply the rule directly without concern for the facts of a case that applied it in the past. Rule-based reasoning is the most common form of reasoning on law school essay exams, where IRAC (Issue-Rule-Analysis-Conclusion) is the preferred organizational approach.

In using rule-based reasoning, the RE paragraphs will normally be short, often without much reference to the facts of a case. (Under the mirror-image approach, we wouldn't need the facts of a case for the corresponding RA paragraph, so we wouldn't include them in the RE paragraph.) When a rule is directly on point for a pending case, the issue the rule pertains to will be immediately resolved by application of the rule.

Think about how most law school essay exams are structured. The facts in the fact pattern give rise to issues. Students are graded in part on their ability to identify the issues. Then they are expected to identify relevant rules that might resolve those issues. Once those rules are recognized, they are applied directly to the facts that gave rise to the issue to reach a conclusion (I-R-A-C). Rule-based reasoning involves the same process.

The beauty of rule-based reasoning is that if the rule is directly on point for the issue being analyzed, it will resolve the issue. Through deductive reasoning, the applicable rule controls the result. The downside of rule-based reasoning, however, is that it rarely resolves the kind of complex issues that are the focus of most legal documents. Again, to repeat the earlier point, if the issue is so easily resolved (by the direct application of a single rule), it probably isn't an issue that merits a full

---

BEST GUIDE TO CANADIAN LEGAL RESEARCH (1987), http://legalresearch.org/writing-analysis/stare-decisis-techniques/.

legal memo or brief. Instead, rule-based reasoning is often used for preliminary issues (issues that must be covered to get to the more significant issues for which no single rule is going to be directly applicable).

However, rule-based reasoning is not so simple when divining the rule itself requires a complex calculus. Consider again the example (from Chapter Two) of the will that was witnessed by two people, only one of whom signed the will. Rule-based reasoning worked there when the rule clearly existed, perhaps in the form of a statute providing that only one witness's signature was required for a will to be valid. If, however, no such statute or other manifestation of a clearly controlling rule existed, the memo/brief writer may have needed to craft a synthesized rule from a series of cases that required several RE paragraphs. The end result of that synthesized rule might then permit a direct application of the rule (rule-based reasoning), but the actual analytic work to get to that rule might involve consideration of a number of cases that address witnesses and signatories to documents. In that instance, the attorney's heavy lifting would be in the RE part of the memo, where the actual rule to be applied would be developed/synthesized. The RA paragraphs would then simply apply the newly synthesized rule.

In its simplest form, lawyers use rule-based reasoning to establish preliminary points in a memo or brief. If a rule is directly on point and immediately resolves an issue, rule-based reasoning is conclusive. For that reason, where it is available as a form of legal reasoning, rule-based reasoning is preferred. And, as noted, it will most frequently be preferred on law school essay exams.

Policy- and rationale-based reasoning both use the same basic approach to resolve issues or to suggest preferred resolutions of issues. With both, the reasoning behind the authority that provides the rule forms the basis for the application of the rule.

These forms of legal reasoning require the writer to understand the rationale for the rule. With rules that come from cases, that rationale will be contained in the court's opinion. In most instances, the way to identify that rationale is to glean the basis for the court's holding on the issue it was considering. A court's rationale can be expressly stated, or it can be implied. Well-crafted opinions will make the rationale for the court's holding evident, but even the best-written opinions might make the reader work to grasp the underlying rationale for the holding.

And in some instances, a court's opinion will leave much to be desired with respect to the basis for the holding. You can gain a good sense of that kind of a problem from reading dissenting opinions, which often attack or criticize faulty reasoning or the lack of a coherent rationale for a holding by the majority in a case.[11]

When a court's rationale is either not evident or is poorly expressed, good lawyers take advantage of the ambiguity or lack of clarity. In such instances, the memo/brief writer can posit alternative reasoning for the court's holding and from those alternatives suggest differing analyses or arguments on an issue in the writer's case. Assume, for example, in the murder hypothetical from Chapter Two, that a court had considered the issue of malice in the shooting death of the victim by the defendant and had held, without providing reasoning, that the shooting was a malicious act.[12] A memo/brief writer in that instance would be able to posit that the rationale for the holding in the case (that the act of shooting the victim constituted malice) was that some acts are so grossly abhorrent as to be malicious as a matter of law. The RE paragraph of that rule would have to explain the court's lack of precision in its holding, but that lack of precision could then be asserted by the writer to be the basis for concluding broadly as to the rationale for the holding.

Of course, most courts will at least indicate some basis for their holdings, but many will leave the rationale ambiguous, and the best

---

11. *See, e.g.*, Justice Stevens's dissenting opinion in *District of Columbia v. Heller*, 554 U.S. 570, 639 (2008). Justice Scalia wrote the majority opinion that held that the Second Amendment of the Constitution confers the individual right to keep and bear arms. The Court overturned a statute banning the registration of handguns in the District of Columbia. In his dissent, Justice Stevens attacked the reasoning of the majority, stating that the "Court stakes its holding on a strained and unpersuasive reading of the Amendment's text."

12. In the hypo from Chapter 2, the victim (V) was shot and killed by either D or T. Which of the two shot V is a factual issue. The legal issue is whether the person who shot V committed murder. Murder is an act done with malice that takes the life of another. Thus, whether the person who shot V murdered him depends on the legal definition of malice, making the murder question a legal, not a factual, issue.

attorneys gain strength from the ambiguities in the law.[13] In fact, without some degree of ambiguity most legal reasoning would be unnecessary, as computers could just as easily resolve issues.[14] It is in making arguments or providing analyses on points of law that are uncertain or ambiguous where lawyers justify their existence (and win cases).

The rationale for a rule can be used to assert the result in "next case" scenarios.[15] Since specific issues only arise from specific facts (see Chapter Two), any change in a material fact can result in a new issue, which may be a "next case" if that particular issue hasn't been addressed before.[16] And when an issue hasn't been considered definitively by prior case law or by statute, it may lend itself to rationale-based reasoning. The RE paragraphs for this type of reasoning will identify the rationale for a court's decision in a similar case (a case dealing with a similar issue). Then, in the corresponding RA paragraphs, the writer will apply

---

13. "The law is full of conundrums and ambiguities.... If you can accept the interplay between those two statements without being distressed at the inherent fuzziness, then you will do well in studying the law. The law is inherently fuzzy in order to be flexible. Although judges attempt to interpret laws that are clear, there is almost always a set of circumstances where applying the rule would be unjust. Consequently, some latitude exists in the law in order to reach a just result." *Four Strategies to Think Like a Lawyer*, LAWNERDS.COM (2013), http://www.lawnerds.com/guide/mind.html#Acceptambiguity.

14. Computers have not replaced lawyers because computer technology cannot yet solve problems with rules that don't exist. It is the lawyer's ability to take the ambiguity in the law and write a persuasive argument that the court adopts, thus creating a new rule, that makes the lawyer's work so invaluable. *See* Anya Kamenetz, *The Four Things People Can Still do Better Than Computers*, FAST COMPANY (July 19, 2013), http://www.fastcompany.com/3014448/the-four-things-people-can-still-do-better-than-computers.

15. The "next case" is a future case that resolves an issue by completing another part of the legal jigsaw puzzle with a new rule. In this sense, a "next case" arises from a change in the facts from previous cases on the same basic issue.

16. Another way that lawyers can use the term "next case" is essentially a case of first impression for a court where there is no precedent that addresses the particular legal or factual issue, thus requiring the court to fashion a rule without the benefit of controlling precedent. Stefanie A. Lindquist and Frank B. Cross, *Article: Empirically Testing Dworkin's Chain Novel Theory: Studying the Path of Precedent*, 80 N.Y.U. L. REV. 1156, 1179 (Oct. 2005). The term "next case" thus can refer either to a new case in which the court applies a rule from a previous case with slightly different facts, or to a case of first impression in which the court has to fashion an entirely new rule for a somewhat different issue. In both instances, the court will create a new piece of the jigsaw puzzle.

that rationale to the issue at hand, thereby providing the basis for the writer's conclusion on the issue.

Policy-based reasoning uses the same approach, but there the rationale is expressed in terms of the legal efficacy or social utility of the rule. Some courts will go to great lengths to justify their holdings in this way. For example, a court might hold that malice needs to be construed broadly to eliminate instances where a defendant could avoid a murder conviction just by showing a lack of specific intent. The court might then go on to point out the social utility of a broad malice rule as a means of reducing instances of violent crime or of enhancing the requisite punishment for those crimes.

Secondary authority can also be a basis for policy-based reasoning. For example, law review articles, or even op-ed columns in newspapers, can provide policy perspectives on issues that come up in litigation. Those articles and columns can be cited for support of a rule that is policy-based. Often, when a "next case" issue is pending, policy-based reasoning can be the most effective way of pushing the envelope and creating new law (or a new piece of the jigsaw puzzle).[17] Again, thinking of ways to support analyses and arguments with any form of authority makes good lawyering better.

So, the RE paragraphs for policy-based reasoning will identify the policy behind a rule, and the RA paragraphs will apply that policy to

---

17. An excellent example of the efficient use of policy can be found in cases that involve new technology. Professor Orin Kerr, an expert on Fourth Amendment jurisprudence, states that courts are "highly attuned" to how the use of technology upsets the balance of police power. So courts "address the role of the Fourth Amendment in regulating these new technologies with a careful eye to retaining the prior balance." Orin S. Kerr, *An Equilibrium-Adjustment Theory of the Fourth Amendment*, 125 HARV. L. REV. 476, 501 (2011). For example, in a monumental Supreme Court decision from 2014, the Court considered whether police officers could search a cell phone without a warrant after they seize the phone from a person they arrest. The Court held that warrantless searches of cell phones violate the Fourth Amendment based on the policy that cell phones are so pervasive in society that almost every person carries one. A cell phone has such immense storage capacity, that allowing the government to search cell phones without a warrant gives the government access to a myriad of highly personal information, even more personal information than is contained in someone's home. Thus, in order to protect privacy interests, the Court declined to extend a warrant exception to cell phones seized incident to an arrest. *Riley v. California*, 573 U.S. 373 (2014).

the pending issue. But beware of the unsupported policy analysis. The tendency for law students (and for some lawyers as well) is to attempt a policy argument based on the writer's personal opinion. The classic example is the first-year student who dives into a controversial legal issue with this kind of statement: "I don't think the rule should be such and such because society will be ill-served by it."

The fundamental problem with that kind of statement is that it isn't lawyer-like. And the reason it isn't lawyer-like is that it isn't based on authority.[18] The most blunt (and obnoxious) way some professors make this point, hopefully without embarrassing a specific student, is by saying, "We don't care what you think, unless you support it with authority."[19] Another way to call out this kind of reasoning, in perhaps a slightly less insulting manner, is to say, "Don't sound like a lay person; it isn't what you came to law school to be."

The point is that policy-based reasoning can be very effective, but it has to be based on what someone has said in a citable document.[20] And, as should be obvious, policy-based reasoning needs to be kept in perspective. Rarely will a policy-based analysis or argument overcome a clearly stated rule of mandatory authority to the contrary. Thus, it is inappropriate (except perhaps in the most uncharted of "next cases") to base an argument or analysis solely on an asserted policy from a

---

18. As explained fully in Chapter Two, in a broad sense, "legal authority" refers to anything that a court or lawyer could cite as a basis for a legal argument, such as a law review article, a case, a statute, or even a newspaper editorial. Legal authority can either be persuasive or mandatory, depending on the source. For example, a California Supreme Court case is mandatory authority, meaning it is binding on lower courts in California, and they must follow it. A treatise on tort law is a persuasive authority, meaning it is not binding and the courts do not have to follow it. Some professors or practicing lawyers may refer to authority only if it is primary authority (encompassing cases or statutes or agency regulations). But secondary authority (writings that only propose or suggest rules, such as law review articles and op-ed columns) is correctly classified as persuasive by all attorneys.

19. Note that even the best legal authority, such as a decision from the highest court in a state or even the Supreme Court, may have flaws. For example, the court may have erred in its legal reasoning or completely failed to address a pending legal issue. This reality highlights the importance of careful reading and of "Shepardizing" or "Key Citing" cases to ensure that all cited authorities are still "good law."

20. Legal citations and the types of documents that need to be cited are discussed in Chapter Seven.

secondary authority. Instead, the far better use of the policy would be to support an analogical or rule-based analysis.

Rationale-based reasoning and policy-based reasoning are added tools for the writer of legal documents. They serve to support well-constructed analogies or counter-analogies and straight rule-based reasoning. And in "next case" scenarios, they can make the critical difference in creating new law.

e. The CREAC Conclusions

The CREAC Cs (the Conclusions) are, of course, what the RE and RA paragraphs support. The first of the Cs can be stated with a heading (discussed in Chapter Four) or with a strong opening thesis sentence. (And consider, as suggested above in Table 2, the option of also indicating the conclusion/prediction in a predictive memo at the beginning of the RA section.) The second C should follow the last RA paragraph. It should be a separate paragraph that may consist of just a single sentence that re-states the first C. (Some writers, space permitting, will re-state their composite or synthesized rule here as well.)

The rest of the traditional predictive memo will include a section that identifies the **issue** addressed in the memo (sometimes called the **Question Presented** section); the **facts** that give rise to the issue—and that are used to resolve the issue (usually referred to as the **Statement of the Facts**); and a **conclusion** (usually in the last section of the memo, appropriately called **Conclusion**), which summarizes the reasoning (the RE-RA paradigm) contained in the body of the memo.[21] Some formats also include a **Short** or **Brief Answer** section in which the analysis of the issue is introduced (usually with an emphasis on the rules that will be considered and applied to resolve the identified issue).

Some law firms and adminstrative agencies use less formal structures for their legal memos, but they all, in one way or another, rely on the basic CREAC paradigm for the presentation of the analysis of the

---

21. The small "c" conclusion at the end of CREAC refers to the single sentence paragraph at the end of a CREAC analysis that summarizes the predictive conclusion. The Big "C" Conclusion refers to the section of the full memo that summarizes the entire Analysis (or Discussion) section. It is the last separate section in the full predictive memo.

issues under review. And the heart of that paradigm will always turn on the identification, explanation, and application of rules.

2. C-RAC

The paradigm for persuasive documents is missing an E. (Otherwise, it is indistinguishable as an acronym from CREAC.) While that missing letter could be significant, it is less so than might appear to be the case. Let's think about what is happening in the two types of documents.

In a predictive memo, the writer is making a prediction on an issue (or multiple issues) in a specific case. The expectation is that the writer has become an expert on the substantive law for that issue (or issues) and is now providing the analysis that supports the prediction that results from that expertise. How does that approach differ from the persuasive document? In a persuasive document, the writer is asserting that a specific result is mandated on a certain issue (or issues). But, again, the expectation is still that the writer has become an expert on the relevant substantive law and is now providing arguments that support the result the writer is asserting.

In both types of documents, the writer's substantive expertise is used to support a resolution of an issue (or issues). One resolution is a prediction; the other is an assertion. But both require legal reasoning supported by the application of rules that come from recognized authority. What, then, is the real difference in the way the two documents should be written?

The answer is that very little difference exists between the two approaches. The persuasive acronym stands for Conclusion-Rule-Analysis-Conclusion, which suggests that the identified rule doesn't need to be explained (the missing E). But, as we've seen, rules only need explanations in CREAC to the extent necessary to allow them to be applied meaningfully. The mirror-image approach eliminates all unnecessary information about the rule (and the case that it came from).

In the persuasive paradigm, the mirror-image approach is also the most effective way to use identified rules. If a particular rule originates in a specific case, we use the case to make the argument regarding the rule (through any of the four methods of reasoning discussed above).

Thus, a rule that is derived from a case will apply the rule as it was explained (or illustrated) in that case, which is the same use we make of the case that gave rise to the rule in our predictive document. Sometimes a rule won't need a case illustration to explain it (most commonly in rule-based reasoning). In those instances, any explanation of the rule will be minimal; similarly, the explanation of such a rule in a predictive document will also be minimal. But when we are going to make an argument based on how a rule was used in a prior case, we still need a case illustration in a persuasive document. In other words, C-RAC assumes the rule will be explained, when doing so is necessary, just as CREAC minimizes the need for the rule to be explained when doing so is unnecessary. So, if the instances of rule explanation in C-RAC are essentially the same as the instances of rule explanation in CREAC, how does C-RAC differ from CREAC?

One primary difference exists in the two paradigms: In the persuasive paradigm, the rules are applied immediately after they have been stated (and explained), instead of having a separate section of the analysis devoted to the rule explanations of each part of a composite rule or of each aspect of a synthesized rule. In the persuasive document, each rule is immediately followed by its application.[22] Thus the relevance of any explanation of a rule will be immediately apparent in the application of that rule.

Consider an example where a defendant enters into a house that was on the market for sale during an open-house sales event and then steals various valuable items from the house. The owners were still living in the house at the time of the theft. An argument made in straight RA fashion about whether the defendant is guilty of burglary might look something like this:

> A person is guilty of burglary if he enters a dwelling house with the intent to commit grand larceny or any other felony. Cal. Penal Code § 459. A person enters a house or structure if he puts any part of his body into it, even just a finger or a hand. *People v. Allison*, 200 Cal. 404, 408 (1927). In *Allison*, the court held that the defendants entered an empty train car

22. The immediate application of the rule that has been stated constitutes the A part of the paradigm (the analysis).

> when they jumped in to sleep in the train car for a night. *Id.* Here, the element of "entry" is satisfied because defendant walked into the home during the open-house sales event.
>
> An "inhabited dwelling house" is a structure where people normally live, and courts look to factors like whether the owner sleeps there, whether the owner keeps personal belongings there, and whether that person intends to continue living there when courts determine whether the house is an "inhabited dwelling house." *People v. Tessman*, 168 Cal. Rptr. 3d 29, 32 (2014). In *Tessman*, the owner of a home was still sleeping in her home and kept her belongings there, even though her home was open to the public for sale when Defendant entered and stole the owner's jewelry. The court held that the house was an "inhabited dwelling house" because it was being used for dwelling purposes at the time of the burglary. *Id.* The case at issue is exactly the same as *Tessman* because, just as in *Tessman*, the victim in the instant case was still living in her home and keeping her belongings there. Thus, the house the defendant burglarized constituted an "inhabited dwelling house."

Most lawyers are more comfortable with this approach. They set out to make an argument on an issue by breaking up the argument into points that they need to make. The totality of those separate points will then constitute the full argument. The burglary example is a simple illustration of how this approach works. The various elements of the crime have to be established to show the defendant committed a burglary. Thus, the writer uses separate rules (all part of the composite rule on burglary) to establish the existence of each element.

More complicated issues will require more extensive explanations of the separate rules, but they will still be directly applied to the facts of the pending case. Thus, if the issue that is argued in a persuasive brief is probable cause, the persuasive writer will still develop the synthesized rule on probable cause from the cases relevant to that issue. And the application of that synthesized rule will still use the separate cases to establish the existence of probable cause in the pending case. But in a persuasive brief, those cases would be applied directly after each is explained, instead of waiting until all of them have been explained as in the predictive document.

Perhaps the best way to understand the difference between the two paradigms is to think of the analysis of an issue in a predictive memo as consisting of two sections—Rule Explanation and Rule Application—and to think of the argument of an issue in a persuasive memo as consisting of only Rule Application, but with lots of rule application paragraphs. In other words, CREAC offers an overall analysis that divides the treatment of the rules into one section where they are explained and one where they are applied, while C-RAC makes lots of mini-arguments (a succession of RA paragraphs) that, taken together, constitute the argument on a particular issue. And those mini-arguments in the persuasive document are each set up as RA paragraphs. So, just as you have RA paragraphs in a predictive memo, you will also have RA paragraphs in a persuasive brief. And they will essentially look and read the same because the rules that are being applied will be explained to the extent necessary (and only to the extent necessary) to make the specific point that needs to be made.

Think about how you organize an argument you will be making in a debate (or even with a friend in a social setting). You'll have an overall point you'll want to make (the ultimate issue in the debate). To establish the validity of your position, you'll need to make a number of points. For each point, you will have an argument (a mini-argument). When combined, these mini-arguments will result in an "ergo" (Latin for "therefore").

Getting to your ergo is what C-RAC is intended to facilitate. We make each mini-argument by using the RA paragraphing for each point in the overall argument. The end result, if you have thought through your full argument and have supported it thoroughly with authoritative rules, will be the ergo that will win the case for your client (or, at least, provide the best chance to win).

So, to clarify the difference between the two paradigms, consider how the acronyms work. As we've seen, CREAC is really CRERAC, with a full RE section (with each rule separately stated and explained) corresponding to a full RA section (where all of the rules are applied in the order they were explained). And C-RAC is really C-RA-RA-RA- . . . C, with mini-RA paragraphs to establish each separate point in the overall argument that resolves the issue.

The C-RAC "Cs" are much the same as the CREAC "Cs." They bookend the arguments with each stating the bottom-line argument that is being made by all of those RA paragraphs. In most persuasive documents the main arguments and sub-arguments will be designated with headings (discussed in Chapter Four). These can and should serve as the opening Cs. The closing Cs should summarize the entire thrust of the RA paragraphs and should be a mere restatement of the opening C.

The typical structure of a persuasive brief (each court will have its own required format) consists of the **issue** or **issues** argued in the brief (usually called the **Questions Presented** or **Issue Questions**), the **facts** that give rise to the issue (**The Facts** or **Statement of the Facts**), the **argument** (usually labelled as **Argument**), and the **conclusion** the writer wants the reader to reach (**Conclusion**), which can be a mere restatement of the point headings.

One absolute no-no exists for the Conclusion section in a persuasive brief: It must never contain anything not covered in the body of the brief. No new thoughts or supplemental points should ever appear in that last part of the brief. If it is important enough to include there, it needs to be argued in the **Argument** section, which, of course, is where (and only where) the C-RAC paradigm should appear in the brief.[23]

Some courts will require additional sections for a full brief. Those may include a **Statement of the Case** (reviewing the procedural history of the case), a **Summary of the Argument** (providing an overview of the most important points in the Argument section), a **Table of Contents**, and a **Table of Authorities** (listing all of the sources of rules that are cited in the brief).

---

23. The same prohibition exists for the Conclusion section in a predictive memo: Never include anything in the Conclusion not covered in the Discussion section of the memo.

Chapter Summary

Paragraphs are to reading what breathing is to exercising. As a general rule, short paragraphs are better than long paragraphs, especially in complex legal documents that require the reader to do considerable heavy lifting. To keep paragraphs from becoming uncomfortably long, new guidelines must be used for the construction of paragraphs in legal documents.

The two basic types of legal documents (predictive memos and persuasive briefs) use strikingly similar constructive paradigms. CREAC is the paradigm for predictive memos. It emphasizes the explanation of a rule in all its component parts before the rule is applied to the facts of the pending case. C-RAC is the paradigm for persuasive briefs. It emphasizes the mini-arguments that are made to construct a full argument on an issue. But it also uses rules and explains them when necessary to establish the validity of each of the mini-arguments.

Rules can be simple, composite, or synthesized. Simple rules can usually be explained with single illustrations from cases. In essence, the description of the case explains the rule. Composite rules consist of component parts, each of which might need its own explanation and illustration. Synthesized rules are developed from the reading of a number of cases or other authorities, with no single one of them providing the ultimate rule that represents the amalgam of all of the cases or authorities. Each of them also needs a separate explanation/illustration.

Each rule must be stated precisely so that it exactly conforms to the explanation of the rule. And each explanation must conform to the application of the rule to the pending case. So we think of the formula A=B=C, where A is the rule statement, B is the rule explanation, and C is the rule application. And we craft our explanations so that they only offer illustrations of the rule we have stated (no spare parts) and we analyze our case be applying exactly what we have explained (no unused parts).

Putting that formula into the written document is best realized by the mirror-image approach, wherein the construction of the paragraphs that explain the rules mirrors the paragraphs that apply those rules. Thus, whatever is explained is applied, and everything that is applied has first been explained. This mirror-image approach will ensure that the reader of the document is never reading anything extraneous to the analysis or argument (again, no spare parts, no missing parts). This approach will eliminate full case briefs in favor of tailored case illustrations.

Four basic types or methods of legal reasoning are commonly employed in predictive analyses and persuasive arguments. Reasoning by analogy and counter-analogy is inductive. It requires drawing tight comparisons (for analogies) or making careful distinctions (counter-analogies) between the facts of the cases. Doing so will suggest either the applicability (analogy) or inapplicability (counter-analogy) of a rule from a prior case.

Rule-based reasoning is deductive and will be best employed when a rule is directly applicable to a case without the need for a detailed explanation or case illustration. The explanation of synthesized rules can be accomplished through rule-based reasoning, but the explanation of each part of the synthesized rule will involve a series of rule explanation paragraphs. The resulting application of the synthesized rule will then be more straightforward.

Policy- and rationale-based reasoning both apply the reasoning behind a rule, often requiring inferences from a court opinion or series of opinions. Such inferences are necessary when the law is ambiguous or when the court's opinion is unclear. The best attorneys gain strength from the ambiguities in the law.

The rationale for a rule or the policy behind a rule can provide the basis for the resolution of "next cases," which are cases for which jigsaw puzzle pieces in The Law do not yet exist. A "next case" can arise from any new fact pattern regarding a previously considered issue since every change in a material fact can result in a new issue and a "next case."

Policy-based reasoning can be most useful in creating new law (or new pieces of the jigsaw puzzle). But all policy-based reasoning (as with all forms of legal reasoning) must be based on (or flow from) existing authority. Good lawyers never argue based on their own opinions or views of how an issue should be resolved. They only argue based on authority. Otherwise, they sound like a lay person, which is not what they went to law school to be.

CREAC is the heart of the predictive memo's Discussion section (where the actual analysis is presented). Other sections in the traditional predictive memo are the Issue Statement, the Short or Brief Answer, the Statement of the Facts, and the Conclusion. C-RAC is the heart of the persuasive brief's Argument section. Other sections in a typical brief are the Questions Presented, the Facts, and the Conclusion.

CREAC and C-RAC are far more similar than they are different. One way to understand the structural differences between the two is to think of CREAC as CRERAC (Conclusion-Rule Explanation-Rule Application-Conclusion, and of C-RAC as C-RA-RA-RA- … C (Conclusion-Rule-Application for each mini-rule in the overall argument-Conclusion). In the end, both paradigms have this basic requirement in common: They apply law (rules) to facts.

Chapter Four

Avoiding Structural and Organizational Confusion in a Legal Document

A. Introduction

B. Headings

C. Umbrella Paragraphs

D. Organizational Devices

E. Organizational Impediments

A. Introduction

Many legal documents are organizationally complex. They consist of separate parts (with sections for issue identification, factual details, and the analyses or arguments that address and resolve the identified issues) that provide a degree of complexity. But within the main body of the documents (the Discussion or Analysis section in a predictive memo, the Argument section in a legal brief), points are frequently made in separate and distinct presentations (the CREAC and C-RAC paradigms discussed in Chapter Three). The result can present the reader of a particular document with something looking more like a maze than a map.

And while the document itself will often deal with complex and even arcane subject matter, understanding how the substance is presented shouldn't be a challenge for the reader. Legal writers use specific tools to clarify most of the structural and organizational complexity.

Headings are the most basic of tools to establish the logical flow of a substantive presentation. In legal documents they are presented in numerical sequence using outline Roman numerals, upper and lower case letters, and Arabic numerals (and Romanettes, if necessary). **Umbrella paragraphs** are also used to provide guidance and direction.

Within the text that comprises the substantive analysis or argument a legal writer is presenting or making, **transitions** (in the form of words, phrases, sentences, or even paragraphs) serve to make the flow of the analysis or argument smooth. And within each substantive point, **non sequiturs**, **irrelevancy**, and **redundancy** should be avoided to keep the reader attuned to the thrust of the writer's analysis or argument.

Finally, the use of **parentheticals** and **signals** can allow for the presentation of necessary information without causing the reader to lose the intended flow of the substantive analysis or argument.

Each of these tools helps the reader of the document by clarifying the organization intended by the writer and by limiting the instances where a reader might lose the flow of the writer's presentation. In the end, the structure and organization of the document should be readily apparent, so that the only hard work required of the reader is to grasp the highly sophisticated or deeply researched analyses or arguments the writer has provided.

B. Headings

Once an issue has been identified as the focus of a legal document,[1] multiple analyses will often address the issue. Legal issues (at least those that require the detailed analyses that comprise most legal documents) tend to require a series of analytical points. Some of these points are sub-sets of a larger point, while others are separate and distinct points.

To maintain coherence in the presentation of these various points, legal writers use headings that serve as signposts for the specific points that will be presented in a particular part of an overall analysis or argu-

1. Many legal documents analyze multiple issues, which in turn may have multiple sub-section analyses.

ment. And when sub-points must be made to support a main point, subordinate headings are used to identify them. So we refer to Point Headings, which identify a main point in an analysis, and Sub-Headings, which identify points that, taken together, comprise or establish a main point.

These headings are designated by numbers and letters that reflect the way the points are organized and how each of them relates to the others in the legal document. The designation follows the standard form of outline denomination, starting with upper-case Roman numerals.[2] Thus, each main point in the document will be designated with a Roman numeral, with the first one noted with the numeral I (upper-case i), the second with II (upper-case ii), and the third with III (uppercase iii). That sequence would continue (IV, V, VI …) in the event more identified main issues are being considered in the document.

And when sub-points exist for a main point, they are first designated with upper-case letters (A, B, C …). If those sub-points are further divided, they are designated with Arabic (common) numerals (1, 2, 3 …). Further divisions then use lower case letters (a, b, c …) and Romanettes (i, ii, iii, iv …). (Any division of points below the lower-case Romans would be exceedingly rare, even in the most intricately presented legal analysis. If such a minute division were necessary, those points would be noted with bullets.)

Sub-headings are common in legal documents because most analyses consist of basic points that must be developed with sub-points. But since no single point can be divided into less than two sub-points, it is never appropriate to have a single sub-heading under a point heading. In other words, you can't have an "A" without a "B" or a "1" without a "2" or an "a" without a "b" (or "i" without "ii").[3]

---

2. An alternative method of "heading numbering" uses only numbers (*e.g.*, 1.1, 1.2, 1.3 … 2.1.1, 2.1.2, 2.1.3).

3. If a brief or memorandum consists of only one main point, meaning the writer only needs one point heading, then no Roman numeral would be used to designate that point. For example, if the only issue in a persuasive brief is that a motion for summary judgment should be denied because there are issues of material fact, the writer would not need to designate that heading with a Roman numeral.

The various levels of headings that will then exist in a document will each have a separate method of presentation. For example, the point headings might all appear in bold (or in upper-case lettering or with the first letter of each word in upper-case). And they might not be indented at all from the left margin. In whatever format the point headings appear, the first level of sub-headings will have a different appearance (perhaps italicized but not in bold, for example). And they might be indented from the left margin.

The particular means by which the various levels of headings are presented in a legal document are determined by the writer, with only one basic rule that is inviolate: The methods used for each level of headings must be consistent throughout the document. The basic structure for the headings in a particular legal document might be denominated as depicted in Table One, "Basic Structure for Document Headings" which appears below.

In Table One, the writer has identified two major points: Point Headings I and II. The first major point consists of two sub-points: IA and IB. Sub-point 1B consists of two sub-sub-points: IA1 and IA2. And each of those contain mini points (IB1a, IB1b, IB2a, and IB2b). The writer has further divided IB2b with the rare requirement for Romanettes i and ii.

The second major point consists of three sub-points: IIA, IIB and IIC. IIB includes sub-points IIB1 and IIB2, and IIB2 contains mini points: IIB2a, and IB2b.

Table One—Basic Structure for Document Headings

I. POINT HEADING ONE.

Umbrella Paragraph (setting out "A" and "B")

A. First Sub-Heading.

Umbrella Paragraph (setting out "1" and 2")

1. First Sub-Sub-Heading.*

2. Second Sub-Sub-Heading.*

B. Second Sub-Heading.

Umbrella Paragraph (setting out "1" and "2")

1. First Sub-Sub-Heading.

    Umbrella Paragraph (setting out "a" and "b")

    a. First Sub-Sub-Sub-Heading.*

    b. Second Sub-Sub-Sub-Heading.*

2. Second Sub-Sub-Heading.

    Umbrella Paragraph (setting out "a" and "b")

    a. First Sub-Sub-Sub-Heading.

        Umbrella Paragraph ("setting out "i" and "ii")

        i. First Sub-Sub-Sub-Sub-heading.*

        ii. Second Sub-Sub-Sub-Heading.*

    b. Second Sub-Sub-Sub-Heading.

II. POINT HEADING TWO.

Umbrella Paragraph (setting out "A," "B," and "C")

A. First Sub-Heading.*

B. Second Sub-Heading.

    Umbrella Paragraph (setting out "1" and "2")

    1. First Sub-Sub-Heading.*

    2. Second Sub-Sub-Heading.

        Umbrella Paragraph (setting out "a" and "b")

        a. First Sub-Sub-Sub-Heading.*

        b. Second Sub-Sub-Sub-Heading.*

C. Third Sub-Heading.*

* Indicates where an actual analysis would follow.

While all of the sub-points can appear confusing at first, they will make sense if the writer has correctly identified the way the writer's analyses or arguments correlate. In essence, the organization can be read verbally in this way: "My argument consists of two main points. For my first point I have two sub-points. And for each of those sub-points, I establish two smaller points. And for one of them, I make two even smaller points. My second main point consists of three sub-points, and for the second of those, I have two additional sub-points. The second of those sub-points consists of two smaller sub-points."

This outline format is precisely what will appear in the Table of Contents to a legal brief if that is the kind of document the writer has drafted. (Legal memos may also have a Table of Contents, but they often will not.) Many readers of legal briefs will look to the Table of Contents to get a sense of the arguments contained in the brief. Obviously, a poorly constructed outline (one that doesn't follow the basic outline rules provided here) will create uncertainty, if not confusion, for the reader before the reader even gets into the substance of the arguments.

Here's the takeaway point: Good legal writing requires attention to form.

But form alone isn't enough. Headings also need to convey substance. The ultimate value of well-constructed headings is that they provide a clear statement of the basic analyses or arguments the document provides in addressing the identified issues.

As regards the construction of the headings in a legal document, let's consider the alternatives. The heading could consist of a key word or a group of words (as might be used to identify an issue on a law school exam), but that method would not fully serve the signpost purpose of the heading. The heading could consist of a phrase (as a newspaper editor might devise in a headline to indicate what an article is about), but that method would only be a tease and would not provide a clear indication of what particular point the writer will be making. The heading could be fashioned as an issue statement, thereby providing the reader with an understanding of what particular point would then be addressed. But that approach would omit critical information: the conclusion on the issue the writer intended to press. This approach would be akin to seeing a sign on a highway that said "Next exit—Springfield" without indicating how many miles ahead the exit was.

Of the several alternatives for the construction of a heading, the best is to use a complete sentence to state the point that will be made in the following text. In most instances, that sentence should state the conclusion of the analysis that will follow. In this respect, it serves as the opening C in the CREAC or C-RAC paradigm (discussed fully in Chapter Three). It then serves the dual purpose of providing the necessary signpost and stating the conclusion of the analysis or argument.

But in some instances, as previously indicated, a point heading will be followed by sub-headings. In such instances, a point heading can become unduly cumbersome and overly long if it specifically includes all of the sub-heading points. Instead, such a point heading should be a single sentence that informs the reader of the answer to the issue the following analyses will provide. Such a heading implicitly and generally includes the separate sub-points that will be specifically stated in the subsequent sub-headings.

These two distinct purposes for headings can be distinguished by considering what immediately follows a specific heading in a legal document.

Those headings that lead directly to an analysis or argument serve as the opening conclusion for the CREAC or C-RAC paradigm. So they are properly referred to as **conclusionary headings**. And conclusionary headings should have this basic structure: *this conclusion because of this law (rule) and these facts.* From a conclusionary heading the writer should then proceed directly to the first rule to be explained (CREAC) or applied (C-RAC). If you understand the purpose of conclusionary headings, you will recognize that they can be either point headings (when no sub-headings follow) or sub-headings (when they are preceded by a heading and frequently by an umbrella paragraph).

Other headings may be followed by sub-headings (and frequently by an umbrella paragraph).[4] Those headings provide the answer to an identified (or implied) issue. We refer to those headings as **primary headings**. A primary heading is not immediately introducing an analysis or argument. Instead, it is announcing that an issue is about to be addressed in a series of separate analyses or arguments (that are introduced by the conclusionary headings that follow). Primary headings do not serve as the opening conclusions for the CREAC or C-RAC paradigms. Instead, they provide an overview of the analyses or arguments that will follow, and they accomplish that purpose by taking a different form.

A properly crafted primary heading should directly answer an issue. That issue may be one that has been expressly stated in the Issue/Question Presented section of the memo or brief. Or it may be one that is implicitly asked by virtue of the way the stated issue is considered.

4. Umbrella paragraphs are fully explained in Section C of this chapter, beginning on p. 95

For example, a stated issue might be, *Was the easement terminated when the dominant tenant changed the way the easement was used?* Assume that to answer that issue, the writer needs to provide two separate analyses or arguments, one regarding possible misuse of the easement, and the other regarding potential excessive use of the easement. Those analyses or arguments would then be announced with sub-headings that would be conclusionary headings. But the lead heading (the point heading in the example) would not introduce an analysis or argument. As a primary heading, it would merely answer the stated issue. In our easement example, the primary heading might, therefore, read as follows: *The easement would be terminated by excessive use and misuse.* (The primary heading might even omit the two termination options, thus shortening it to *The easement would be terminated.*)

Note how that heading serves to indicate (or tease) the separate analyses or arguments that will follow rather than identifying the specific conclusion that would flow from those analyses or arguments.

To further clarify and understand these two types of headings, consider that primary point headings and primary sub-headings only serve to introduce (or suggest) conclusionary headings. They do so by answering stated or implied issues without stating the reasons.

Stated issues are those that are indicated in the Issues or Questions Presented portion of a memo or brief. An issue would be implied when a sub-heading is followed by further divisions—into sub-subheadings, as when an A sub-heading is followed by sub-heading 1 and sub-heading 2 in this example:

I. Point heading (Primary heading)

    A. Sub-heading (Primary heading)

        Umbrella paragraph

        1. Sub-sub-heading (Conclusionary heading)

            Analysis or argument

        2. Sub-sub-heading (Conclusionary heading)

            Analysis or argument

II. Point heading (Conclusionary heading)

    Analysis or argument

Now review the Sample Outline of Headings (Table Two).

Table Two—Sample Outline of Headings

I. The easement will be available for use by the new owner of the dominant tenement.

  A. The easement was not abandoned when it was not used for sixteen years.

    1. Intent did not exist in the letter sent by the dominant tenant because the period of projected non-use was not specified.

    2. Intent did not exist in the dominant tenant's placement of the fence that obstructed entry to the easement because the fence was non-permanent and could easily be removed.

  B. The easement was not terminated by extinguishment when it was used by the hotel's guests.

    1. The easement was not terminated because the use by the hotel guests did not constitute a non-conforming use.

    2. The easement was not extinguished because the use by the large number of hotel guests did not amount to excessive use.

    3. The easement was not extinguished because the damage to the servient tenement was minimal.

II. The expansion of the hotel will not require the production of an environmental impact report (EIR).

  A. An EIR will not be required because the bird species that nests on the property is not protected by treaty.

  B. An EIR will not be required because the state regulations are not controlling on matters of U.S. treaty law.

III. The hotel has met all other statutory and regulatory requirements to construct the additional rooms for occupancy.

  A. The state's land use restrictions are not violated because the hotel is exempt from the code's provisions.

  B. The county's ordinance is not violated because it was enacted after the permit was granted by the county's land use director.

Note that the headings (those for point headings I, II, and III as well as sub-headings IA and IB) are all stated as primary headings in that they answer issues, either those for I, II, and III that are stated in what would be the Questions Presented in the full memo or are implied from the way the basic issue is interpreted (for sub-headings IA and IB). And also note that the headings for IA1, IA2, IB1, IB2, IB3, IIA, IIB, IIIA, and IIIB are all stated as conclusionary headings because they would directly lead to the full CREAC analyses that would immediately follow them. The primary headings are direct answers to specific issues. The conclusionary headings state the prediction for the issue followed by the "because clause" that refers to the law (rules) and facts that would be used in the following analyses.

To summarize this explanation of the different types of headings, here is how the headings would be crafted in a hypothetical fact pattern.

Example of primary heading—**The defendant exhibited malice in firing the gun randomly in the movie theater.** That heading answers this issue: Did the defendant exhibit malice in firing the gun randomly in the movie theater? It will be followed by an umbrella paragraph that provides a roadmap of separate arguments in support of the statement in the heading.

Example of conclusionary heading—**The defendant exhibited malice because of his willful misconduct in shooting his gun in the crowded movie theater.** That heading announces the conclusion of an analysis or argument that will be made immediately following the heading. That analysis or argument will state and apply rules from cases in standard CREAC or C-RAC structure.

So conclusionary headings will always follow this structure: this conclusion because of this law (rule) and this fact/these facts. Conclusionary headings are always followed by full CREAC analyses (or C-RAC arguments). Primary headings will only answer the issue the subsequent analyses or arguments address. Primary headings are immediately followed by umbrella paragraphs or another heading.

So, again consider the difference between the primary headings and the conclusionary headings in the Sample Outline of Headings table (Table Two). The headings for Roman numerals I, II and III, as well as those for IA and IB are all stated as direct answers to issues. They do not explain the answers (with a "because clause") because they are followed by lower-ordered headings (IA1, IA2, IB1, IB2, IIA, IIB, IIIA, and IIIB) that provide specific conclusions with reasons (because clauses).

As the foregoing discussion suggests, headings should not be afterthoughts or tossed-in parts of a well-crafted legal document. In many respects, the careful construction of them can be the most important work for the writer in the drafting of the document. To constitute a meaningful signpost, headings must state the substantive point clearly. As we know now, primary headings will be simple declarative answers to expressly stated or implied issues. Conclusionary headings require more detailed construction because of the need to indicate the reason for the conclusion (the because clause). The ten requisites for conclusionary headings are provided in Table Three.

Table Three—Rules for Conclusionary Point Headings

1. They should consist of a single sentence. If more than a single sentence is required to set out a signpost for the text that follows, the text probably consists of separate sub-points that require separate sub-headings (and separate paradigm presentations).
2. They should relate to an identified issue or part of an identified issue that is stated in the Issue section of the document. Point headings are meant to set out the basic analytical points that address the issue or issues that prompt the legal document. If a point heading doesn't relate directly to an identified issue, query whether the text that follows is truly relevant.
3. They should be stated affirmatively as a declarative conclusion. The point heading should serve as the opening C of a CREAC or C-RAC paradigm presentation. Stating the point as a question or a matter to be pondered defeats the signpost purpose of the heading. It should state what the text that follows is going to establish.
4. They should be single-spaced. Whether they are typed in upper-case or as a normal sentence, they need to stand out, and single-spacing serves that purpose.
5. They should be preceded by a Roman numeral (or letter or number for sub-headings), unless the heading would be a single heading for the entire document, in which case, a heading may not be necessary.

6. They should never include a citation. Citations in a point heading are redundant, since they will be part of the text that follows. And citations are burdensome for the reader, who is only looking for a signpost, not a detailed topographical map.
7. They should include a case name only in the rarest of instances. The rare exception applies when the case name is representative of a well-known rule or legal principle that is most easily identified by a case name (*e.g.*, *Miranda* warnings or *Chevron* deference).
8. They should never contain a footnote. If a footnote is appropriate to the subject matter in the text that follows the heading, it should be in that text, not in the heading.
9. They should only include abbreviations or acronyms if those identifications are universally known (*e.g.*, Inc., ACLU.)
10. Taken together, in order, the headings in a document should provide a complete overview of the analyses (or arguments) contained in the document. And they should completely answer the issue or issues identified in the document.

Deciding what sub-headings are necessary should be a simple matter of identifying what substantive points, taken together, constitute the point heading. These will be the A, B, and C points in the Table of Contents. And each may then have sub-sub-points that will be the 1, 2, and 3 points (and so on through each of the possible sub-divisions of finite specificity that are represented by the a, b, and c and the i, ii, and iii sub-headings; again, we follow the basic pattern of outlining that is standard in academic work).[5]

But the inclusion of sub-headings also affects the text that follows the point headings to which they relate because the analyses or arguments that substantiate the point heading will appear in the text following the sub-headings, not in the text following the point headings. In other words, when a legal document has sub-headings, the analysis or argument that substantiates the point heading must appear following those sub-headings, not before them.

5. Some writers are now favoring "Heading Numbering" as identified in Footnote 2 to denominate the headings in a document.

Re-read and think about that last paragraph. The key to making sense of all of this division of points into sub-points and headings into sub-headings is that the actual analysis or argument is almost always made in the smallest of the sub-points. In other words, apart from setting out a fundamental rule or principle that is necessary for each of the following sub-points, no actual CREAC analysis or C-RAC argument will be made in any but the smallest sub-point for each of the divisions. The Basic Structure for Document Headings table (Table One) notes, with an asterisk (*), where actual paradigm analyses or arguments would be made in the sample organization provided there. If you understand the difference between primary and conclusionary headings, the reason for the placement of those asterisks will be self-evident.

And as explained in the foregoing text, the way the headings are stated will depend on whether they are serving as conclusionary headings or primary headings. If they are primary headings, the subdivisions that follow will often be introduced with another organizational tool that we use in legal documents: the umbrella paragraph.

C. Umbrella Paragraphs

Umbrella paragraphs are the roadmaps that assist a reader in understanding the structure and organization of a legal document. They are included anywhere in a legal document where multiple analyses or arguments are going to be made to substantiate a more basic point. Thus, if a point heading is going to be followed by two or more sub-headings, an umbrella paragraph will follow the point heading (and precede the sub-headings). And that paragraph will essentially tell the reader what separate analyses or arguments are about to be provided.

Compare the two organizational tools (headings and umbrellas) by thinking of their distinct purposes. Headings (and sub-headings) are signposts that tell the reader what is going to be presented in the section of the document that the heading introduces. Umbrella paragraphs are roadmaps that tell the reader how the next part of the document is going to be divided and structured. Headings are relevant to the section of the document that immediately follows. Umbrella paragraphs are relevant to the divisions in the text that follow.

In addition to serving as roadmaps, umbrella paragraphs can also be used to introduce basic substantive points that are needed for the sub-points that follow. For example, if the issue to be analyzed concerns when *Miranda* warnings must be given,[6] an umbrella paragraph following the point heading (which would be a primary point heading as explained above) and preceding the sub-headings would identify and explain the circumstances that must exist for *Miranda* warnings to be required. That paragraph could actually be multiple paragraphs (see Chapter Two on the requisites for paragraph length) depending on the complexity of the explanation.

But umbrella paragraphs are only used to introduce basic substantive points if or when those points will not be explained again in the text following any of the sub-headings that the umbrella precedes. In other words, umbrellas can and should be used to cover basic substantive points, but only if the points are necessary to, but not part of, the analyses or arguments that are contained in the sub-points.

Again, think about the *Miranda* example. The basic requirements for *Miranda* warnings could be identified in the umbrella paragraph following the point heading, but they then wouldn't be identified again in the separate A and B sections that followed. Instead, those sections would be devoted to showing that the specific *Miranda* requisites were or were not met.

That second use of umbrella paragraphs (introducing a basic substantive point) only applies when the first reason to use one (to provide a roadmap of the sub-points that will follow) exists. In instances where a basic substantive point needs to be made as to a single analysis or argument, the basic substantive point should be made in the full text of the argument. Or, if the basic substantive point is necessary to understand a single specific argument, the point should be included in that argument.[7] In other words, if you aren't looking at an A and B

---

6. Law enforcement must provide a *Miranda* warning of the right to remain silent and right to obtain counsel after a person is placed in a "custodial interrogation" setting. *Miranda v. Arizona*, 384 U.S. 436, 444 (1966).

7. In the instance of a basic point that needs to be understood for a single argument, the basic point can be set out in a simple RE paragraph that leads to the actual rule that is the basis for the particular argument being made.

sub-heading, you should not have an umbrella paragraph. (Umbrella paragraphs can be helpful, but they lose their utility if they are used excessively.)

Summarizing the use of headings and umbrella paragraphs, consider the example in the "Basic Structure for Document Headings" table (Table One on page 86).

In this example of a fully organized brief, umbrella paragraphs are needed after each heading or sub-heading that precedes a further division of points to be made. And actual C-RAC arguments are made where the most finite point is indicated (*) for each of the sub-divisions in the outline. Review this structure until you understand why the umbrellas appear where they do and why the actual arguments are made where they are. Understanding these organizational tools and how they fit with the substantive points made in a legal document will enhance your ability to effectively communicate the analyses and arguments you want your reader to appreciate.

D. Organizational Devices

Headings and umbrella paragraphs are the primary organizational tools in a legal document, but good legal writers also use other devices to make the documents less structurally dense and more reader-friendly. Each of the following devices assist readers by reducing the amount of reading (parentheticals), giving an immediate sense of why a citation is included (signals), or providing comfortable bridges from one thought in the document to the next (transitions).

1. Parentheticals

Parentheticals are used to shorten the amount of reading required to make a substantive point. They condense what would otherwise be a full in-text illustration of a case or a detailed review of a previously introduced case. They reduce to the barest of essentials the information the reader needs. When properly used, they aid in the organization and structure of the document by eliminating redundancy and irrelevancy (two impediments to organization that are discussed below).

Parentheticals are easily understood by readers when they are constructed in the manner that has become commonplace in legal writing. In most instances, the parenthetical will be introduced with a participial phrase (a phrase that begins with a present participle), which includes the key facts that explain the rule in the case. When referring to a specific case, the participial phrase will follow the name of the case, as in the following example: (*People v. Smith*, citation, holding that when Defendant intentionally started the fire that spread to the adjoining property, malice existed as a matter of law).

Compare that example with this in-text illustration using the *Smith* case:

> In *People v. Smith*, citation, the defendant deliberately started a fire on the property directly adjoining the victim's property. The fire then spread to the victim's property, consuming the victim's residence in its flames. The court held that even though the defendant did not intend to burn down the victim's residence, his act of deliberately setting fire to the immediately adjoining property constituted malice as a matter of law.

Obviously, the full in-text illustration is longer and would take more time to read. Is any of the information in that paragraph necessary for the point the parenthetical alternative addresses? The answer to that question will determine whether the parenthetical is appropriate. In most instances, parentheticals are desirable and appropriate where the reference is supplemental to a point already made by a previous full-text illustration or when the point for which the case is used is secondary in importance to a more significant rule contained in the analysis.

Thus, as in many other decisions in legal writing, the use of a parenthetical is a judgment call for the writer of the document. Properly used, parentheticals make the reader's work easier by making the document shorter (and less burdensome). And because legal readers are accustomed to seeing parentheticals in a legal document, they know how to read them and what purpose they serve. But to use a parenthetical where more details are needed (as when an analogy will be created) can be counter-productive. You aren't helping your reader if you leave out key information that is necessary to the analysis or argument you are going to make.

The mirror-image approach is a valuable check in deciding to use a parenthetical. (The mirror-image approach is presented and explained in Chapter Three.) If the information in the parenthetical mirrors (matches) the information used in the analysis or argument, the parenthetical will be an effective tool. But if the information in the parenthetical either exceeds or omits information used in the analysis or argument, the use of the parenthetical will be counter-productive. If, for example, a parenthetical only mentions Fact A from a case when Facts B and C are also used in the analysis or argument that follows, the parenthetical has not been useful. Similarly, if the parenthetical refers to both Facts A and B, but only Fact B is used in the analysis or argument that follows, the parenthetical has not been helpful.

Parentheticals can be used at any point in a CREAC or C-RAC paradigm. Thus, you may use a parenthetical in the RE portion of a legal memo and then refer to the information contained in it in the RA portion of the memo. Or you may use a parenthetical in the RA portion of the memo to summarize the full in-text illustration of a case you provided in the RE portion of the memo.

Here are some more specific rules regarding the use of parentheticals (both as to the form they should take and the ways in which they might be abused):

1. Most parentheticals will begin with a present participle and a lower-case letter and end without punctuation (because they are generally part of a longer sentence). But "holding" need not be the participle in every instance. (In fact, as explained in Chapter Two, "holding" refers to the court's reasoning for its conclusion on an issue in the case, and, thus, may not be the correct designation of the reference to the case.) Many other possible present participles exist to begin a parenthetical, including these: adopting, allowing, analyzing, applying, approving, awarding, considering, construing, denying, determining, discussing, explaining, finding, indicating, interpreting, issuing, limiting, overruling, permitting, reasoning, recognizing, re-

jecting, relying, remanding, requiring, ruling, suggesting, upholding, and vacating.[8] Note, however, one participle that would not normally be appropriate: arguing. Attorneys "argue" to courts, but courts do not "argue" in their opinions.

2. Parentheticals should not be used to hint at rules. The rule should be stated before the parenthetical, which should then illustrate the rule.[9]
3. Parentheticals should not be redundant.[10] If the point has been stated in the preceding text, a parenthetical should not be used to restate the point. Instead, the parenthetical should provide an illustration of the point.
4. Parentheticals must be relatively short and definitely should not include what would essentially be a full in-text illustration from a case.[11]

---

8. Example: A dog owner will not be liable for injuries caused by a dog when the owner does not have possession and control of the premises where the dog is kept. *Morris v. Cordell*, 608 N.E.2d 809, 811–815 (Ohio Ct. App. 1992) (affirming summary judgment for defendant because defendant's dog injured plaintiff on plaintiff's property while defendant was not on the premises).

9. Identify the violations of this rule in the following examples:

> A plaintiff must prove four elements to prevail on a claim for intentional infliction of emotional distress. *Christensen v. Superior Court*, 54 Cal.3d 868, 903 (1991) (requiring plaintiff to show that the defendant acted with extreme and outrageous conduct with the intention of causing, or in reckless disregard of causing, emotional distress, the plaintiff suffered extreme emotional distress, and that the defendant's conduct was the actual and proximate cause of plaintiff's injuries).
>
> Several exceptions exist to the requirement that police need a warrant to search a home. *Kentucky v. King*, 536 U.S. 452, 459 (2011) (holding that police may enter a home without a warrant to provide medical care to an occupant based on "exigent circumstances").

In both examples, the rule is stated in the parenthetical, not before it.

10. Example of a violation of this rule: In order to recover for a claim of negligent infliction of emotional distress, a plaintiff must be immediately related to the victim. *Molien v. Kaiser Foundation Hospitals* (1980), 27 Cal.3d 916, 918 (requiring plaintiff to be immediately related to the victim).

11. Example of a violation of this rule: The veterinarian's rule prevents a plaintiff from succeeding on a strict liability claim against a dog owner when the dog bites a trained professional entrusted to care for the dog. *Priebe v. Nelson* (2006) 39 Cal.4th 1112 (a kennel technician sued the defendant, an owner of a pit bull, after the dog bit

5. A parenthetical should not be used when greater detail about the case will be provided immediately following the parenthetical. In that instance, the parenthetical becomes a distraction for the reader instead of a time-saver. Rather, the information provided in the parenthetical should just be presented in the in-text description of the case.

Because parentheticals are recognized as "tools of the trade," a well-constructed parenthetical makes reading the document easier. Parentheticals serve to assist the reader in understanding the purpose of the reference contained in the parenthetical and by saving the reader time and effort that would be required to get through a full in-text illustration. Their usefulness is further enhanced by the use of a companion tool: signals.

2. Signals

Signals are used to tell a reader why a citation is being provided. They lighten the load for the reader much as symbols do in mathematics, where we use the equal sign (=) in lieu of the word "equals" and the plus sign (+) in lieu of the word "plus." In providing citations, the comparable savings in words is considerably greater, and, since the signals are universally understood in the legal profession, they have the same degree of utility and efficacy as symbols do in mathematics.

The actual rules for specific citations require the use of manuals (*e.g.*, the *Bluebook*, the *ALWD* manual, or the *California Style Manual*). They are discussed in Chapter Seven. At this point, you just need to know that this form of "abbreviation" exists and is available as an organizational device. The following chart lists the ten most commonly used signals in legal writing.

---

the plaintiff while the dog was being housed at the kennel where the plaintiff worked; defendant argued that the "veterinarian rule" absolved him of potential liability for injuries that his dog inflicted while boarded; the court held that the defendant assumed the risk of being bitten by dogs by the nature of her job).

Frequently Used Signals

1. *e.g.,*—used when the cited authority is representative of, or merely an example of, many authorities that stand for the same proposition but are not cited in the document.
2. *Accord*—used when two or more authorities state or support the proposition but the text quotes or refers to only one; the others are then preceded by this signal. (This signal can also be used to show that the law of one jurisdiction is essentially similar to that of another jurisdiction.)
3. *See*—used when the cited authority only implicitly supports the stated proposition.
4. *See also*—used to cite authority, in addition to that previously cited, that supports the proposition. But using this signal indicates a weaker (less compelling) reference than either the *see* signal or no signal would indicate. (See below for the significance of the lack of any signal.)
5. *Cf.*—used when the cited authority supports the stated proposition only by analogy. (When this signal is used, it is often accompanied with an explanatory parenthetical.)
6. *Compare ... [, and ...] with ... [, and ...]*—used to compare authorities or groups of authorities that reach different results concerning the stated proposition. (An explanatory parenthetical will often accompany the use of this signal.)
7. *Contra*—used when the cited authority directly contradicts the stated proposition.
8. *But see*—used when the cited authority implicitly contradicts the stated proposition. (If this signal is used immediately following a *contra* signal for the prior citation, the *but* would be eliminated so that it would be interpreted to indicate that the previous *contra* signal also applies to this citation in its effect.)
9. *But cf.*—used when the cited authority contradicts the stated proposition by analogy. (If this signal is used immediately following a *contra* or *but see* signal, the *but* would be eliminated so that it would be interpreted to indicate that the previous *contra* or *but see* signal also applies to this citation in its effect. An explanatory parenthetical will often accompany the use of this signal.)

10. *See generally*—used when the cited authority provides helpful background information related to the stated proposition. (An explanatory parenthetical will often accompany the use of this signal.)

In addition to these ten signals that can be used to identify the purpose of a citation, the default option exists to use no signal. The lack of a signal with a citation can mean one of three things, however. It can indicate that the cited authority is the source of a general reference in the text preceding it. It can also indicate that the cited authority provides direct support for the stated proposition that immediately precedes it. And it can indicate that the cited authority is the source of the quotation that directly precedes it. In almost every instance, which of these three meanings will attach to the lack of a signal with a cited authority will be readily apparent from the text preceding the citation.[12]

Because everything asserted in a legal document must be based on authority, citations are a critical part of any legal document. Signals (or the decision not to use a signal) tell the reader how the impact and significance of the cited authority is to be understood. In this respect, they are a valuable organizational device, saving the reader from burdensome reading and giving the reader a clear understanding of why a citation appears at a particular location in the text.

3. *Transitions*

Transitions are the footbridges of a well-crafted legal document. They take the reader from one thought to the next, and they can be as subtle as a single word ("therefore" is a commonly used transition

---

12. Below are examples of the three times where a signal is not needed before a citation:

> The Fourth Amendment protects people from unreasonable searches and seizures by the government. *Katz v. United States*, 398 U.S. 347, 353 (1967).
>
> The government, by attaching a device to a phone booth to listen—without a warrant—to a suspect's conversation, violates the Fourth Amendment. *Katz v. United States*, 398 U.S. 347, 353 (1967).
>
> "... the Fourth Amendment protects people, not places." *Katz v. United States*, 398 U.S. 347, 351 (1967).

word) or as obvious as a full sentence, as in this example: "The rules from those cases resolve the issue presented by this case."

Transitions are most commonly used at the start of a paragraph or at the beginning of a new section of a legal document, but they can also be effective at the end of a paragraph or as a stand-alone paragraph bridging two sections of a document. On a smaller scale, transitions can also bridge thoughts within a paragraph, sometimes even within a sentence. As with all legal writing, choosing to use a transitional word or phrase (or sentence), apart from the separate question of which one to use, is a judgment call. We do, after all, want to keep our document shorter rather than longer, and words and phrases add up, especially when, by themselves, they add nothing of substance to the document.

But transitions do serve a valuable function in helping the reader stay connected with the substance that the writer is presenting. Think about your own reading experiences. You probably find yourself drifting from the document on occasion. Many factors can cause that momentary loss of focus, but one might be a sudden shift by the writer from one point to the next. Those segments of a legal document cry out for a transitional word or phrase as a way to say to the reader, "Stay with me; we're just moving from that last point to a new one."

These helpful words and phrases can be useful in a variety of particular points in a typical legal document. The following chart lists eight different instances where the right word or phrase can be an effective organizational device.

Purposeful Uses of Transitions

1. To show agreement or similarity from one point to the next. The writer in this instance has more to say on the same subject. Here are just a few of the words or phrases that might keep the reader focused: "by the same token," "in like manner," "another example," "moreover," "similarly," "additionally," "not only ... but also," "again," "and."
2. To reflect an opposing perspective or to offer a contradictory point. These areas in a legal document are dangerous because the reader can easily become confused if the new thought isn't indicated with a transition. Some of the possible words or phrases are "in contrast," "on the

other hand," "to the contrary," "nevertheless," "nonetheless," "be that as it may," "notwithstanding," "and yet," "but."

3. To indicate a cause of something or a condition or purpose in something. Here the writer seeks to provide a reason or intention for the presentation of a point (one just made or about to be made). Again, the risk is that without a bridge to ease the reader into the point, the reader's thoughts may drift and come back only to be uncertain or confused. Good words or phrases for this circumstance include these: "with this point in mind," "inasmuch as," "for the purpose of," "so that," "provided that," "due to," "while," "if."
4. To provide examples of a point or support for a point. In this instance the writer has made a point but now wants to emphasize or clarify it with an example. Appropriate words or phrases include these: "for example," "to explain," "for instance," "specifically," "particularly," "especially," "such as," "including," "like."
5. To clarify the effect or consequence of a condition or factor. Often in a legal document, a rule must be explained by providing the likely result of its violation. Just as frequently, the effect or consequence of an event must be provided. These words or phrases are some of those that can be useful bridges in these instances: "as a result," "consequently," "therefore," "accordingly," "for this reason," "hence," "thus."
6. To introduce a conclusion or summary of a previous thought or series of thoughts. Legal documents will regularly include summaries or restatements of points just made. Transition words and phrases in these instances often serve as identifications to a reader who may only want to read the summary, or they may alert the reader that the end of an exposition of a point or series of points has been reached. These words or phrases might work in such instances: "as shown by the foregoing," "in conclusion," "to summarize," "in essence," "restating," "ultimately," "all in all."
7. To indicate chronology or sequential relationships. Often in a legal document, the writer will need to provide a sequence of events or show how events relate to each other with respect to time. These words or phrases may be helpful in such instances: "to begin with," "in the meantime," "meanwhile," "as soon as," "from time to time," "as long as," "occasionally," "after," "since," "then."
8. To indicate relative spatial locations. Not infrequently, geographic and other space perspectives can require definition in a legal document.

Here are some words and phrases that may be useful in such instances: "in the middle of," "from a distance," "viewed closely," "regarding the space," "alongside," "between," "nearby," "around," "adjacent to," "there," "here."

In each of the foregoing instances, the lists provided are only partial. In fact, transitions should flow naturally in the text so that they are hardly even noticed by the reader. They are most effectively used when they are least evident, since their purpose is not to add substance to the document but to make the reading of the document easier, like a footbridge over a narrow creek makes a walk in the park easier.

E. Organizational Impediments

Since so much attention is given to making the legal document's organization easy to understand (as all of the above-discussed organizational tools and devices indicate), anything that makes the reader's task in following that organization more difficult also merits attention. Organizational impediments can occur when the flow of an analysis or argument is interrupted with a non sequitur, when a point irrelevant to the issue being discussed is injected into the text, and when a point is unnecessarily repeated.

1. Non Sequiturs

A **non sequitur** (Latin for "it does not follow") destroys the flow of an analysis or argument by injecting a point that is logically disconnected from what has preceded it. In mathematical terms, it is the equivalent of D=E in this formula: A=B; D=E; B=C; therefore: A=C. In that series of equations, D=E has no logical connection to the prior (or succeeding) equation. Its inclusion in the series serves no purpose, even if, on its own, it is a true mathematical statement. Instead, it is an impediment to understanding the otherwise clear flow of the equations.

Similarly, in legal reasoning, the insertion of a point that serves no purpose in the logical flow of the analysis or argument is an impediment to understanding the analysis or argument that is being presented. When non sequiturs appear in legal documents, they are usually the result of poor editing. Typically, the offending sentence (or series of sentences) was included in an earlier draft and then was not caught and removed in the process of editing the document.[13]

Consider the logical flow in the following paragraph. Which sentence constitutes a non sequitur?

> If a dog is provoked, its owner will not be liable for injuries suffered by the person who provoked it. (*Siewerth v. Charleston*, citation.) In *Siewerth*, the plaintiff kicked the dog several times. The defendant's son also kicked the dog. The defendant told the plaintiff to go home. When the defendant's son again kicked the dog, the dog bit the plaintiff. The court held that the plaintiff had provoked the dog by kicking it and held that he could not recover from the defendant for his injuries.

The offensive sentence is pretty easy to spot, isn't it? Why do we care in the context of the RE paragraph the writer is providing that the defendant told the plaintiff to go home? It might be a relevant point for a separate rule, but it does nothing to further the illustration of the rule stated to begin the paragraph.

Now identify the non sequitur in the following comparable RA paragraph.[14]

> The issue in the instant case is whether the plaintiff provoked the dog. If he did, pursuant to the rule from *Siewerth*, the defendant will not be liable. In *Siewerth*, the plaintiff and the defendant's son both kicked the dog. The court held that the plaintiff had provoked the dog, and the defendant was not liable. In the instant case, the plaintiff did not kick or abuse the dog physically. The dog was normally peaceful and friendly. When it bit the plaintiff, it had not been provoked.

---

13. In a properly white-gloved legal document, the offending sentence would be caught and edited in the ten-step process. Non sequiturs would be caught in Step Three.

14. See Chapter Two for the discussion of the RE (Rule Explanation) and RA (Rule Application) paragraphs in a predictive memo.

Why is it necessary to include the sentence about the dog's normal temperament in that RA paragraph? It might be a relevant fact for a different analytic point, but it has nothing to do with the rule from *Siewerth* or the illustration of the rule provided from that case. In that paragraph, and the previous RE paragraph, including the non-sequitur sentence only serves to impede the reader's understanding of the logic of the analyses provided in them.

2. Irrelevancies

Irrelevancy is related to non sequiturs in that both identify points that are not related to the basic point of discussion. Irrelevancies, however, are more glaring and can, therefore, be more serious impediments to the reader's understanding of the organization of the legal document. An irrelevancy in a predictive memo would be the identification, explanation, and application of a rule that had no effect on the issue analyzed in the memo.

In the dog-bite illustration above, for example, if the issue is whether the dog was provoked, a rule identifying whether the plaintiff was lawfully present when a dog bit him may be irrelevant even if lawful presence is also required under the statute for a plaintiff to recover.[15] It would only be relevant if the writer's analysis identified and explained a way in which lawful presence affected the provocation of the dog. But absent such a connection, the fact that lawful presence is also required to establish liability in Illinois dog-bite cases would not be relevant to an analysis of an issue that only concerned whether a dog had been provoked.

Most irrelevancies in a legal document are the result of inadequate substantive expertise. Some attorneys, for example, fall into the trap of using a shotgun approach in drafting a brief. Instead of studying the

15. The Illinois Code states, "If a dog or other animal, without provocation, attacks, attempts to attack, or injures any person who is peaceably conducting himself or herself in any place where he or she may lawfully be, the owner of such dog or other animal is liable in civil damages to such person for the full amount of the injury proximately caused thereby." 510 Ill. Comp. Stat. Ann. 5/16 Lexis Advance through P.A. 99-506 of the 2016 Regular Legislative Session, formerly Ill.Rev.Stat., Ch. 8, ¶ 366.

legal issue and conducting sufficient research to understand it, they will load up the brief with any argument that they think might be on point.

The professional and proper approach is to correctly identify the appropriate legal arguments and to limit the brief to those arguments. Failing to understand the issue and the law applicable to it is a likely reason for irrelevancies to be included in a legal document.

Irrelevancies in a legal memo or brief can be severe impediments to a reader's understanding of the organizational structure of the document. They are likely to cause the reader to ask, "why am I reading this?" This question is usually the last one a reader will ask before putting the document in the reader's read-later pile.

3. Redundancies

Redundancy is perhaps the most irritating of impediments to clear organization in a legal document. It occurs whenever a point is restated unnecessarily. Redundancies can be found within a paragraph and even within a sentence, as in this example:

> The dog-bite statute protects dog owners from liability when their dog was provoked by a plaintiff who engages in an act of provocation.

Here's an example of redundancy in a short paragraph:

> Dog owners are protected from liability under the state's dog-bite statute. The statute protects dog owners in a variety of ways. Dogs that are provoked cannot subject their owners to liability because the statute provides that dog owners are not liable when their dogs have been provoked. In this way, the statute protects a dog owner from liability.

How many paragraphs like that one do you suppose a reader would read before deciding to put the document in that dreaded read-later pile? Most redundancy is the result of sloppy writing and poor white-glove work, but redundancy also exists in some of the common phrases that many writers all-too-easily slip into using. Here are some of them:

Actual fact—as opposed to a made-up-fact?

Forever and ever—as in beyond infinity?

Past history—not present or future history?

Postpone until later—can you postpone something to any other time?

Accidental mistake—in contrast to a purposeful one?

10 a.m. in the morning—can 10 a.m. ever not be in the morning?

In all honesty (or candor)—isn't "honestly" (or "candidly") enough?

Everyone slips into some of these on occasion, especially in casual conversation. But they shouldn't appear in a legal document. If nothing else, they make the document longer than it needs to be. Brevity is to legal writing what cleanliness is to a chef's kitchen.

Chapter Summary

The organization of a legal document should be evident to the writer of the document since legal writing is intended to present a logical flow of analytic thoughts that respond to a legal issue. But that organization should also be apparent to the reader of the document if those analytic thoughts are going to be appreciated and understood. Specific organizational tools and devices exist to aid the reader in understanding the writer's organization. Specific impediments also exist that make that understanding harder to convey.

Headings are the signposts that a writer uses to announce to the reader that a new topic or subject is about to be discussed. Those topics or subjects can be sub-divided (numerous times) and each time they are, a new signpost (a sub-heading) should appear to announce the new sub-topic.

Headings and sub-headings in a legal document are presented in a common outline format that identifies the level of division and subdivision with standard denomination tools (*e.g.*, Roman numerals, upper-case letters, Arabic numbers). These markings (the numerals, letters, and numbers) follow a specific pattern that mirrors the pattern in the document's Table of Contents (as in most persuasive briefs).

Conclusionary headings should state affirmatively the point that the following text will make or address. They should serve as the opening C of a CREAC or C-RAC paradigm presentation. But those substantive presentations (the actual analyses or arguments) should only be made after the most finite of the sub-headings under a given heading. Primary headings answer stated or implied issues; they do not directly introduce analyses or arguments and are often followed by umbrella paragraphs.

Umbrella paragraphs should follow all headings and sub-headings (primary headings) that are further divided into more finite sub-headings (conclusionary headings). Umbrella paragraphs should serve as roadmaps for the reader, describing how a particular topic is divided into sub-topics. Umbrella paragraphs can also be used to introduce basic legal concepts or principles that will be referred to in the substantive analyses that are contained after the sub-headings that follow.

Taken together, the headings and sub-headings in a legal document should provide a complete overview of the analysis contained in the document and they should read in logical order with one point either divided into sub-points or clearly distinguishable from the next point in the writer's organization.

Parentheticals, signals, and transitions are organizational devices. Each of them can help the reader to understand how the writer intends a part of the legal document to be understood in relation to the rest of the document. Parentheticals simplify a reference to a rule from a case or the illustration of a rule. They are written in a specific format that begins with a present participle (*e.g.*, holding, explaining, indicating, ruling). Signals are used to identify why a particular citation is included in the text of a document. They are the equivalent of symbols in mathematics and serve much the same purpose (*i.e.*, reducing the number of words that would be otherwise needed to convey the significance of the citation that follows). Transitions are footbridges in a well-crafted document. They help the reader cross from one section of the document to another (or from one thought to another thought). They can be full sentences, phrases, or just single words, but, in each instance, they smooth out what might otherwise appear to be sudden jumps from one point to the next.

Organizational impediments in a legal document can appear as non sequiturs, in irrelevancy, and in redundancy. Non sequiturs are thoughts that do not flow logically from previous thoughts or do not relate meaningfully to following thoughts. Most non sequiturs in a legal document result from inadequate editing (white-glove inspection) work. Irrelevancy in a legal document occurs when a rule is included that is unrelated to, and can have no effect on, the issue that is being analyzed. Most irrelevancy in a legal document results from inadequate substantive expertise. Redundancy in a legal document occurs when a point is unnecessarily restated. Redundancy can appear within a paragraph or a sentence. Even commonly used phrases can contain redundancy. Most redundancies result from careless, thoughtless writing.

The goal of the organization of a legal document must be to make the reading of it easier. A dense substantive document needs to be structured clearly with full use of the basic tools and devices that make that structure easier to understand and without the organizational impediments that have the opposite impact.

Chapter Five

The Perfectly Constructed Sentence in a Legal Document

A. Introduction
B. The Elements of a Sentence
C. The Basic Structure of a Sentence
D. Compound and Complex Sentences
E. Barriers to Good Sentence Structure
F. False Alarms—Alleged Barriers that Aren't
G. Specific Parts of Legal Documents that Require Special Attention to Sentence Construction

A. Introduction

Consider the perfection of a simple sentence.

"Jesus wept."[1] It's the shortest verse in the Bible, and yet it conveys so much information and provokes so much thought. And, most importantly, it makes the reader want to read more.

Compare that sentence with this one: "Jesus, having seen the suffering of Lazarus and the sorrow that those who loved him were experiencing (and having full knowledge of the fate that awaited him as ordained

1. John 11:35. This verse occurred in the context of the death of Lazarus, and amidst the Jews pleading with Jesus, both misunderstanding the necessity of Lazarus's death and hoping that Jesus could remedy this impossible and unjust situation. These two words, at once, brought to light Jesus's emotional attachment to Lazarus and his remorse, and also provided the transition toward the resurrection of Lazarus.

by his heavenly father), and even though he knew he was about to raise Lazarus from his death, shed tears along with those around him."

What is wrong with the second sentence? Grammatically, it is perfectly fine. It is properly punctuated, contains all the requisite elements for a complete sentence, and provides information that the writer wants to convey (and does convey in the rest of the actual Biblical verses). But, unlike the actual two-word sentence, it is difficult to read, difficult to understand, and unlikely to make the reader want to read what follows. Simply stated, it tries to do too much, to convey too much specific detail, to squeeze too much information into the space between the capital letter that starts it and the period that ends it.

Now think back to those three piles that are on every lawyer's work desk. Which pile will a document end up in if the document is laden with sentences upon sentences that are equally difficult to digest?

Legal writing is not meant to be literary. We aren't trying to be John Updike[2] when we write a legal document. Updike was a marvelous writer; he was a wordsmith and an artist with the language. He could write sentences that contained multiple thoughts and amaze his readers with the beauty of the way he constructed those sentences, let alone the brilliance of the thoughts contained in them. But Updike (or Dickens or Shakespeare, if you prefer) wrote for a very different audience than lawyers. They wrote to entertain. Lawyers write to inform.

Legal documents are the lawyer's means of transmitting information. The substantive information contained in the documents is information the lawyer (on behalf of the lawyer's client) needs the intended recipient to read. And since each sentence represents potential substantive difficulty for the reader, every sentence must be written with care. The writing must be easy to read, so that every sentence states as simply, as clearly, and, as precisely as possible, the information the writer wants the reader to receive.

Good legal writing starts with reader-friendly sentences.

---

2. John Updike was one of three people to win the Pulitzer Prize for fiction more than once. He was praised for his lucid depictions of the American middle class, and he was also a literary critic who critiqued nearly every major literary author in the twentieth century.

Think back to the first books you read. They were most likely primers in grade school that had sentences like, "Jane ran. John ran with Jane. They ran together." Later you read books that had more meaningful information, but the likelihood is that they were also comprised of simply constructed, short sentences. Why? The object of those how-to-read books was to teach you how to understand the way letters combine to form words and how words combine to form sentences.

Legal writing is similar in this respect: The words that are combined to form sentences should convey a specific thought, maybe not one as simple as that Jane ran, but one that is as easy to understand as that thought we understood back in first grade from that first primer.

B. The Elements of a Sentence

Every sentence must contain a subject and a verb. Subjects are things (or persons or places). They are identified by words that we call nouns or pronouns. Every sentence has to have one of these (or imply one in rare instances[3]), and it has to be shown doing something.

The "doing something" is the other required element for every sentence. It is called a verb. Verbs are what subjects do. Verbs indicate some kind of action or state of being. Thus, "Jesus wept" satisfies the two requirements, having both a subject (Jesus) and a verb (wept). But if we move the noun (Jesus), we might not have a sentence, as in "Wept, Jesus seeing the mourners." In that construction "Jesus" is still a noun, but not a subject. (He could be the intended subject of the intended sentence, but a noun (or pronoun) can only qualify as the subject of a sentence if it is followed by a verb.) So, the simple lesson to understand in constructing a sentence is that you must have a noun (or pronoun) doing something. (In our non-sentence, above, "seeing" does not suffice as a verb, because, as the sentence is written, it would have to be a

3. In imperative sentences, the subject "you" is understood, as in, "Leave her alone!" In that sentence, it is understood that the speaker is saying "'you' leave her alone!'"

participle.[4] "Wept" is a verb, but it is not connected to a noun in that construction.)

As simple as properly constructing a sentence sounds, all too often non-sentences appear in legal documents when the writer is trying to explain a point or make an argument. For example, "Finding that the facts did not suffice for burglary" would be a non-sentence that could mistakenly be written in this kind of paragraph:

> "The court considered and rejected the prosecution's argument. Finding that the facts did not suffice for burglary."

As will be explained shortly, the offensive non-sentence is actually a dependent clause (also called a participial phrase)[5] of what would be a complex sentence if it were constructed as follows: "Finding that the facts did not suffice for burglary, the court considered and rejected the prosecution's argument."

The other element that is often found, although not required, in a complete sentence, is the object of the sentence.[6] Objects in sentences are also usually nouns or pronouns, but the object in a sentence can also be a phrase. The standard way to think of objects in sentences is by asking to whom the subject did something, as in this construction: *She reprimanded him.* In that sentence "him" would be the object of the reprimanding.

Other elements of a standard sentence are always optional. For example, a prepositional phrase (a phrase beginning with a preposition) can add meaning to a sentence, as in this construction: *She reprimanded*

---

4. A participle is a form of verb that functions as an adjective to modify a noun or pronoun.

5. A participle phrase is a group of words containing a participle, modifier, and pronoun or noun phrases.

6. The subject of a sentence is the "who or what" that does the doing in a sentence. The object is the person or thing that the doing is done to. A common mistake is to consider the subject to be the main idea of the sentence. For example, in the sentence "The investigator looked for the evidence," one may identify "the evidence" as the subject. In normal discourse, that interpretation may be accurate (the speaker may be focusing on the evidence), but grammatically, "the investigator" does the doing, and so that person is the grammatical subject of the sentence. "The evidence" is the object, because that is the thing for which the investigator does the looking.

the entire class for behaving badly. There, "for behaving badly" is a prepositional phrase, beginning, as it does, with a preposition (for). ("The entire class" would be the object of the sentence.)

The Nine Parts of Speech

1. Noun

   Nouns are the person, places, and things that we speak of when we form sentences.

   Example: The murder *weapon* was bloody.

2. Pronoun

   Pronouns are the words we substitute for names and specific identities.

   Example: *I* need *them* to cooperate in order to get a conviction.

3. Verb

   Verbs describe an action, a state, or an occurrence.

   Example: Travis *murdered* the victim, and then we *prosecuted* him.

4. Adverb

   Adverbs modify a verb with the manner, place, time, or frequency of the action.

   Example: Travis *quickly* left the scene after the murder.

5. Adjective

   Adjectives indicate attributes that describe a noun.

   Example: Travis was caught with a *bloody* knife at the scene of the crime.

6. Preposition

   Prepositions show direction, time, location, or introduction.

   Example: Travis was caught *near* the train platform.

7. Conjunction

   Conjunctions join phrases or clauses together. The commonly used conjunctions are denoted by the acronym FANBOYS: for, and, nor, but, or, yet, so.

   Example: Originally, we thought that the murderer was Diane, *but* we discovered that it was Travis.

8. Interjection

   Interjections are added to sentences to convey an emotion or sentiment.

   Example: *Oh*, we didn't know that Travis had a licensed firearm.

9. Articles and Determiners[7]

   Articles and determiners specify and identify nouns. The commonly used articles are a, an, the. Commonly used determiners include *these, that, those, enough, much, few, which, what.*

   Example: *The* most violent crimes are *the* most heinous acts that are committed by only *a* few people.

C. The Basic Structure of a Sentence

When we read, we want to know who (subject) did what (verb) to whom (object), as in this example: She reprimanded the class. We might want to know additional information (for behaving badly), but the most important information is who did what to whom.

Thus, in constructing a sentence, the three basic elements are best presented together and at the beginning of the sentence. Additional information can then follow. Think about the optional ways the sample sentence we've been using could be written:

A. She reprimanded the class for behaving badly.

B. For behaving badly, she reprimanded the class.

C. She reprimanded, having observed the students behaving badly, the class.

D. She, having observed the students behaving badly, reprimanded the class.

E. The class, having behaved badly, was reprimanded by her.

---

7. Articles and determiners are not always included in parts of speech lists. Some lists only identify eight parts of speech while others identify nine, including articles and determiners.

"A" follows the preferred structure and is most reader-friendly because it provides the essential information right away. "B" makes the reader wait to find out whom we are talking about and what she did to someone else. ("B" also contains a misplaced modifier in that the sentence appears to indicate that "she," not "the class," had been behaving badly. Misplaced modifiers are barriers to good sentence construction, as noted later in this chapter.) "C" and "D" are likely to create frustration in the reader, as the object of the reprimanding is removed from the action by the insertion of the intruding phrase (in "C") and what she did and to whom is placed at a distance from "she" with the intruding phrase (in "D"). And in "E" we have completely inverted the structure and made "the class" the subject when in fact it is the object of the teacher's action. We call that kind of sentence a passive construction because the actual actor has been hidden and placed in a passive position. (Passive construction is another barrier to good sentence construction, as also noted later in this chapter.)

When properly employed, this preferred structure forces the writer to consider the fundamental purpose of each sentence in a legal document. The result is almost always going to be reader-friendly sentences that make the receipt of the intended information almost automatic. Sentences, for example, that begin, "The court held ..." are going to deliver the necessary information efficiently and quickly, with little or no work required by the reader to receive that information. The sentence that immediately follows could then provide the court's reasoning, as in this construction: "It considered prior case law and analyzed the relevance of key facts in the instant case." Thus, in two sentences, both of which follow the preferred structure (subject-verb-object), the reader receives easily understood and quickly grasped information.

Contrast that construction with this kind of sentence (intended to provide the same information): "After carefully considering prior case law and analyzing the relevance of key facts in the instant case, the court held...." The writer who writes this sentence is hiding the critical information behind secondary information. The reader will get the information, but getting it will be a little harder because the sentence construction is slightly less reader-friendly. And note the other problem with this construction: It results in a single long sentence that provides the reader with the information the writer wants to convey instead of two shorter sentences that provide the same information. In terms of reader-friendliness, short is better than long with respect to sentences (and paragraphs, as discussed in Chapter Two).

Note how different the reader-friendly approach for legal documents is to what someone like John Updike might have had as his fundamental purpose in constructing the sentences he wrote. Part of the lure of an Updike novel is the mastery of his use of grammar. He is not trying to make it simple. He isn't writing to inform. He is writing to entertain. He is writing to enthrall. He is writing to create an image or to convey a sense of a character or to explore the dimensions of an emotion. His writing is to grammar what Picasso is to drawing.

But legal documents are not written for that purpose. Remember what we are doing in a legal document: We are passing information to the reader that is intended to inform or persuade the reader of an analysis or an argument regarding a legal issue. The substance of that document is very likely going to be difficult and complicated. It will require the reader to understand legal principles and to appreciate how those principles apply to a set of facts. The process of understanding that substance is demanding. The way in which it is presented should not be.

Good writing is hard. It requires careful construction of each sentence so that the reading of each sentence is easy. The information provided will be demanding enough in an analysis of a complex issue. Presenting the information should not make the reader's task even more difficult.

Here's the bottom line: Think deeply; write simply.

D. Compound and Complex Sentences

Occasionally in legal writing, thoughts can be best expressed in longer sentences. For instance, some thoughts might be so closely connected that separating them into two sentences might make their connection less apparent. In creating an analogy, for example, the writer might better show the comparison between two facts from separate cases in one sentence instead of two. So the writer might convey the comparison in this way: *Just as in* Smith, *where the plaintiff suffered injury when the boulder struck his car, so in our case Mr. Jones was injured when the tree fell on his truck.* To make that point in separate sentences would make the comparison less compelling, as in this construction: *In* Smith, *the plaintiff suffered injury when the boulder struck his car. In our case, Mr. Jones was injured when the tree fell on his truck.* Adding a transition word (as explained in Chapter Four) can make the two sentences fit more convincingly, but showing the analogy in a single sentence still might be preferable.

Combining thoughts in a single sentence can be accomplished by creating sentences that are referred to as either compound or complex. The difference between these two types of sentences is in the type of clauses that are joined within the single sentence. We refer to clauses as being either independent or dependent.

1. Compound Sentences

Compound sentences consist of two **independent clauses** that are joined by a conjunction. An independent clause is a part of a sentence that could stand alone as a complete sentence. In other words, independent clauses are wholly contained thoughts that satisfy the grammatical requirement of containing a subject and a verb. When we put two independent clauses together in the same sentence and join them with a conjunction, we have created a compound sentence. Such sentences always require a comma before the conjunction. The comma serves as the notation that alerts the reader to the compound sentence.

Now consider these two attempts to create a compound sentence. Which one is correctly written?

A. The court applied the rule from *Smith*, and decided in favor of the plaintiff.

B. The court applied the rule applied from *Smith*, and it[8] decided in favor of the plaintiff.

---

8. Courts are always referred to with the pronoun "it," not "they." A court is always assumed to speak with one voice (concurring and dissenting opinions notwithstanding). In common discourse, lawyers may frequently say "they held" when referring to a court's opinion. But in legal documents the correct pronoun is always "it": "it held."

"B" is a compound sentence. It consists of two independent clauses ("The court held that …" and "it decided in favor …"). Both clauses would be separate sentences if they were not joined by the conjunction.

"A" is a simple sentence with two verbs ("held" and "decided"). The comma in "A" is inappropriate. What is missing in "A"? Look carefully at the phrase that follows the conjunction. Can it stand alone as a sentence? Because it lacks a subject, "decided in favor of the plaintiff" is not, by itself, a complete sentence.

Why is the comma inappropriate in "A"? It adds nothing to the sentence and creates potential confusion by its presence. Consider a similar sentence, stripped of the added words: "The court applied and decided." That sentence would look silly with a comma before "and." The comma there would serve no purpose. Similarly, in "A" the comma serves no purpose. But in "B" the comma serves to tell the reader that the sentence is a compound sentence. The comma can have more meaningful significance when the two clauses contain different subjects as in this example: The court applied the rule in *Smith*, and the plaintiff prevailed.

So, compound sentences are pretty easy to identify (and to write). They just require independent clauses that are joined with a conjunction that is preceded by a comma. What about complex sentences?

2. Complex Sentences

Complex sentences join two clauses, only one of which is independent. The other clause in a complex sentence is a dependent clause. **Dependent clauses** cannot stand alone as complete sentences. They always contain a verb, and sometimes contain a subject as well, but they are not joined to the other clause in the sentence with a conjunction. Here are several examples of complex sentences with the dependent clauses in bold:

> **While he was driving to school**, he listened to a tape of last week's lecture.
>
> He went to class, **even though he was unprepared**.
>
> **If the test includes negligence issues**, he will be ready for them.

The professor's lecture was boring, **though the topic was interesting.**

Complex sentences can make a point easier to understand by joining two thoughts that make up the point, but they also create the risk of making the meaning of the sentence more difficult to grasp. Remember the value of keeping the subject and verb in the sentence (*the who did what* part of the sentence) connected. Doing so makes the sentence easier to understand. Positioning the subject and verb at or near the beginning of the sentence also aids in providing the reader with an immediate way to focus on the writer's intent in the sentence. But in many complex sentences (particularly those that begin with a dependent clause) the subject and verb will appear later in the sentence. Thus, the reader will be less likely to immediately grasp the significance of the point made by the sentence.

Compound and complex sentences have a place in legal documents. Properly and judiciously used, they can aid in creating compelling arguments and effectively communicated analyses. But remember that you aren't writing a novel and that your reader is not reading your document for pleasure or entertainment. The sentences in your legal document should be easy to read and understand, and, most often, that requirement will mean that they should be short.[9]

---

9. The more words and punctuation you put into a sentence, the more opportunities there are to make errors. Here are some examples of unnecessarily long sentences containing errors:

First example: There was no reason for the Defendant to go to the store so late at *night, he* had everything he needed in his fridge and his alibi did not make sense. (Note that this sentence contains a "comma splice" and could easily have been broken into two sentences.)

Second example: The defendant was accused of murdering his girlfriend, and he was not responding to calls from the police or his family so everyone assumed that he was guilty of committing the crime, but, in reality, he was also a victim of the *bloody killer's spree.* (Note that the modifier, "bloody," is misplaced. The "killer's bloody spree" is not only more proper, but also more aesthetically pleasing to the reader. These errors are easily avoided when a sentence is made shorter and more manageable to contemplate during the white-glove inspection.)

Third example: The violent offender was found on the third floor of the building, hiding from police, attempting to take the female resident of the apartment hostage, attempting to destroy evidence, and her clothes torn suggesting that an assault had taken place. (Not only is this sentence overly long, but the final clause does not fit

E. Barriers to Good Sentence Structure

Whether they are constructed as simple, compound, or complex sentences, all sentences can fall prey to construction difficulties that result in grammatical errors. Poorly constructed sentences can also be harder to comprehend or easier to ignore, depending on the willingness of the reader to work through them. Most of the errors that slip into sentences in a legal document are the result of internal complexities in the sentences that take the writer's attention away from the construction as the writer focuses on the substantive point the writer is trying to make. The resulting construction then presents the reader with the opposite problem: focusing excessively on the structure of the sentence (to figure out what it is saying) at the expense of the substantive point the writer was trying to make.

The following construction errors can be avoided by viewing each sentence as a separate work of art, or, more practically, by focusing on how the sentence is constructed as much as on what the sentence purports to say.

1. Passive Constructions

Passive construction or writing with a passive voice is a great way to avoid socially awkward scenes. It's a way to be tactful, and tact has its place in much social intercourse. Passive constructions can be also beneficial if the writer or speaker is trying to hide the thrust of the statement. A politician, for example, might say, "Mistakes were made, which I regret," when the person really means, "I made mistakes, and I'm sorry." Or, in a social setting, a speaker might say, "Statements were just made that are hurtful," instead of, "You hurt us by making those comments." And consider how unromantic it would be to say, "Love is felt by me for you," instead of "I love you."

Sentences written in the passive voice misdirect the reader's attention and force the reader to work a little harder to understand the intended point of the sentence. They are, therefore, undesirable in legal

with the subject of the sentence. The writer's thoughts here could and should be broken into two, three, or even four sentences.)

documents (because we want the reader to grasp the writer's intent as easily as possible).

Compare these two sentences:

A. The defendant exhibited malice in shooting the gun.

B. Malice was exhibited in the defendant's act of shooting the gun.

In sentence A, the verb (exhibited) and the object (malice) immediately follow the subject in classic sentence construction, and the verb indicates immediately what the subject did, with the object identifying what resulted. In sentence B, a phantom subject, malice (which is really the object of the writer's intended sentence) separates the verb and the intended subject. The reader now must struggle momentarily to determine what the writer really intended to convey in the sentence.

Passive constructions are easily identified by the use of a form of the verb "to be" (am, are, is, was, were, had been, has been, have been), which, existentialism aside, is about as passive a verb as the English language contains.[10] If the sentence contains any of those variants of "to be" immediately following the subject, the sentence has most probably been stated in the passive voice. Such sentences are also easily identified because they hide the actor (the person or entity the displaced action verb is really intended to be paired with).

Compare these two sentences:

A. Reasoning was provided for the holding in the case.

B. The court provided reasoning for its holding in the case.

"A" doesn't even mention the court, leaving it to the reader to figure out what entity provided the reasoning. The sentence appears almost apologetic in tone, as if the writer doesn't want to offend the court by naming it as the entity responsible for the holding in the case. "B," on the other hand, credits the court for the reasoning it provided in support of its holding.

---

10. Not all usages of the infinitive "to be" are passive. For example, the declaratory statement, "she is a suspect in the murder," utilizes a form of the "to be" infinitive, but it is not used in the passive voice as it does not displace the real subject of the sentence.

The basic problem with passive sentence construction is that it hides who did what. And since we have already identified (earlier in this chapter) that the best construction identifies those two elements quickly and definitively, passive construction is immediately undesirable. Consider how much less dramatic and meaningful the Biblical verse would have been if the writer had said, "Weeping was an indication that Jesus was sad."

Good legal writers avoid those constructions in most instances, unless, of course, they are insulting the judge to whom they are submitting the document. In such instances, a phrase like "errors were made in certain rulings" may be preferable to "this court erred in certain rulings."

2. Mixed Constructions

Mixed constructions in sentences occur when the writer begins with one form of construction and ends with a different form of construction. These errors can appear in simple sentences.

Consider this example: In writing, sentences, being the basic unit in a paragraph, require attention to detail.

The writer of that sentence hasn't constructed the sentence to say what the writer wants to convey since it's the writing of sentences that require attention, not the sentences themselves.

Mixed constructions occur when the writer's thought gets ahead of the way the writer needs to convey the thought. The writing of the sentence does require attention to detail, lest the sentence create potential confusion for the reader because of a mixed construction error. Certain writing tools that are otherwise helpful in conveying intended thoughts can create mixed constructions. In the above example, for instance, notice how the inclusion of the modifier—"being the basic unit in a paragraph"—leads to the mixed construction error. Without the modifier, the writer would have more easily noticed the error in the sentence. Indeed, what the writer really wanted to say was probably something as simple as "Writing sentences requires attention to detail," but by seeking to add the thought about how integral sentences are to paragraphs, the writer has made a mixed construction error.

Subject-verb disagreements are errors in sentence construction. They can also result from the inclusion of added thoughts to the basic point the writer seeks to make in the sentence. The error that results will render either the subject or the verb incorrect in the constructed sentence, as in the following example: *Sentences, especially when constructed like this one, is likely to contain an error.* The error occurs in the sentence because the writer has lost track of the subject. The simple rule is that subjects must match their verbs in number and person. In this example, the subject (sentences) is plural in number, but the verb matches with a singular subject.

Here is an example of a subject-verb disagreement where the person doesn't match: *Bill, when he is with his friends, have fun.* Again, the writer has lost track of the subject of the sentence. Friends do have fun, but in this sentence, Bill is the subject, and he *has* fun.

As these examples suggest, subject-verb errors are most likely to occur when the writer places a clarifying or modifying phrase between the subject and verb.

Subject-verb disagreements also occur when multiple subjects appear in the sentence. In such instances, specific rules apply. They can be memorized or, with access to the Internet, they can be quickly researched. Here are a few of those rules:

- When multiple subjects are joined by the word "and," the plural verb is required.
- When multiple subjects are joined by the word "or," the verb that matches the last listed subject is required.
- When a "neither … nor" or "either … or" construction is used to identify the subjects of a sentence, the verb that matches the last of the subjects is required.
- When "there" takes the place of the subject in a sentence, the verb must match the entity that "there" refers to in the sentence. If the entity is a plural, as in this sentence—*There are many reasons for this rule*—the verb must be the plural form. (But note, as explained later in this section, how using *there* as the subject of a sentence creates an undesirable passive voice construction.)

Subject-pronoun disagreements are also easily made when clauses or phrases intervene between the subject of the sentence and the later reference to the subject with a pronoun. Consider this example: *Sentences, like this one, can be mistakenly constructed when it contains a pronoun that doesn't match the subject of the sentence.* In the sentence, the pronoun "it" is singular, but the subject "sentences" is plural. Again, the culprit/cause of the mistake is the intruding phrase that places a singular reference in between the plural subject and the following pronoun.

Similar rules exist for the pronoun that should relate to multiple subjects as we saw in the subject-verb agreement rules. They also can be easily researched on the Internet, but here are a few that are commonly encountered:

- When multiple pronoun subjects are joined by the word "and," the plural pronoun is required.
- When multiple pronoun subjects are joined by the word "or," the pronoun must match the last listed subject.
- Titles as subjects of sentences are always singular and thus require a singular pronoun. (Thus, Chaucer's *The Canterbury Tales* is (not *are*) a good read, and it (not *they*) merits (not *merit*) your attention.)
- Compound pronoun subjects in the "neither … nor" or "either … or" constructions must be matched by the pronoun that agrees with the last of the subjects.

The largest area for subject-pronoun errors is in gender identification. In the bad old days when the default gender was always male, neutral subjects, such as a person, an employee, or an executive, were always indicated by the male pronoun (he, him, his). That view, thankfully, is no longer acceptable. Gender-neutral subjects must be viewed as either male or female (or, perhaps, non-binary, but that issue raises other questions that must be addressed separately[11]), but this rule can

11. The usage of they, them, and their to refer to a singular person is becoming more acceptable, primarily when referring to unknown individuals or the general public as in "a person may be tired when they haven't gotten enough sleep." This common grammar faux pas has appeared in the works of many famous authors, in-

create problems when word count limitations are a concern. Consider this sentence as a rule statement in a brief: *A person has committed an assault when he/she causes apprehension in another of a harmful or offensive touching.* The use of *he/she* to show gender neutrality is the less desirable way to deal with the gender-neutral issue as it is essentially a contraction of "he or she." The better approach for that sentence is either to use *he or she* (two more words for word count purposes) or to pluralize the gender-neutral subject as in this alternative to the example: "Individuals have committed an assault when they cause...." The third option, which is the "easy" way to handle the problem is to use the plural pronoun (they, their, theirs) for the singular gender-neutral subject. However, this alternative is grammatically incorrect and should be avoided even if word count is a concern.[12]

3. *Nominalizations*

Nominalizations occur when a verb is made into a noun, as in this example: *They held a meeting to discuss the plan.* The writer of that sentence has made the sentence longer than it needed to be. The preferred construction would avoid the nominalization of the verb "to meet": *They met to discuss the plan.* Most nominalizations have an adverse effect similar to the problem that passive constructions create. In both instances, the intended point of the sentence is deflected. As we have seen in passive constructions, the intended subject is misplaced (mistakes were made, instead of I made mistakes). In nominalizations, the action is masked or made less obvious. In most legal writing the goals are to address points directly and to state ideas clearly. Nominalizations do not facilitate those goals.

---

cluding Lord Byron, Chaucer, and Jane Austen, and of course is common in everyday speech. However, legal work is meant to be precise. So, those pronoun uses should be avoided, except as the method of identifying gender-fluid and gender-dysphoric references may require, assuming that "they" either becomes universally accepted for such individuals or is the pronoun of choice for a particular individual. In legal documents, "singular they" usage is still not universally accepted. Stay tuned.

12. *Id.*

Most nominalizations are accomplished by adding a suffix to the verb.[13] Here are just a few examples:

investigation (investigate)

irritation (irritate)

movement (move)

failure (fail)

refusal (refuse)

Nominalizations are common in everyday speech, which is why they so easily slip into many legal documents. As with many other barriers to good sentence structure, they often must be corrected through careful white-glove work.

4. Misplaced Modifiers

Misplaced modifiers are an even more pernicious kind of sentence-construction error. They occur when modifying words or clauses are misplaced in a sentence so as to appear to be modifying something other than what the writer intended. At best, they can be viewed comically, as in the sentence: *Convinced that he had been driving while intoxicated, the judge sentenced the defendant.* At worst, they can cause the reader to lose the flow of the text and perhaps the thrust of an important analysis or argument.

The use of modifiers is perfectly appropriate in legal writing. In some instances, they are essential to convey the writer's intended meaning, as with the inclusion of the modifier "excessive" in this example: *The attorney's excessive reaction to the judge's ruling caused the judge to hold him in contempt.* But even when not essential, they can add color and helpful detail to an otherwise less illuminating sentence.

Most misplaced modifiers appear in the form of phrases or clauses, as in the "driving while intoxicated" example above. In such instances,

---

13. Adjectives and adverbs can also be nominalized. For instance, typically "blind" is used as an adjective to describe someone, but "the blind" can be used as a noun to refer to a group of people. Adverbs are less frequently nominalized, but the adverbs "here" and "now" could also be used referring to "the here and now," a noun used to describe the present.

modifiers can appear in one of three possible incorrect constructions. One incorrect construction occurs when they appear next to a person or entity the modifier is not intended to modify and at a distance from the person or entity it is intended to modify. The judge who really wasn't the intoxicated individual is a good example of that kind of erroneously placed modifier.

A second incorrect construction occurs when, by their location in a sentence, the modifier could be interpreted to modify either of two words. Squinting modifiers, as they are called, can be especially troublesome in a legal document where precision is critical. For example, what was the writer's intended meaning in the following sentence? *The court's order adopting the attorney's argument substantially destroyed the prosecution's case.* Is "substantially" intended to modify the order that adopted the attorney's argument or is it intended to modify how badly the prosecution's case had been destroyed?

As confusing as they can be, at least squinting modifiers give the reader an option as to which of the two words or phrases the writer intended to modify. The third incorrect construction that constitutes a misplaced modifier occurs when the modifier does not relate to any word in the sentence. Called "dangling modifiers," these modifiers are misplaced in the sense that they are homeless, as in this example: *By providing detailed reasoning, the result was wholly justified.* As written, the sentence indicates that the result provided detailed reasoning, which, of course, is nonsense. The writer, in haste (and by doubling down on errors in using a passive construction), omitted the likely entity the detailed reasoning was intended to apply to. A more carefully constructed sentence would have avoided the dangling modifier by using active voice construction: *By providing detailed reasoning, the court wholly justified the result it reached.*

Misplaced modifiers, in any of their forms, make the reader's job more difficult. They detract from the effectiveness of the writer's analysis or argument, and they do so irrespective of the brilliance of the substantive analysis or argument the writer wants to present. As with all barriers to effective legal writing they are avoidable if the construction of the sentence is undertaken with the same degree of care that was used in devising that brilliant analysis in the first place.

5. *The Nowhere "There" and the No Thing "It"*

The nowhere "there" and the no thing "it" are undesirable ways of creating a passive construction (which, as we have already seen, is an undesirable way of making a point or stating a fact or a rule) and of avoiding an active voice. Compare these sentences:

A. There was a reason given for the court's decision.

B. The court gave a reason for its decision.

C. It is indicated in the court's opinion that the trial judge erred.

D. The court indicated in its opinion that the trial judge erred.

In sentences "A" and "C," passive construction must follow from the use of "there" and "it" as the subjects of the sentences. When "there" or "it" are used as fill-in subjects, as they are in those sentences, they are not indicating anything specific as the proper use of those words would. "There" is a noun, referring to a specific place. "It" is a pronoun, referring to a specific thing. But in sentence "A," "there" doesn't refer to a specific place, and in sentence "C," "it" doesn't refer to a specific thing. Sentences "B" and "D" are far more preferable ways of saying what is intended in "A" and "C," as they state directly (active voice) what is stated passively in the weaker sentences.

Any sentence that uses a nowhere "there" or a no thing "it" can be written more effectively by rephrasing the intended meaning so that those words are not used. The bottom line on "there" and "it" is that they should only be used in sentences where their meaning is clear and specific.

6. *Misuse of "This" and "That"*

"This" and "that" also have the potential of being misused. Compare these sentences:

A. This follows logically from the court's reasoning.

B. The result follows logically from the court's reasoning.

C. The court's reasoning clearly establishes that.

D. The court's reasoning clearly establishes that conclusion.

In sentences "A" and "C," the references are incomplete because "this" and "that" are being used as nouns (persons, places, or things) instead of adjectives (determiners of nouns).

In casual speech, we will often use these words without their nouns ("This is what I meant"; "I thought you were going to take care of that"). And, occasionally, in legal documents the missing word (the noun) is understood or can be easily inferred by the reader. But in hastily making an argument or presenting an analysis, continued use of "this" and "that" without the nouns they refer to can hide the writer's intended meaning and leave the reader confused and working harder than necessary to overcome the confusion.

7. Double Negatives

Double negatives are difficult to comprehend. Perhaps they shouldn't be, and maybe to mathematicians they aren't. But most readers, like most people, get flustered when a thought is stated with multiple negatives. Consider these sentences:

A. The absence of reasoning did not make the attorney's argument easy to follow.

B. The attorney's argument was hard to follow because it lacked reasoning.

C. Never reject the truth.

D. Always accept the truth.

Sentence "A" presents the double negative of "absence" and "did not." A typical reader of that sentence will pause momentarily and recalculate the sentence so that it reads more like sentence "B." So why not write it as "B" and make the reader's work easier? Sentence "C" contains the negative "never" immediately followed by the negative "reject." It isn't a hard thought to understand, but doesn't "D" state it more effectively, more pleasingly, more positively? Which of those sentences is likely to have more impact for the reader?

8. Double Possessives

Double possessives can also be problematic for much the same reason as double negatives. They just require more mental gymnastics than many people/readers are accustomed to performing when reading. Consider these sentences:

A. The plaintiff's home's damages were severe.

B. The damages to the plaintiff's home were severe.

C. The judge is a friend of the attorney's.

D. The judge is a friend of the attorney.

Sentence "A" takes a second or two to unravel because of the double possessive, while sentence "B" says the same thing without requiring the added calculation. In most instances, the added second of time is a trifle, and many writers will opt to save the extra word or two in favor of the extra second or two. But numerous double negatives of the type in sentence "A" can become more burdensome and so should be avoided in legal documents.

The difference between sentences "C" and "D" is the sense of the double possessive created by the word "of" in both sentences. Grammarians are split as to whether the use of the apostrophe in "C" is optional, preferable, or just plain flat-out incorrect. The argument in favor of "C" flows from the use of "mine" as opposed to "me" in a comparable sentence ("The judge is a friend of mine"/"The judge is a friend of me"). Most people use the possessive form of the pronoun in that sentence; hence the reasoning suggests that the possessive should also be used when the possessor is someone (or something) else. With respect to this form of the double possessive sentence, the key is to be consistent throughout the document.

9. Contractions

Contractions are not grammatically incorrect (assuming they are correct in and of themselves; "it's" is not the possessive of "it" and "ain't" is not a recognized word in formal verbal or written communication). But they are problematic at best in legal documents. The best approach is to avoid them in court documents like briefs and to follow the culture of the firm in internal documents like legal memorandums. The exception to avoiding use of contractions would be where the full use of the term sounds stilted or overly dramatic. Then again, sometimes sounding dramatic is exactly what the speaker or writer might want, as in, "This decision just won't stand."

F. False Alarms—Alleged Barriers that Aren't

Some old rules never were really rules, and others that may have at one time been considered "best practices" are no longer given much attention. The following list contains such "rules." As we'll see, in most instances, they aren't rules at all and may not even merit consideration in the most vigorous white-gloving.

1. Split Infinitives

Split infinitives were traditionally avoided by good writers, but the rules have softened considerably. (An infinitive is the "to" form of a verb, as in "to work," "to study," "to practice.") In only a few instances should split infinitives be avoided. One such circumstance is when the infinitive is split by a long phrase, as in this example: *The rule allowing writers to, except in rare instances, split infinitives should not be abused.* A preferable way to write that sentence would place the intervening phrase at the start of the sentence. Another split infinitive to avoid is the negative of the infinitive, as in this sentence: *The rule to not split infinitives is only rarely recognized.* The better way to construct that sentence would place the "not" before the infinitive.

2. Ending Sentences with Prepositions

Ending a sentence with a preposition is another rule that has been largely discarded by even the best writers. Most sentences that end with a preposition are perfectly acceptable in almost all instances.[14] Gram-

14. In one oft-quoted instance, an editor rearranged one of Sir Winston Churchill's sentences so it would not end with a preposition, to which Churchill replied, "This is the sort of bloody English up with which I will not put!"

matical pedants may still raise an eyebrow if a sentence does happen to end with one of the many prepositions (*e.g.*, of, with, in, from, to, about) that normally introduce parenthetical phrases. But the modern view is that sentences that are otherwise grammatically correct may most certainly end with a preposition.

3. Beginning Sentences with Conjunctions

Beginning a sentence with a conjunction is a presumed rule that has really never been a grammatical rule. It certainly is not a recognized rule in legal writing. Conjunctions (*e.g.*, for, and, but, or) are frequently used to join two separate complete thoughts into a single sentence, as noted above in the discussion of compound sentences. They have that purpose and save many sentences from being grammatically incorrect when so used. But (notice the word that starts this sentence) they can also start a complete thought that also results in a grammatically correct sentence. In fact, in legal writing, starting a sentence with "but" or "and" can, in certain instances, have an especially dramatic effect by calling attention to what follows in the sentence, as in this example: *But, here, the defendant's confession was coerced in direct violation of the rationale behind the* Miranda *rule.*

G. Specific Parts of Legal Documents that Require Special Attention to Sentence Construction

Every sentence in a legal document should be written with care, using all the rules and preferred approaches already noted in this chapter. But some parts of a legal document absolutely demand the most careful attention to detail.

1. Rule Statements

Because so much of our reasoning in legal documents is based on rules, the sentences that we write stating those rules are critically important. Rules must be stated precisely, and they must be stated clearly.

A reader should never have to struggle to understand what the rule is or, even worse, whether the sentence is even stating a rule at all.

Constructing a rule statement so that it satisfies those basic requirements—precision and clarity—can be best accomplished by focusing on the purpose of the specific rule in the specific legal document in which it will be used. And since most rules in a legal document are intended to support an analysis or an argument, the subject of the sentence that states the rule should identify the point in the analysis or argument that the rule will support.

Suppose, for example, that the rule is going to support an analysis of one of the issues addressed in the document. What is that issue? Most often, legal issues involve whether something exists or is satisfied by a factual occurrence. Let's use our murder example from previous chapters. The legal issue was whether the defendant exhibited malice in shooting a gun into a crowded movie theater. So the basic issue concerns malice: whether it existed in the defendant's action. Our rule statement is then going to be about how malice can be found. How can we best state that rule precisely and clearly?

Consider these alternatives (assume that all of them flow from a case that will be used to explain the rule):

1. *Acts that are performed in reckless disregard of the consequences are malicious.*
2. *Defendants who act in such a way that their conduct is reckless and in disregard of the likely consequences have exhibited malice when the victim dies as a result.*
3. *When a defendant causes the death of another through reckless conduct, the defendant has exhibited malice.*
4. *Malice is a requirement for murder.*
5. *Malice exists when a defendant engages in reckless conduct that causes the death of another.*

Which one states the rule clearly and precisely? Number one can't work. It doesn't even use the word malice, which is our issue. Number two buries malice two-thirds of the way into an overly long and cumbersome sentence. Number three is a complex sentence that hides the key word until the end of the sentence. Number four starts with the key word, but it doesn't provide the definition that is necessary for the issue the document is going to address.

Number five is the best attempt to state the necessary rule for malice clearly and precisely. Let's analyze what it does to satisfy those requirements. First of all, it makes malice the subject of the sentence. If we are stating a rule that defines malice, malice should appear as close to the start of the sentence as possible, and making it the sentence's subject is a great way to accomplish that goal. Second, the sentence is a simple sentence with the verb immediately following the subject. Thus, the reader quickly knows that this sentence is going to state when malice exists. And the rest of the sentence clearly and precisely states what the requirement is to find malice.[15]

To summarize, when stating a rule, make the subject of the sentence the key word in the issue the rule addresses. Follow the subject with the verb that identifies how the word is being described in the sentence. Keep the sentence in simple sentence form. Only include in the definition those details that will be used in the analysis that flows from application of the rule.

2. Headings

Headings are discussed more fully in Chapter Four. We review their importance here in the context of the specific requirements that exist in writing them.

Headings serve a valuable purpose in a legal document. They are signposts that inform the reader of what will be discussed in the text that follows. Headings that introduce major sections of a legal document are called point headings. As the term implies, they address major points in the document. More specifically, they notify the reader

---

15. In Chapter Three, we discussed the CREAC paradigm and introduced the A=B=C conceptualization. In this case, the preferred rule statement, number five above, would be the "A" that would be the first sentence of the RE paragraph. This concise and clear rule statement would then be explained, the "B," in the rest of the RE paragraph, and it would be applied, as stated and explained, in "C," the RA paragraph.

that the following text will address a major issue that is at least one of the reasons the document has been written.

Headings that are specific to an argument or analysis that follows are called sub-headings. We can further identify two types of sub-headings. Sub-headings that are further sub-divided in the document are *primary sub-headings*. These sub-headings introduce a part of the document that addresses a sub-issue of a primary issue.[16] Sub-issues often will be inferred, but making the inference should not be difficult. A sub-issue is, essentially, what is being specifically addressed in the following analysis or argument. For example, if the main issue in your case is whether the defendant is guilty of murder, a sub-issue might be whether malice existed in the facts of the case. And since a number of ways exist to establish malice, separate analyses (or arguments) might be presented to establish each particular form of malice. The analyses (or arguments) would then be introduced with a primary sub-heading addressing the malice sub-issue. The primary sub-heading would then be followed with an umbrella paragraph (described in Chapter Four) and then by separate conclusionary headings as the opening Cs for each form of malice that will be considered.

The second kind of sub-headings are those that serve to introduce the specific analysis or argument that will be offered or made. In the CREAC and C-RAC paradigms, these sub-headings serve as the opening Cs—the introductory conclusions—for the analysis or argument that follows. These sub-headings are *conclusionary sub-headings*.[17] Point headings can be either primary—if sub-headings follow—or conclusionary—if they are not followed with sub-headings. Thus, in instances where the point heading is serving as the opening C of the CREAC or C-RAC paradigm, the analysis or argument will be offered

16. An example of a primary sub-heading might be "Adjudicating Appellant's Claims Does Not Excessively Entangle the Court with Religion." It would provide a general answer to the issue regarding excessive entanglement under the Establishment Clause. It would then be divided further into conclusionary sub-headings for each of the three prongs of the "Excessive Entanglement" test.

17. For a visual of conclusionary sub-headings, review Table One, "Basic Structure for Document Headings" on page 86. The asterisks on that table indicate where a substantive argument would be made. Thus, the headings introducing those arguments would be conclusionary sub-headings.

immediately following the point heading. As should also now be apparent, if a heading, either point or sub, is followed by an umbrella paragraph that introduces more finite sub-headings, the heading will be a primary heading.

All headings in a legal document should be stated as sentences. The kind of sentence—the purpose of the sentence—will differ depending on whether the heading is a primary heading or a conclusionary heading. Primary headings should be structured so as to provide a direct answer to the issue or sub-issue the text following them addresses in the legal document. Conclusionary sub-headings, on the other hand, since they offer the initial C in the CREAC or C-RAC paradigm, should be structured so that they provide the conclusion of the analysis or argument that will follow. They will then have a specific form, which is as follows: Conclusion because of this Law and this/these Fact(s).

Here is an example of a primary heading:

I. The defendant exhibited malice in the act that caused the death of the victim.

This heading is primary because it directly answers an issue that is addressed in the legal document. That issue, presumably, would be as follows: Did the defendant exhibit malice in the act that caused the death of the victim?

Here is an example of a conclusionary heading:

A. The defendant exhibited malice through an act of willful and wanton misconduct in shooting his gun in the crowded movie theater.

This heading uses the above-mentioned form, stating the conclusion because of applicable law and corresponding facts. It would then be followed by the specific analysis or argument that supported the conclusion stated in the heading. (Hence, the heading would then suffice as the opening C in the CREAC or C-RAC paradigm.)

Note that both examples are full sentences. All headings in a legal document should be stated as full sentences. Only in the rarest of instances would single words or phrases suffice to serve as the signpost the reader needs to indicate what will follow in the document.

And, as with most writing in legal documents (see previous discussion of barriers to good sentence construction), the sentences should be stated in the active voice. Stay away from passive voice constructions in headings. They make the signpost that the heading is intended to represent harder for the reader to comprehend.

3. Conclusions

The CREAC and C-RAC paradigms have two Cs. As we have indicated, the first of those Cs should be stated in the conclusionary heading that is the signpost for the text that follows. But what about the closing Cs? They should also be single (or multiple) sentences at the end of the analysis or argument.[18] And, because they represent a separate and distinct thought, albeit a summary of previous thoughts, they should be stated as a separate paragraph.

Depending on the complexity of the analysis or argument that these conclusions are summarizing, they can be stated as single sentences. (A paragraph can consist of a single sentence. Review the rules for paragraphs in Chapter Two.) Such sentences would commonly begin with the phrase, "For these reasons" (or "From these cases"). Often, such an allusion to the detailed analysis/argument that has preceded the sentence will suffice. The reader, having just read the preceding substantive presentation, has those points in mind and will understand that "for these reasons" refers to them and that the phrase is introducing the restatement of the conclusion that was first stated in the conclusionary heading that started the analysis/argument. The balance of the sentence will then be a scaled-down summary, such as (referring to our murder/malice example), "Malice existed in the defendant's act of shooting the gun in the crowded theater."

These concluding paragraphs can certainly be longer than a single summary sentence, but, when they are longer, they should only restate the points in the presumably detailed analysis or argument that pre-

---

18. These closing Cs from the C-RAC and CREAC paradigms discussed in Chapter Three are distinguished from the "Conclusion" section of a memo or a brief. The "Conclusion" section of the entire document can simply be a restatement of your headings and sub-headings, assuming the headings have effectively stated the points covered in the brief.

ceded them. Thus, a concluding paragraph might consist of three sentences that might take this form: restatement of the controlling rule; restatement of the controlling fact to which the rule has been applied; summary sentence.

Using our malice example, such a concluding paragraph might be drafted as follows:

> From these cases, the rule is definitively established that malice exists in the willful and wanton action of an individual that causes the death of another individual. Here, the defendant acted willfully and wantonly in firing his gun in the crowded theater. Therefore, the defendant exhibited malice in his action.

Whether a single sentence or a short paragraph as in the example above, the concluding C for the CREAC and C-RAC paradigms should consist of carefully constructed sentences that say no more than necessary to summarize the analysis or argument that has followed the conclusionary heading that introduced the analysis or argument.

4. Lists

Lawyers must be entirely comfortable with lists as they either encounter or use lists regularly. Some lists are provided in statutes and regulations, others arise from court-generated rules, and many result from intricate analyses that might produce a complex synthesized rule or from an argument that has a number of sub-points. In each instance where a list appears in a legal document, the challenge for the writer is to provide the list in a comprehensible sentence that is relatively easy to read and is punctuated properly.

Regarding the punctuation of these sentences (we'll call them "list sentences"), legal writers need to know how and when to use two dreaded punctuation marks: the colon and the semi-colon. The colon is the mark that indicates that specifics will follow the mark to illustrate what has preceded it. Look at the sentence that started this paragraph for an example. The colon appears in the sentence after the general reference to "two dreaded punctuation marks." Immediately following the colon in that sentence are the specific punctuation marks that were just referred to generally.

Okay; so colons appear to be pretty straightforward. They have a specific purpose. But they can still be misused if they are indiscriminately used to indicate that a list will follow their insertion in a sentence. Consider these two examples:

A. Two dreaded punctuation marks are used in sentences that provide lists. These marks are: the colon and the semi-colon.

B. The following two dreaded punctuation marks appear in sentences that provide lists: the colon and the semi-colon.

The sentence in "A" that uses the colon only consists of the subject ("marks") and the verb ("are") before the colon. The sentence in "B" includes the object ("in sentences that provide lists") of the subject ("marks") and verb ("appear"). The use of the colon in "A" is incorrect; its use in "B" is correct. So the punctuation rule for the use of colons is that they are only appropriate in sentences where they are preceded by the subject, verb, and object of the sentence that precedes the list.

Knowing that basic rule should clarify when colons must (and must not) be used to introduce lists. What about semi-colons in a list sentence? Semi-colons can be used to separate the items in the list, but they are not always used to do so. Consider these two examples:

A. Some of the colors artists frequently use in paintings include the following: red; green; and blue.

B. Some of the colors artists frequently use in paintings include the following: red, especially to show emotion; green, often to suggest nature; and blue, frequently to indicate tranquility.

The use of the semi-colons in "A" is inappropriate because they serve no purpose in substituting for commas. Their use in "B," however, does serve a purpose because each of the items in the list is further identified with a modifier. Since the modifiers are properly set out with commas, the use of semi-colons serves to clarify where each item in the list ends, thereby making the reading of the list easier to comprehend.

So the punctuation rule for the use of semi-colons in a list sentence is that they should be used when the items in the list contain commas or when the items in the list are of considerable length.[19]

The punctuation rules for list sentences are relatively simple to use once you learn them. Learn them now, and you will never have to concern yourself with that aspect of constructing a list sentence again.

The more difficult task in constructing list sentences involves what is called parallel construction. "Parallel" may not be the best word to describe what is involved; "equivalent" might be better. The idea is to set out each item in the series (the list) with the same form of construction. This part of the writing can be a little artistic if done well. Consider these two list sentences:

A. List sentences are easy to read when the following tasks have been accomplished: the items in the list all relate to the same point; correctly punctuated throughout; and uses parallel construction as to each item in the series.

B. List sentences are easy to read when the following tasks have been accomplished: the items in the list all relate to the same point; the items are all punctuated with the same marks; and the items in the list are all constructed in the same manner.

Both sentences provide the tasks that need to be accomplished, but in "A" they are constructed without regard to how the structure of each relates to the others in the series. The result is a sentence that reads awkwardly, if not ungrammatically. In "B," the items are substantively the same as those in "A," but each item is constructed in the same manner (specifically, each is basically written in the form subject-verb-prepositional phrase: items ... relate ... to the same point; items ... punctuated ... with the same marks; items ... constructed ... in the same manner).

19. Example: Due to the negligence of the defendant, Michelle fractured her neck, back, and leg; suffered a concussion and facial lacerations; and has been diagnosed with post-traumatic stress, a brain injury, and neuropsychological issues.

Constructing list sentences in parallel form is a mechanical task that requires attention to the flow of each item in the series. It takes work to do it well, but the result is a list that will be easier for the reader to negotiate. With practice, constructing list sentences in parallel form will become more natural and, occasionally, will even leave you feeling like a word artist when you make a complicated list of items easy to read.

Chapter Summary

Every correctly constructed sentence must contain a subject and a verb. Sentences that place the subject and verb next to each other (or very close to each other) are easier to read since the "who did what" is the essential information in every sentence. Placing the object (the "to whom") close to the subject and verb provides the reader with the critical information the writer intends to convey. And placing all three at or near the start of the sentence makes the reading even more reader-friendly.

In legal documents, short sentences enhance readability. A simple sentence contains a single clause that conveys a single thought. Occasionally, multiple thoughts can be conveyed with compound or complex sentences. Compound sentences contain two independent clauses that are joined by a conjunction. Complex sentences contain an independent clause and a dependent clause. If the dependent clause comes first, it is followed with a comma; if the independent clause comes first, it is not usually followed with a comma.

Well-constructed sentences are easy to read even when they contain complex thoughts. Numerous barriers to good sentence structure exist. Passive construction is one such barrier. It places the intended subject of the sentence in the place of the object of the sentence. Passive constructions are built off of a variant of the verb "to be." Mixed constructions attach the verb to the wrong subject. Subjects that don't match the verb to which they are intended to attach and subjects that don't match the pronouns later in the sentence that they are intended to match are internal disagreements that result in poorly constructed sentences. Pronouns that do not match with the gender of the subject of the sentence should be avoided without defaulting to a generic gender.

Nominalizations exist when a verb is made into a noun. They make a sentence longer than it needs to be and deflect the intended point of the sentence. Misplaced modifiers can be comical at best and confusing for the reader at worst. The "nowhere there" and the "no thing it" should be avoided in sentences. They are usually traps for passive constructions. The use of the "this" and "that" as nouns can leave the reader wondering what word they were referring to. Double negatives and double possessives can also make a reader's work more difficult and should be avoided. Contractions are generally inappropriate in legal documents.

Some formerly considered barriers to good sentence construction are not so recognized in legal writing. Most split infinitives are acceptable. Ending a sentence with a preposition and beginning a sentence with a conjunction are also perfectly acceptable.

Certain parts of legal documents require special attention in sentence construction. Rules should always be stated precisely and with clarity. Focusing on the purpose of the rule in the document promotes proper construction of rule statements. Headings should always be stated as complete sentences. Point headings should answer major issues that the document is addressing. They should be written as the answer to the issue. Sub-headings can be either primary sub-headings or conclusionary sub-headings. Primary sub-headings address sub-issues in the document. They should be stated as answers to the sub-issues. Conclusionary sub-headings introduce analyses or arguments. They should state the conclusion with the reasoning summarized (specific law applied to specific facts).

Conclusions to specific analyses or arguments can be as short as a single sentence. Rarely should they be longer than three sentences. These conclusions are not the Conclusion section of a full memo or brief. They are only intended to summarize the analysis or argument just provided in the document. They can often begin with the phrases "for these reasons" or "from these cases."

Lists are ubiquitous in legal documents. They should always be written in parallel form so that each item in the series (that comprises the list) is structured in the same way. Correct structuring of list sentences requires proper use of colons and semi-colons. Colons are only used to introduce a list when what precedes the list is the subject-verb-object part of a complete sentence. Semi-colons are only used between the items in the series when the items are long or contain internal commas.

Good sentence construction is reader-friendly writing. It does not reduce the complexity of the thought; it just makes the thought easier to read.

Think deeply; write simply.

Chapter Six

Correct Grammar and Punctuation in a Legal Document

A. Introduction
B. The Punctuation Marks
C. Putting Them All Together—Colon, Semi-Colon, or Comma
D. Results of Incorrect Usage
E. Parts of Sentences
F. Potential Pitfalls
G. Complex vs. Complicated

A. Introduction

You may have heard that even a missing comma can make a big difference in legal writing. It is not an exaggeration, as certain food industry workers in Maine discovered a few years ago.

In *O'Connor v. Oakhurst Dairy*,[1] the drivers of the dairy's food delivery trucks claimed that they were mistakenly left out of a state law solely because of the absence of a comma. In the case, the particular comma that was omitted from the legislation is called the Oxford comma (also called the serial comma), which is the comma that some writers include at the end of a series of things. The grammatical world is divided on whether this comma is necessary, preferable but unnec-

1. 851 F.3d 69 (1st Cir. 2017).

essary, or just plain inconsequential, but in *O'Connor* the question was one the court could not avoid.

Here is the specific provision of the legislation that provided the crux of the issue: "The canning, processing, preserving, freezing, drying, marketing, storing, packing for shipment and distribution of...." The key phrase is "packing for shipment and distribution," which the employer company argued should be interpreted to mean "workers who pack for shipment and distribution" as opposed to "workers who pack for shipment and workers who distribute."

The absent comma forced the court to go through a belabored review of dictionary definitions and the guidance provided to legislation drafters by the Maine Legislative Drafting Manual in attempting to resolve this issue of statutory construction. The court ultimately ruled for the truck drivers, but it only did so after deciding that the ambiguity created by the missing comma allowed the court to revert to an entirely non-grammatical canon of statutory construction (simply entitled, "liberal construction"). Under that canon, the court held that the statutory language was meant to provide the workers with the overtime pay that the truck drivers sought.[2]

Did the court get it right in *O'Connor*? It did unless the Maine legislature decides to re-visit the issue by amending the original statute. But as it stands, *O'Connor* is a good example of the importance of punctuation in legal writing. Commas matter, as does their absence.

In this chapter, we'll cover all seven major punctuation marks as well as some of the less frequently used ones. We'll also explain those nasty punctuation rules that can bedevil even Bill Gates (and the infamous green underlining that is supposed to point out punctuation and grammatical errors but is often incorrect on Word's infamous Gram-mar Check function). We will also review some essential grammar rules and distinguish run-on sentences, comma splices, and non-sentences, all of which are unacceptable white-glove glitches in any legal document.

2. *Id.*

B. The Punctuation Marks

Thirteen separate punctuation marks are available for use in legal documents. They are the period, comma, exclamation point, question mark, colon, semi-colon, dash, hyphen, parentheses, brackets, apostrophe, quotation marks, and ellipses. Some of these are far more ubiquitous in their usage than others. But they each have rules that govern when they must be used, when they may be used, and when they must not be used. Happily, even if you never learned these rules before you started law school, none of them will tax your brain nearly as much as the Rule Against Perpetuities or the Felony-Murder Rule. And, even more happily, a simple Google search will almost always provide the answer to a question about the usage of a particular punctuation mark. So, let's get into them.

1. The Period

The purpose of this punctuation mark is, simply stated, to note the end of a sentence. And in legal documents, the key to the use of a period is to identify that what it (the period) follows is a complete sentence. Unlike what is sometimes seen in literary writing, the period should not be used to create a "staccato tone or cadence."[3] The period is not a stylistic mark. Stylistic writing can have its place in legal documents, but the proper use of the punctuation mark must be followed in creating the style or tone the writer seeks to convey.

Of course, the period can also be used at the end of abbreviations. Abbreviations such as "Jr." and "Sr." always require periods. They may also be required in abbreviated titles, times of day, and other commonly used terms, but be careful not to create your own abbreviations or to use esoteric abbreviations. Only use abbreviations that are universally understood and recognized. The citation manual and style manual your office or court use is your best guide.

3. The following is an example of a staccato: He hit her. But not him. In legal writing "But not him" would need to be included in the single sentence, as in "He hit her but not him."

2. The Comma

The comma is probably the most utilitarian of the punctuation marks. In its most basic sense, the comma is used to set apart phrases or terms within a sentence. Commas are used in lists of items, and also between adjectives that are interchangeable. A comma can be used to remedy the misplaced modifier error discussed in Chapter Five. And the comma can both avoid and create misunderstandings as discussed in the introduction to this chapter regarding the "Oxford Comma."

Commas bind together independent clauses that are linked by a conjunction (the seven words that are identified by the acronym FANBOYS[4]). Commas are not used to join two independent clauses without a conjunction. Doing so creates a dreaded "comma splice," where the comma is incorrectly used to make what should be two separate sentences into one.

Commas are also used for sentences that start with a dependent clause or an introductory word or phrase.

Commas also set off non-essential phrases in writing that are used as descriptors or asides. The comma should sit on both sides of these phrases to make clear to the reader that the phrase is supplemental to the thrust of the sentence. A good test to determine if the commas are necessary is to omit the phrase and ask if what is left of the sentence expresses the basic point that was intended. If the answer is yes, the commas are necessary on either side of the phrase.

A comma can also set off other non-essential words at the beginning of a sentence, like "well" or "why." These are colloquialisms, though, and should not be used in legal writing. As exemplified by the word "though" in the previous sentence, words that break the flow of the sentence should also be bracketed by commas.

Commas are also used to set off titles, degrees, and the words Sr. or Jr. after an individual's name. A common mistake, one even sometimes made by professionals, is the placement of a comma outside of quotation marks in a sentence. The American rule (contrary to the English

4. For, and, nor, but, or, yet, so.

rule) is to place the comma (and, when appropriate, the period) inside of the quotation marks. Compare the following examples:

1. "He hit me", she said.
2. "He hit me," she said.
3. "He hit me".
4. "He hit me."

The punctuation marks are correctly placed in 2 and 4; they are incorrectly placed in 1 and 3.

One last point bears mentioning: Commas are not used solely for the purpose of indicating a pause in a spoken sentence. (This misunderstanding seems to be the default way commas may have been taught in lazy sixth grade grammar classes.) In some sentences, the point of a natural pause may be where a comma would be placed, but it would be placed there because of one of the grammatical reasons noted above, not because the sentence sounds like it needs a comma there. The point to remember is that commas serve to clarify how a sentence should be understood, not how it might be read aloud.

3. The Semi-Colon

For reasons only psychologists can fully fathom, this punctuation mark is often the bane of many writers' efforts. When used properly, this punctuation mark is effective in denoting the way a writer intends a pair of coherent points to be understood. However, when used incorrectly, it can serve as a signpost that the author is not an experienced writer or has not carefully edited the text. Repeated incorrect use of the semi-colon can detract from a reader's appreciation of the quality of the document and of the professionalism of its author. Indeed, a reader's overall appreciation of a substantive analysis or argument can be diminished by these kinds of errors.

The practice most often botched by inexperienced writers is the use of the semi-colon to join two independent sentences. Those sentences must be linked in some way in order for the unification to make sense. An example might be something like, "He accepted the plea bargain; there was ample evidence to convict him." Those sentences flow out of and into one another due to their subject matter and because one can be considered a cause or consequence of the other. The semi-colon is properly used there to reflect the coherence of the points; in effect, it makes one sentence out of two.

For that reason, the semi-colon should not be used to join what would otherwise be two sentences that are substantively unrelated or are only tangentially so. The substantive link needs to be genuine to justify the use of the semi-colon for this purpose. And the two clauses that are joined by the semi-colon must be "independent" grammatically, meaning that they could otherwise stand alone as complete and separate sentences (each with at least a subject and a verb).

Where the semi-colon is often incorrectly used (even by MS Word's Grammar Check) is when a phrase is being joined to an independent clause, as in this sentence:

> The sentence was complete as written; including the added point.

The phrase that begins with "including" in that sentence cannot stand alone as a separate sentence as it is not a separate independent clause. Thus, the sentence should not have a semi-colon to denote the added phrase. The same erroneous use of the semi-colon occurs when it is used to separate dependent and independent clauses. Avoid these mistaken uses of the semi-colon by properly identifying phrases, dependent clauses, and independent clauses[5] (all of which are explained later in this chapter).

Semi-colons are also used to join what would otherwise be a second sentence that begins with words like "however" and "therefore." Those words when used in that way are called transitional expressions or "conjunctive adverbs."[6] With that usage of the semi-colon, a pair of

5. A dependent clause is a group of words that contains a subject and verb but does not express a complete thought. A dependent clause cannot stand alone as a sentence. An independent clause contains a subject and verb and expresses a complete thought. An independent clause can stand alone as its own sentence.

6. A conjunctive adverb is a word that joins two sentences or independent clauses. The purpose of a conjunctive adverb is to link ideas in two sentences or clauses. Some of the many common conjunctive adverbs are however, consequently, therefore, also, furthermore, incidentally, indeed, likewise, meanwhile, nevertheless, nonetheless.

sentences that are clearly related can be joined as one sentence, as in this example: *Semi-colons can be very useful; however, they must be used correctly.*

That sentence could also be written as two sentences: *Semi-colons can be very useful. However, they must be used correctly.* But the flow of the thought is probably easier to grasp with the semi-colon.

Semicolons are also used in extended lists that contain complex terms or items, especially if any of those terms or items contain commas themselves. In such lists, the items in the list will be preceded by a colon. The specific items can then be separated by semi-colons, especially if one of the items in the list has commas within it. In such instances, the semi-colon serves to clarify the separate items that might otherwise be difficult to distinguish. Because so many legal rules consist of lists, the semi-colon is frequently used for this purpose.

4. The Exclamation Point

This punctuation is one of the most overused marks in today's society. In the age of social media, messenger applications, and Internet commenting, the exclamation point has become a ubiquitous sign of outrage, emphasis, and excitement. Those emotions are rarely, if ever, appropriate in legal writing. As a result, this form of punctuation should, with the fewest of exceptions, only appear in quotations that are included in a legal document.

The intended readers for most legal documents will not be persuaded by emotion. They will, instead, be almost exclusively interested in the legal analysis that supports the reasons for the resolution of a legal issue. Any emotion a reader feels in reading a legal document should come from the legal reasoning conveyed in the document, not from the hints of emotion that an exclamation point may suggest. In those rare instances where a writer seeks an emotional response, the legal analyses presented by the writer should elicit that response. Specific analytic points can be emphasized in a legal document far more effectively with the impenetrable logic of the reasoning rather than with the artificial emphasis that an exclamation point might otherwise provide.

One final point on this particular punctuation: In those very rare instances where an exclamation point is deemed useful, one, and only one, will suffice. Multiple, successive exclamation points at the end of a sentence are never appropriate in any legal document.

5. The Question Mark

The question mark is also self-explanatory. Like the exclamation point, its use should be primarily limited to where it appears in quotations. Noting questions can be appropriate in a legal document (especially in stating issues), but rhetorical questions (such as would require a question mark) should be rare in a legal document.

Questions should also be rare in headings in a legal document. As explained in Chapter Four, headings should be written as complete affirmative sentences. The use of questions in headings is more appropriate for scholarly legal writing (*e.g.*, law review articles) than in legal memos and briefs.

And, of course (as also noted in Chapter Four), questions should never appear in the conclusion of a legal document. Even as a rhetorical device, the placement of a question at the end of a legal brief or memo is likely to be more distracting than beneficial to the reader.

6. The Colon

Colons may be thought of as demonstrative marks in that they are used to note the presentation of something that was introduced by the immediately preceding text. The colon can be used to introduce a series of items, but the clause before the colon should include what would be the subject, verb, and object of a complete sentence, as in this example: "We will need to research the law in many areas: torts, contracts, and real property." If the preceding clause lacks the object of the would-be sentence ("the law" in the sample sentence), the use of the colon would be incorrect, as in "We will need to research torts, contracts, and real property." The first word following the colon should only be capitalized if it would normally be capitalized, as with proper nouns or where what follows is a complete sentence (although some grammarians do not capitalize letters that would be the first word in a complete sentence following a colon).

When colons are used to introduce lists (as is often the case with legal rules), the items in the list will usually be separated by semi-colons (as noted above in the section on semi-colons), unless the items in the list are very short, as in the "torts, contracts, and real property" example above. The combined use of colons and semi-colons in this manner is ubiquitous in legal writing. Gaining comfort with the technique is essential for anyone engaging in the drafting of legal documents.

Another use of the colon is to introduce a block quotation. Block quotations are a tool to be used sparingly, but they occasionally appear in legal treatises, judicial opinions, and other academic writing. Block quotes present large (in excess of fifty words) quoted sections of text, usually because they say something in such a perfect or particular way that paraphrasing will not do them justice or provide the same effect as simply reproducing the words.

7. The Dash

Dashes are the marks that appear to simply be longer hyphens with spaces around them. In some word processing programs, they will appear as two successive hyphens, which may be joined automatically as you type or may remain separate. Either form is acceptable provided that form is used consistently.

Dashes are like commas and parentheses in that they are used to set apart pieces of a sentence that are otherwise unnecessary but add context to the substance of the sentence. Anything contained between dashes should be able to be excluded without affecting the substantive purpose of the sentence. Of course, the point of having the phrase inside the dashes is that it adds something. That point may very well add a great deal to the cadence or feel of the sentence, though it is grammatically superfluous.

Most dashes in legal writing are "em dashes," so called because their length more approximates the length of the letter m. Em dashes are used to indicate a break in the main thought of a sentence. In that respect they are similar to parentheses or the use of commas to set off a parenthetical phrase, and they would be placed both before and after the phrase. They can also be used in lieu of a colon, introducing a thought that expands on or further explains what has preceded it.

In some publications (newspapers and magazines, in particular), em dashes are preceded and followed by a single space. In most instances when they are used in legal documents (and literary works), they are not separated from the text with spaces.

En dashes are shorter dashes (more like the size of the letter n). Their use is mostly limited to separating dates or times or numbers, as if to say, between X date and Y date or from page X to page Y.

8. The Hyphen

The hyphen is the baby cousin of the dash. The hyphen is not for emphasis, and usually does not have a space on either side of the word or numbers it connects. In fact, that is the purpose of the hyphen, to connect. A hyphen is used for compound words, such as "off-campus." Some terms take the form of words by being hyphenated. "Vis-à-vis" is one example of such a term. Hyphens can even be used to form new terms, in order to avoid the appearance of an incorrectly worded sentence.

Hyphens are also used, as a rule, when writing out numbers and terms with numbers attached to them. A "two year statute of limitations" may well be clear enough, but a "two-year statute of limitations" ensures that the terms "two" and "year" are never taken to refer to two separate year-long statutes.

Compound numbers and spans of time or numbers also require a hyphen. Fractions written out should also be hyphenated, such as in the sentence, "He received a one-third reduction from his probation due to good behavior." Some people's names will even be hyphenated. This little mark pops up everywhere. When used properly, it adds clarity in the joining of words or phrases.

9. Parentheses

Parentheses in legal writing are not used in the same way—as an aside—as they are in simple prose. Using parentheses in legal writing for information that is unnecessary to the sentence is rare. For this purpose, dashes are preferable.

Parentheses do have a significant use in legal writing, in the form of a parenthetical citation (discussed in Chapter Four). In some citation manuals, the citations themselves are usually enclosed by parentheses.

When parentheses are used in a legal document to add secondary information or thoughts, certain punctuation rules must be observed. If a parenthetical aside occurs inside a sentence, it should appear without a capitalized first letter and, usually, with no added punctuation at the end of the sentence. If an entire sentence is in the parentheses, the first letter of the first word will be capitalized and punctuation will be included within the closing parenthetical mark.

Finally, the language inside the parentheses is excluded from the formulation of grammar outside of the parentheses. Consider this next sentence as an example. *The murderer (and his accomplices) was convicted of the crime.* In such a sentence, the clause inside the parentheses (despite how it sounds when read) is not part of the sentence for grammar purposes. Thus, in the sample sentence, the correct verb is "was," not "were."

10. Brackets

Brackets are most frequently used inside quotations to note a change made to the wording that makes the quoted language fit more naturally into the written sentence. If the quote reads, "then he said he stole the bracelet," the sentence may be repurposed to read, "then [you] said [you] stole the bracelet" if the quotation were being placed into a paragraph directed at the speaker of that original quote. If a quote from the internal section of a sentence is used at the beginning of one of the writer's own sentences, the brackets will then be placed around the first letter, which will be capitalized. "[G]et it?" Brackets also have uses "such as flagging mispelings [sic][7] inside quotes." Other specialized uses for brackets, as in string citations, are also common (depending on the citation rules that are being followed).

---

7. "Sic" means "exactly as written." It is placed after a quoted word or passage to indicate that the quoted material has been transcribed or translated exactly as it was found in the original text, including any typos, grammatical errors, or non-standard spellings. It can also apply to a surprising assertion, faulty reasoning, or other material that might appear as an error. It is derived from the Latin word of the same spelling.

11. The Apostrophe

This simple mark is all too easily overlooked when it should be used and is all too often used incorrectly when it shouldn't be used. The rules are not confusing, which makes the frequent errors in usage bewildering. An apostrophe before or after the letter "s" that ends a noun indicates the noun's possession of whatever follows the noun in the sentence. If the apostrophe is before the "s," the noun is singular; if the apostrophe is after the "s," the noun is plural.

Apostrophes are also used to show contractions, although the traditional rule has been that contractions should not be used in legal documents. (That rule is becoming somewhat archaic and may not be as strongly held currently, but the general view that continues to be recognized by some is still that contractions that are common in speech should not be used in a legal document.)

Where apostrophes should not be used because the usage is incorrect is to show the plural of a noun. This mistake is apparently the equivalent of a typo (discussed fully in Chapter Eight), as the appearance of the misuse is equally ubiquitous. Thus, the apostrophe error in the following sentence can appear all-too often and can be overlooked in white-gloving all too easily: The attorney's agreed to continue the trial. The mistake is egregious for two reasons. First, it indicates sloppy writing and editing skills, and second, it can be momentarily off-putting, if not confusing, for the reader.

One use of the possessive apostrophe does require some added knowledge of usage. That usage is when a word ends in "es'" to show both plural and possessive, as in this sentence: The Joneses' lawsuit was dismissed without prejudice. In the sentence, the "es" is used to indicate more than one member of the Jones family, and the apostrophe is added to show the family's possession of the lawsuit.

Apostrophes are also accepted after numerical terms made plural and single letters made plural, as in "Hopefully, the student will receive straight A's this semester." And, finally, apostrophes are not single quotation marks, even though they look the same and appear by pressing the same key on a keypad. The difference between the two is discussed briefly in the next section.

12. Quotation Marks

Quotation marks must always be used when directly quoting language from another authority within the text of a legal document. The capitalization and punctuation rules are similar to those that apply for text inside parentheses (capitalize and punctuate a complete sentence). The overall text flows better when the quote is made part of the written sentence, but an entire sentence in quotes within a sentence of text can be awkward and difficult to grasp quickly.

An exception to the use of quotation marks exists when using a block quote. Block quotes are used in those rare instances when the language is so famous, important, specific, or provides such clarity that, despite its length (at least fifty words), it is desirable to include it.

Including statutory language in the text of a legal document is desirable when the statute is integral to the reasoning or analysis of an issue. If the reader will need to refer repeatedly to the statutory language, including that language in the text of the document (as opposed to placing it in a footnote) is preferable. For block quotes of a statute, the quoted section of the statute will appear two single-spaced lines down from where the text ends. The quote will be single-spaced, indented a half-inch on each side, and will *not* use quotation marks, as in this example:

> All persons born or naturalized in the United States, and subject to the jurisdiction thereof, are citizens of the United States and of the state wherein they reside. No state shall make or enforce any law which shall abridge the privileges or immunities of citizens of the United States; nor shall any state deprive any person of life, liberty, or property, without due process of law; nor deny to any person within its jurisdiction the equal protection of the laws.

U.S. Const. am. XIV

The text will then resume another two single-spaced lines below the citation.

Direct quotations from authorities should be used sparingly. The better approach is to use them only to supplement an argument or analysis, rather than to suffice entirely in and of themselves. Thus, paraphrasing what the authority says and then citing to that authority is preferable. In most instances, whether to include a direct quote is a judgment call for the writer. If the language is especially poignant or helpful to your case, a quote can enhance an analysis or argument. The writer's judgment must determine whether a quote is necessary, helpful, or gratuitous and perhaps even distracting.

Quotations can be used for terms that you are coining, or that are terms of art not commonly known to all legal practitioners. They should not be used for legal terms of art that are known to all, such as the levels of scrutiny, reasonableness standards, and the other rules that are common knowledge for most lawyers and jurists. Quotations can frame letters and numbers that should be read as those letters and numbers themselves, as opposed to the sounds that they create in spoken language.

Single quotation marks (as opposed to the standard double marks) are used to show quotations within quotations. If, for example, a brief includes a quote from a police report, and that police report in turn contains a quote, single quotation marks would denote the quote contained in the report, as in this example: The report read, "Officer Alhambra responded to the scene, and found an intoxicated suspect screaming 'They're out to get me!'" Notice that the same rule for internal punctuation applies: If there is a complete sentence within the single quotation marks, capitalize and punctuate the sentence as if it stood alone.

13. Ellipses

Ellipses will rarely be used in a legal brief. They can be used in the middle of a quote in order to signify that some text has been omitted. They should not be used, as they often are in non-legal prose, to demonstrate cadence, or hesitation in the thought pattern the writer is seeking to convey. Legal writing is not the place for dramatic stylization. Instead, the words themselves must convey the desired impact of the point being made.

Closing Thoughts on Punctuation Usage

All of the rules on punctuation usage detailed above are ultimately adaptable to the specific context of the writer's individual style. At the start of a legal career, the rules are a foundation and baseline. As attorneys develop their own sense of their professional self, they invariably find their voice. That voice may be molded by early mentors (indeed, even legal writing professors) or by the strictures and dictates of the first firm or agency where attorneys begin their careers. Ultimately, each attorney's voice will allow for flexibility in some of these rules regarding punctuation usage so that violating the rules are perceived not as mistakes, but as purposeful and stylistic writing choices. But until that point of confidence (and seniority) is reached, the rules should be respected. They provide the baseline for perceived competence in legal writing, which is how, in part, every attorney's professional reputation will be formed.

The following sections provide more specific examples of situations where the punctuation rules can enhance competent legal writing.

C. Putting Them All Together—Colon, Semi-Colon, or Comma

We've already briefly discussed the correct usage for each of these marks individually. But in practice, the real question is which mark must be used in each particular circumstance. Usually, just knowing the specific rules will make the decision relatively easy. With respect to the colon, semi-colon, and comma, however, the choice indicated as technically correct by a specific grammar error algorithm may be incorrect for the purposes of the actual intended sentence.

The colon is one of the marks that are less frequently used in non-legal writing. Hence, the tendency may be to use a comma in its place in a legal document. But its purpose in a legal document is different and distinct. The colon is used in a demonstrative fashion to signal a point directly related to the point just made, whereas a comma just indicates separate sections of a sentence. Adding a comma in a place that should be inhabited by a colon will create an awkward second half of the sentence as in this example:

> There are certain elements in common law burglary, a breaking and entering into a dwelling house, at night, and with the intent to commit a felony therein.

A colon clarifies the list that follows as in this version of the sentence:

> There are certain elements in common law burglary: a breaking and entering into a dwelling house, at night, and with the intent to commit a felony therein.

In the first sentence, using a comma creates the impression that burglary is the first term in a list, instead of burglary being defined by a list that follows. Because of the comma, the reader may have to go back and scan the sentence again to glean the correct meaning. Whereas, using a colon immediately sets the first part of the sentence apart from the following portion and denotes an explanation or elucidation of sorts.

Using a semi-colon in the place of the comma is also problematic, as in this example:

> There are certain elements to common law burglary; a breaking and entering into a dwelling house, at night, and with the intent to commit a felony therein.

Although this construction seems to distinguish the second part of the sentence more clearly as an explanation, the result is that the list appears as a sentence fragment, which most readers will recognize as such. They will take note of each incidence of incorrect grammar, and too many such notes will create a negative overall bias against the writer's work as a whole. Yes, the error can be ignored, but, over time, the reader's ultimate opinion of the writer will suffer.

Two common sources of confusion in the use of these three marks are in their utility in complex lists and in the joining into one sentence of otherwise complete sentences.

In lists, using a comma instead of a semi-colon can leave the reader confused and forced to re-read the list to determine where each term of the list begins and ends.

A rule of thumb for punctuating lists is as follows: If the individual components of the list vary greatly in length as between each other, or if all of them are made of several words so as to comprise a phrase, then semi-colons are usually appropriate to separate the items in the list. Commas used in such a sentence will give the reader the initial impression that the list terms are clarifications rather than parts of a complete concept or rule.[8]

The same can be said of the use of a comma instead of a semi-colon to join two otherwise complete sentences. The brain does not like to digest long strings of complex thoughts. Two sentences may be very closely related, and they may be correctly joined; however, commas are associated with the ongoing enterprise of a single thought, merely partitioning different parts of that thought so as to clarify its expression. But the semi-colon, as it is used in the prior sentence, shows that two thoughts are complete in their own right but that they should be considered together due to their relationship. The difference is subtle, but it can be meaningful in interpreting a rule in a legal document.

The goal of choosing the correct punctuation in a sentence is to ensure that the reader correctly and quickly comprehends the thoughts the writer wants to convey. The result of the incorrect usage of punctuation is often confusion, and that confusion can obscure (or make more difficult to appreciate) the valuable (perhaps even brilliant) ideas the writer is offering.

In the next section, we will go over the most common grammatical errors that result from the incorrect use of punctuation.

D. Results of Incorrect Usage

The rules of grammar exist for reasons beyond forcing elementary school children to diagram sentences. We speak in patterns. Actually, we speak in layered patterns. The words that we use can be understood, individually, by other animals (a pet dog, for example), but the sentences that we speak cannot be so understood. We take individually defined terms, organize them into patterns, and then organize those smaller patterns into larger frameworks that are used to build complex expressions of thought. In architecture and structural engineering, not only must one understand the ways to fasten individual pieces to one another, but also the forces exerted by larger structures, the weight that

8. Most lists in legal documents provide the parts of a rule, as is common in legislative or court-created rules with elements or factors.

can be borne by certain angular combinations, and the aesthetics of the entire building as an overarching consideration. Legal writing, such as in briefs and legal memos (or even statutes and regulations), is subject to the same interrelatedness and complexity.

The effect of having established rules of grammar is to begin with an understanding between the reader and the writer that ideas will be conveyed via the typical means, and this understanding allows the reader to focus on the merit of the argument instead of spending time figuring out what the writer is trying to express. If readers wanted to puzzle over how to express a thought, they would write a brief or scholarly work themselves. Thus, good legal writers build their thoughts to the specifications of proper grammar by policing their work to avoid the following errors of construction.

1. Run-On Sentences

These errors occur when what would otherwise be two complete sentences are joined as one without either a properly punctuated connecting word or the simple intrusion of a semi-colon. Here is a simple example of a run-on sentence:

> The writer had a single thought it was mangled in its writing.

The run-on would be corrected in any of the following alternative constructions:

1. The writer had a single thought; it was mangled in its writing. Here, the semi-colon is used correctly to separate the would-be sentences.
2. The writer had a single thought, but it was mangled in its writing. This correction uses the conjunction "but" to create a compound sentence.
3. The writer had a single thought; however, it was mangled in its writing. This correction would also work with a period in place of the semi-colon (followed by upper-case H for "however").
4. The writer had a single thought. It was mangled in its writing. Here, the writer is reverting to the two separate sentences as, possibly, were originally intended.

2. *Comma Splices*

The word "splice" is a throw-back to the days of reel-to-reel recording tapes when adhesive tape was used for tears in the recording tape. Comma splices are grammatic errors because the comma is used incorrectly to join what would otherwise be separate sentences, as in this example:

> The writer had a single thought, it was mangled in its writing.

To avoid this kind of error, the writer needs to insert a conjunction after the comma to create a compound sentence—The writer had a single thought, but it was mangled in its writing. (The writer could also insert a semi-colon, as noted previously.)

3. *Fragments/Non-Sentences*

Any phrase that stands alone as if it were a sentence is a fragment and a non-sentence, as in this example that starts with a complete sentence: The writer had a single thought. Just mangled in the writing.

Fragments as would-be sentences are fairly common in literary writing, where authors have an implicit allowance to allow for dramatic effect. Not so in legal writing. (Notice the fragment in that last non-sentence.)

E. Parts of Sentences

Complete sentences can be constructed in a variety of ways. They can consist of as few as two words, as we noted in Chapter Five with the Biblical verse, "Jesus wept." (In fact, one word can constitute a complete sentence if the subject is unstated but understood, as in "Listen!" where the subject "you" is understood in the context of the statement.) But a complete sentence can also consist of a mix of phrases and clauses that total multiple words.

To be able to use those phrases and clauses correctly and effectively, a writer must know how they are different and appreciate what punctuation requirements attach to each.

1. Clauses

Clauses are combinations of words that contain a subject and a verb. In some instances, those combinations can be complete sentences in and of themselves. In others, they serve to supplement another clause that would, on its own, be a complete sentence.

Independent clauses are those combinations of words with a subject and a verb that could stand alone as complete sentences. That they do not in a specific sentence is because they are supplemented (or modified) with another clause or other combination of words (a phrase, as explained below) that gives the independent clause more meaning.

Let's again consider the Biblical verse. "Jesus wept" is an independent clause. It can stand alone as a complete sentence. But if another combination of words supplemented those two words, the sentence would still be a complete sentence; it would just include more information, as in, "Jesus wept, having seen the sorrow around him." In that sentence, the independent clause is followed by a group of words that would not, by themselves, be a complete sentence. (Those words, in that sentence, are a participial phrase (discussed below).)

Independent clauses can obviously be longer than two words, and they usually are. For example, "Jesus wept openly and without shame" is still just an independent clause that can be a complete sentence. Punctuation rules are rarely a problem when an independent clause constitutes a complete sentence. In such instances, the sentence ends with a period.

Punctuation issues arise, however, when the independent clause is followed (or preceded) by another clause or phrase.

Dependent clauses are combinations of words that include what would be a subject and a verb but that also include other words that make those words reliant (dependent) on other words (most commonly an independent clause). If the Biblical verse was "Jesus wept when he saw the sorrow around him," the portion of the sentence beginning with "when" would constitute a dependent clause. It is dependent on the independent clause that precedes it. In such sentences, the dependent clause follows the independent clause without punctuation (*i.e.*, no comma). The sentence is complete with the two clauses joined naturally wherein the second provides context for the first and the first gives meaning to the second.

Introductory clauses are clauses that introduce independent clauses. They are also dependent in that they are not able to be complete sentences even though they contain a subject and a verb. "When he saw the sorrow around him" would be an introductory clause if it preceded "Jesus wept" in our re-written Biblical verse. But in that sentence, the dependent clause introduces the independent clause and, as such, it must be followed with a comma. Thus, the words can be the same, but the punctuation rule is different: a comma if the dependent clause introduces the independent clause; no comma if the dependent clause follows the independent clause.

2. Phrases

Phrases are combinations of words that appear in a complete sentence but do not contain both a subject and a verb. Phrases are common to most sentences since any combination of words that doesn't constitute a clause is a phrase. Various terms are used to describe the different ways that words can form phrases. Here are a few particular types of phrases that merit special attention.

Introductory phrases are those few words that can start a sentence. They are almost always followed by a comma. (Occasionally, the comma can be optional if the phrase is clearly connected to the subject.) If the Biblical quote had said, "On arriving that morning, Jesus wept," the words preceding "Jesus" would constitute an introductory phrase that would be followed by the obligatory comma. (If, on the other hand, the sentence had read, "That morning Jesus wept," no comma would be required.)

Participial phrases are phrases that begin with a participle. (A participle is a form of a verb that acts as an adjective in that it modifies a noun or pronoun.) The phrase "beginning a sentence" is a participial phrase. If the phrase starts a sentence, it is followed with a comma. If it follows an independent clause, it is not preceded with punctuation. If it is part of a dependent clause, it is punctuated or not punctuated in the same way as restrictive and non-restrictive phrases (discussed below).

Parenthetical phrases are phrases that are placed somewhere in the middle of a sentence to provide additional, non-essential information regarding something more central to the purpose of the sentence. They are always set off with commas, much as a parenthetical would be set off with parentheses if it appeared in the middle of a sentence.

Parenthetical phrases can begin with prepositions (in which case they are also *prepositional phrases*) or with other words that indicate a break from the main point of the sentence. They are parenthetical if the sentence can be read and understood without them. Returning again to our Biblical sentence, if it read, "Jesus, after seeing the sorrow around him, wept," the phrase between "Jesus" and "wept" would be a parenthetical phrase (which would also qualify as a prepositional phrase since it starts with the preposition "after"). (Note also that in the previous sentence, "Returning again to our Biblical sentence," is a participial phrase and that it is followed with a comma.)

Restrictive phrases consist of a number of words that are essential to the meaning of the sentence. They are not preceded by a comma and usually start with the word "that" instead of "which." Determining whether a phrase is essential is largely dependent on the context of the phrase relative to the subject or object it relates to. Thus, if the sentence concerns the quality of a man's jacket, the phrase is most likely restrictive as in this sentence: The jacket that the man was wearing was wrinkled and dirty. There, the quality of the jacket is integral to the purpose of the sentence. Hence, the phrase is restrictive and is led with the word "that" without a comma preceding it.

Non-restrictive phrases consist of a number of words that add to the meaning of a sentence without being necessary to the meaning of the sentence. They are usually introduced with the word "which" and are preceded with a comma. In the sentence, "The wrinkled jacket, which the man was wearing, was also dirty," the man wearing the jacket is not essential to the purpose of the sentence (to describe the quality of the jacket). Hence, the phrase is non-restrictive (it is not essential to the meaning of the sentence) and is introduced with the word "which" and is preceded by a comma. The phrase is then ended with a comma to set it off from the rest of the sentence.

The simple rule of punctuation for restrictive and non-restrictive phrases is that restrictive phrases start with "that" and are not preceded with a comma, while non-restrictive phrases start with "which" and are preceded with a comma. Deciding whether a particular phrase is restrictive or non-restrictive will often depend on the writer's purpose in constructing the sentence.

F. Potential Pitfalls

Even with complete knowledge of how all the punctuations work and how and when they should and should not be used, writers can create errors in their legal documents in a number of ways. Here are a few of the potential causes of errors that can occur even when specific punctuation marks have been used correctly.

1. Length

The *length* of all sentences should be carefully considered in legal documents. Some manuals even recommend a limit of twenty-five words for every sentence. While the actual number of words may have its own significance, the problems with overly long sentences ultimately relate to the reader-friendliness of the document. As we stressed in Chapter Five, ease of reading is paramount for documents that present substantively complex analyses. And overly long sentences make the reader's task more difficult when that reader is working through a less-than-straightforward argument.

Most long sentences contain more than one substantive point. And while a well-crafted complex sentence can be its own reward, if that sentence contains multiple points, the burden on the reader may detract from that reader's ability to grasp the nuanced point the sentence contains. Consider for a moment that last sentence (the one just preceding this one). It is thirty-six words long and contains three clauses and several separate phrases. It probably required more than one reading to fully grasp the main point it was making.

Now consider the same sentence broken up into four smaller sentences: A well-crafted sentence can be its own reward. But that sentence may contain multiple points. When it does, the burden on the reader may be too great. The result might then be that the nuanced point the sentence contains won't be grasped.

In four shorter sentences, the writer expresses the same point, and the reader more than likely grasps that nuanced point more easily. In legal writing, short is better than long.

2. Tails

Tails are an unfortunate result of some overly long sentences. They occur when, in the writing of the sentence, the writer loses the subject of the sentence as the number of words mount. Consider this example: James, in his efforts to construct perfect sentences while also including several substantive points, combined a complex and compound construction, and they were unappreciated by his readers.

The example sentence consists of twenty-eight words, so it is probably too long anyway. But its "tail"—"they were unappreciated by his readers"—makes the sentence essentially incomprehensible. Does that clause refer to the "complex and compound construction" that immediately precedes it? Or does it refer to the "several substantive points" earlier in the sentence? Or might it refer to the "efforts" James made in constructing the sentence? Obviously, the writer has lost the thread of the writer's intended thought. And the reader's resulting appreciation of the effort is problematic at best.

Sentence tails are common by-products of overly long sentences. They are decidedly reader-unfriendly and can be eliminated by avoiding overly long sentences in the first place.

3. Parentheticals and Parentheses

Parentheticals and parentheses can also create problems in legal documents. Legal parentheticals have a definite place in legal documents. Because of the formalistic way they are constructed (with a present participle introducing them), they will be immediately identified and appreciated by most readers. But their use can be abused, as when they intrude so heavily on the actual text of a document as to become a distraction.

Other parenthetical inserts can also be overused. As explained in Chapter Five, the best sentence construction places the subject, verb, and object of the sentence together near the start of the sentence. Readers look for who (subject) did (verb) what (object) in every sentence.

And they most appreciate those three elements when they don't have to hunt for them. Parentheses disrupt the flow when they are placed between any two of the three elements. Parenthetical phrases (discussed above) are also intrusive, but less so for the reader (as in this sentence).

Often, the use of parentheses indicates a secondary thought that may be presented more effectively in a footnote or, perhaps, not presented at all. Again, if the goal is reader-friendliness, parenthetical inserts should be carefully considered and not abused through overuse.

4. Quotations

Quotations can also be intrusive for a reader as they present a potentially different "voice" in the reader's head. Some quotes say perfectly what the writer might otherwise take more words to say less clearly. But others are a lazy substitute for the writer, allowing someone else's words to say, perhaps less precisely, what the writer really wants to say.

Block quotes (quotes of fifty or more words that are placed in block form within the text of the document) are especially difficult for most readers and may even be unread at worst or merely skimmed at best. Block quotes can be useful when they summarize a point previously made in the text. At their worst, they are used to make a separate point beyond what is stated in the text of the document. And, however useful they may otherwise be, their mere appearance invites a reader's inattention, which can be disastrous when the text is already substantively complex.

Every quotation, however long, should be considered carefully before inclusion in a legal document. Some will survive the scrutiny and serve their purpose well. Others will be better replaced with the writer's carefully constructed more precise prose.

5. Citations

Citations are certainly ubiquitous in legal documents. Readers want and need to know where a specific piece of information first appeared, and providing attribution is every attorney's fundamental responsibility in any legal document. But the **placement of citations** within the text of a paragraph can make a big difference in the quality of the reader's appreciation of the substance of the text.

Compare these two sentences, both of which make the same substantive point with almost the same words:

> The court held in *Smith v. Jones* (2 Utop. 43 (2014)) that a negligent killing can be the basis for a wrongful death claim.
>
> Negligent killing can be the basis for a wrongful death claim (*Smith v. Jones*, 2 Utop. 43 (2014)).

Note how easily the citation can be ignored in the second sentence and how burdensome it is in the first. The citation itself is necessary as it provides the basis for the rule, but the reader will probably appreciate its placement at the end of the sentence when the substantive point has already been understood.

Good legal writing makes the placement of citations as unobtrusive as possible.

6. Footnotes

Footnotes are certainly one way to make citations unobtrusive as they essentially hide the citations entirely out of the text of the document. But that advantage can be largely defeated if the footnote itself appears within a sentence, thereby causing the reader either to stop reading the sentence to check the citation or to have to re-read the sentence to remember why the footnote was placed where it was placed within the sentence.

Footnotes definitely have their place in legal documents. But, like the citations they often contain, they should not intrude on the reader's attempt to grasp the substantive point of the principal text to which they are appended.

G. Complex vs. Complicated

Obviously, the two words are similar. But they have a very different meaning in practice. No writer of a legal document is seeking for it to be beautiful because it is so marvelously complicated. Instead, the challenge is to express complex thoughts in an easy-to-read manner. The way to accomplish that result is largely by using the tools of the trade correctly and effectively.

Complexity is manifest in the law. Rules, in the form of statutes, regulations based on those statutes, ordinances, agency rules and regulations, and judicial interpretations of all those rules can make any legal issue complex. The philosophical justifications inherent in the law themselves are the subjects of entire treatises, even the lifelong pursuits of many legal scholars and lay observers, and yet they are rarely addressed directly because to do so would make legal writing too cumbersome.

"Complicated" is used as a synonym for complex in common parlance. However, it means "burdensome" to the legal writer. Good writers of legal documents do not burden their readers with the task of discerning the meaning of a jumbled mass of seemingly related words. Burdensome reading can occur when the structure of sentences is convoluted. When a simple and direct sentence will do, additional clauses, introductory phrases, adverbs, or extraneous adjectives become burdensome. These extra parts weigh down—they complicate—the sentences. The danger is that the thought gets lost in the trappings of what a brief or memo writer might think of as a more aesthetically pleasing sentence.

Complexity follows from the interrelation of various components and considerations involved in resolving the issue that is the focus of the document. Complexity is a reflection on the concept as a whole. Complicatedness is a problem within a sentence, paragraph, or partial section of the full document.

Complicated writing is not necessitated by complex reasoning. In fact, the opposite is the better way to think of the relationship. Thus, as the amount of complexity in an analysis or argument increases, the writing should become less complicated. Adhering to that approach does not mean that each sentence in a legal document must be a simple declaratory sentence. But it does mean that the cadence in the structure of a full paragraph or series of paragraphs should be appropriate to the likely difficulty the material itself will present for the reader.

For example, foundational principles and the rules that an analysis relies on may be more effectively presented in shorter sentences in the beginning of a paragraph. Longer sentences with multiple clauses that illustrate the initial rule may then follow. The paragraph could then conclude with a short, declarative, summary sentence.

A good default approach to enhance a reader-friendly document would be to inversely treat complicated analyses with unencumbered prose. In other words, as an analysis becomes more complicated substantively, the prose that explains it becomes less cumbersome for the reader. Think deeply; write simply.

Chapter Summary

Considerations of punctuation and grammar have not ended because of the green or blue underlining that is now generated by our computers, especially since, as noted previously, some of the underlined sentences are perfectly fine as written. Syntax, diction, grammar, and punctuation are all still as relevant as ever in crafting legal documents. Substance is always of paramount importance, but how that substance is delivered, how the analyses are presented, and how the arguments are structured should never detract from the ease with which that substance can be understood.

Properly used, punctuation can make the substance of an analysis easier to understand and make the task of gaining that understanding less burdensome. Legal documents that are cleaned of any punctuation errors are more likely to hold the reader's attention.

Good punctuation and good grammar go hand in hand. Perfectly punctuated sentences that are crafted to say precisely what they need to say in the minimum number of words necessary are the path to reader-friendly writing. They ensure that the reader's focus will be on the substance that supports the resolution of an issue that is the reason for the document.

Competent legal writing requires adherence to these mechanical writing rules. And competent legal writing is a requirement for those who strive to be successful in the work of the profession.

Chapter Seven

Proper Citation to Authority in a Legal Document

A. Introduction

B. The History of Citations

C. A Guide to Research

D. The Research Outline

E. The Citation Triggers

F. Signals

G. Citation Manuals

A. Introduction

"We don't care what you think, unless you cite to authority."

One of your professors may have jolted you (or some other student in the class) with that harsh statement early in your law school career. While the tone may suggest disdain, the actual meaning of the remark is far less obnoxious. What your professor was emphasizing is that everything asserted in a legal argument or analysis must be supported with a reference to the source that supports the assertion. And in most instances, that source is a rule that has been stated in written form by someone (or some entity). Thus, we "cite to authority" to show where the rule that is the basis for our assertion can be found.

In this chapter, we will provide a way to systematize the research that can lead to the discovery of authorities that will then be cited in a legal document. We will then explain when citations are required (the triggers that dictate inclusion of a citation) and how citations are prescribed in the principal citation manuals. We will conclude by comparing and contrasting the citation rules in the three main manuals. They are the *Harvard Bluebook* (*Bluebook*), the *Association of Legal Writing Directors' Manual* (*ALWD*), and the *California Style Manual* (*CSM*).

B. The History of Citations

Rules have been cited for centuries. The earliest formal use of citations probably dates to the sixth century when Justinian's *Corpus Juris Civilis* was compiled. Justinian's digest of Roman law was eventually updated in Italy to include cross-references and notes. Around the eleventh century, a new citation system was developed in Western Europe.[1]

Over the course of succeeding centuries, English courts worked with the early citation system, as the sources of rules expanded beyond the edicts from the ruling monarch to statutes enacted by parliament and to recognition of the writings of scholars of the law. Even then, case citations were only used infrequently, and previous decisions were not considered binding.

But during the Middle Ages, English courts began to keep records of the names of litigants and the courts' decisions in litigated cases. And as lawyers began to extract the reasoning of similar cases (as early as the 1220s), the need for a method of citing to those decisions became apparent. Beginning in 1292, and continuing through 1535, reports of proceedings in court were compiled in Year Books.[2]

By the fifteenth century, it had become more common to cite cases by referencing the calendar year and the term, but citations remained vague until the advent of the printing press and the introduction of printing to England. After printing was introduced, citations were able to contain more precision and volumes of citations were more easily able to be compiled. And, as those citations became more accessible, their usage increased.

---

1. Cooper, Byron D., "Anglo-American Legal Citation: Historical Development and Library Implications" (1982).

2. *Id.*

From 1571 to 1865, reports were cited by the name of the reporter. A set of reports could contain cases from several years, and some years might not be included at all. Overlaps in the years covered by each reporter also occurred. During the seventeenth century, the practice began of placing a volume number before the title or author's name.

The pre-independence American colonists followed English citation practices, which they were familiar with from their experiences in England and from imported English legal works. American colonial laws were originally organized by the English calendar year, but because of the possibility for confusion with English statutes, the practice developed of giving the colony name and the page of printed work, for example "Laws of Virginia p. 437."

In the 1800s, states began providing for official reporters and recognizing official reports. These reports continued to be cited by the name of the reporter, but the practice eventually evolved to citing reports by the title of the case or statute.

As the states continued to publish the cases and statutes from their own jurisdictions, private publishers entered the field. Several of these private publishers developed extensive coverage of cases and statutes in the various states until one publisher ultimately developed an interconnected system for identifying how specific issues have been addressed in all of the states. That publisher is West Publishing, and it added federal cases and codes to essentially take over the task of publishing all of the primary authority in all of the jurisdictions in the country.[3]

In some states, the West reporters are recognized as the jurisdiction's official reporters. In other states, the official reporters are still published by the states' governments. But even in those states, West reporters publish all court opinions that have been officially published as well as all statutes that have been enacted into law.[4]

3. *Id.*

4. *Id.*

C. A Guide to Research

Legal documents (be they legal memos or briefs that are filed with the court) seek resolutions of issues through the application of rules. Those rules must be cited in the document, but to be able to cite them, they first have to be found. Thus, legal research is often the first step in finding an authority to cite.

Back in the day when some of your professors were sitting in your seats, much legal research was a laborious process that started with digests that were the finding tools for actual authorities. Then, once a relevant case or statute was found, a series of books called Shepards had to be studied to determine if the particular authority was still good law (meaning it had not been overruled or otherwise circumscribed by a later opinion or statute). The entire process, just to find one set of cases or statutes, could take an hour or more (not counting the time required to actually read a case or study a statute).

But with the advent of computers (and the placement of almost all cases and statutes online), finding authorities to include and cite in a legal document has become a lot easier (and faster in terms of the time it takes). The immediate access to cases, statutes, and secondary sources can be of great benefit to an attorney if the attorney has a process for conducting the research. Two primary methods are available. One can be of good value when used rarely; the other is likely to be beneficial in more instances even though it is usually more time-consuming. The pros and cons of both methods must be understood before deciding which one to use in any research session.

In the first (let's call it the rifle approach), the attorney focuses immediately on the identified issue and uses a tightly crafted set of search terms that lead directly to a case or statute that appears to be right on point for the identified issue. With the rifle, the target of the research has been assumed to be correct and the hits will then also be assumed to be germane to the identified issue. The result can then be a case or statute that appears to lead to a winning argument or highly persuasive analysis.

The potential benefit of the rifle approach is that it is a great time-saver. Authorities are found quickly that can then be cited in the legal document as they are used to construct the argument or analysis that most favorably resolves the identified issue. But the danger with the rifle approach is that it immediately narrows the potential field of authorities to a single analytic point. To use the jigsaw puzzle concept (introduced in Chapter Two), the research has focused on one piece of the puzzle without considering other parts of the puzzle and the pieces outside of that single piece. And narrowing the scope of inquiry too quickly runs the risk of missing alternative ways of considering the issue (and other ways of approaching the resolution of the issue).

The rifle approach is best suited to issues that an attorney is already conversant with or, ideally, already has a good level of expertise about. In those instances, the attorney can safely explore a specific "piece of the jigsaw puzzle" to find the best cases without spending time in learning the law or figuring out what the overall "puzzle" looks like.

On the other hand, the rifle approach works poorly when an attorney identifies an issue the attorney is not conversant with or has never dealt with before. In those instances, the rifle approach may narrow the field of inquiry too quickly, with the result being missed authorities that could have led to a better argument or a more well-reasoned analysis.

The second approach (the shotgun approach) presumes that the attorney is not well-versed in the substantive law of the issue at hand (or at least is not an expert). Thus, the attorney needs to get a complete understanding of what the entire part of the jigsaw puzzle looks like. That attorney will want to develop a wide range of search terms that can lead to a number of possible areas of focus. As each of those areas is explored, the attorney will learn some law that might not be of ultimate value in the memo or brief the attorney is preparing to write. But it will also provide the kind of education that the attorney probably needs to identify what particular rules or concepts need to be developed into the winning argument or persuasive analysis the attorney will want to make.

The shotgun approach can lead to those exciting moments in the law that the best attorneys most appreciate: when ideas arise from newly discovered concepts. Some attorneys refer to finding needles in a haystack, but the shotgun approach allows for the exploration of multiple haystacks in which multiple needles might be found.

Obviously, exploring all of those haystacks takes time (even when new haystacks are just a click away on the computer), and that reality makes the shotgun approach only desirable if time allows for the search. Exploring multiple haystacks (or looking at different parts of the jigsaw puzzle) can be educational, but most attorneys are on the clock (or are on their client's clock). Thus, the shotgun approach can be counter-productive if time is spent exploring what end up being rabbit holes that never end.

D. The Research Outline

Whichever research approach is used will be most effective if what the research revealed is preserved, which requires the use of an efficient note-taking system. And the creation of a continually developing research outline is the best system for any research that is intended to develop an analysis of an issue. In many respects, a good research outline is similar to the outlines law students prepare for their substantive courses. Those outlines, when they are most effective, result from the student's developing understanding of how the substantive law of the particular course fits together (or how the jigsaw puzzle looks). Thus, instead of random rules and concepts that are loosely listed on a computer file, a good outline reflects a student's understanding of how those rules and concepts flow and are related to each other.

A good research outline does much the same thing. Thus, as new cases are found, they are put into the outline where they best fit with the other cases that have been found. And, critical to every research outline, each case (or other authority) is noted by the rule that it provides, by a brief note on the facts that gave rise to the rule, and by the pinpoint cite to the page within the case where the rule was stated. And in the process of creating that research outline, much the same thing happens as when the law student puts together the outline of the substantive course: To wit, the attorney learns (becomes an expert in) the substantive law on the issue the legal document will seek to resolve.

Here is an example of a simple, but effective research outline. Assume that in creating this outline, the attorney had been retained to represent a client who had been charged with larceny and that the attorney had never had a larceny case before and had forgotten everything from the first-year course in criminal law many years before. (The cases and citations are fictional.)

Larceny requires:

A trespassory taking

State v. Smith (7 Utop. at 43; D took control of victim's purse w/o her consent)

People v. Adam (68 Nirv. at 268; D took victim's TV w/o victim's consent)

And carrying away

State v. Smith (7 Utop. at 56; D removed victim's purse from her car)

People v. Adam (68 Nirv. at 273; D carried victim's TV to his car)

Of personal property

State v. Jones (23 Utop. at 156; D took victim's wallet)

People v. Butler (98 Nirv. at 401; D took victim's car)

From another's possession

People v. Davis (46 Nirv. at 234; D took victim's horse from victim's stable)

State v. Bolton (38 Utop. at 332; D took V's diamond ring from V's jewelry box)

With the intent to permanently deprive the victim of the property

People v. Davis (46 Nirv. 247; D sold victim's horse to T)

State v. Bolton (38 Utop. 346; D fenced victim's diamond ring)

In this imagined example, the attorney has researched larceny and found the five elements that comprise the crime. The attorney has systematized the notes from that research in the outline. The outline reflects the cases the attorney found for each element of the crime. The cases are noted with their citation (to the page where the element of larceny is explained or illustrated) and with a basic summary of the facts relevant to the element identified in the case. The attorney now has an easy way to review the results of the research and, potentially, to use those results in crafting a brief or memo.

The other decision that must be made for any meaningful research relates directly to which of the two methods (rifle or shotgun) are used. Cases will most often be where good research will end (because case law is often the linchpin of persuasive arguments and analyses). But are cases always the best place to start?

Again, the difference between the two methods is instructive. If an attorney is already well-versed in the substantive law of the particular issue that is the reason for the research, the attorney may not need the broader education that a good law review article or other secondary source might provide. But if, as in our example above, the attorney is dealing with a new area of the law (larceny), then the attorney might benefit from a treatise on criminal law or a good *ALR* article on larceny. Hence, the range of sources that are searched must be part of a good research plan.

And finally, because some research will take place over more than one session or period of time, a valuable technique can add to the efficiency of the continuing research. At the end of each session, the attorney should briefly summarize what substantive understanding the attorney has as a result of the research completed to that point. This final step for each session serves two purposes. First, it assists the attorney in gaining a full understanding of what knowledge has been gained for that session of research. And second, it provides a review of what that knowledge is (and, perhaps, of what the attorney needs to explore beyond that point) when the attorney recommences the research a day (or several days) later.

Time is precious, especially when a client is paying for that time. Thus, a fully systematized method of research makes the use of time more efficient and provides a process for attacking every research task. Viewed in this way, a research outline is really just an efficient and effective way to take notes while engaging in the research.

E. The Citation Triggers

The goal of the research is, of course, to find authorities that can be used in the legal memo or brief. And in most instances, the citation to those authorities will be included. In some instances, a cite is not required, even though the authority may be the basis for an analysis. The times when a cite is required are directly related to how clearly the authority is referred to.

The absolute rule is that a citation must be included whenever an authority is specifically mentioned or referred to in the text of the document. Hence, if the case of *Smith v. Jones* is mentioned, the cite for that case must be included immediately after the reference. But a cite should also be provided to *Smith v. Jones* if the text only suggests the reference to *Smith.* If, for example, the text read, "Some courts have required application of X rule in these instances," and *Smith* was one of those courts, the cite to *Smith* would be appropriate.

Perhaps the most common need for a citation occurs when a rule has been stated. After reading the rule, the reader of the document will immediately want to know where the rule came from (what authority provided the rule). Thus, many legal memos and briefs will feature paragraphs that start with this basic format: State the rule, state the authority that provides the rule, and give the citation for that authority.

And, because many rules come from cases, and because those cases are often lengthy and cover a number of different points (with a number of different rules), the citation should always be precise. Therefore, many case citations in a legal document will include both the first page on which the case appears in the reporter where it is published and the specific page where the rule is stated or otherwise noted. These pin/pinpoint cites spare the reader the considerable time it might otherwise take to find the part of the case that actually presents the rule that the writer has included in the document. Obviously, then, pinpoint cites must be accurate. A senior partner or judge (or the judge's law clerk) is not likely to be pleased when a pinpoint cite is inaccurate. The result of such "errors" can be that the value of the rest of the document is discounted (or worse).

F. Signals

A signal in connection with a citation informs the reader about the relationship between the point in the text that precedes the citation and the authority that the citation indicates. The various signals that are used in legal writing each have a different meaning (or provide a different understanding of the significance of the citation). Signals are not used when the cited authority directly states the point that the citation follows. They are also not used if the citation identifies the source of a quotation that immediately precedes the citation or identifies the authority immediately referred to in the preceding text.

The rules for the use of signals vary slightly between citation manuals. The chart below notes the primary distinctions in the use of signals with the *ALWD Manual* and the *California Style Manual* (*CSM*). (Note, also, that signals are always italicized in the *ALWD* and *Bluebook* manuals but are not in the *CSM*.)

Obviously, some degree of judgment exists in the choice of which signal might be most appropriate for a particular citation. In those instances where a choice must be made, the thought should be to align with how the reader would be expected to understand the signal.

G. Citation Manuals

The two most commonly used citation manuals are the *ALWD Manual* and the *Bluebook* manual. In California, the *California Style Manual* is also commonly used. Citations for briefs filed in California state courts generally follow the *California Style Manual.* Briefs filed in federal courts generally follow either the *Bluebook* manual or the *ALWD Manual.* The *Bluebook* manual is the most well-known and has historically been the default manual for many jurisdictions. But the *ALWD Manual* is also used by some offices and courts. The formats for citations are largely the same in both manuals with minor differences for specific kinds of authorities. The formats for citations in the *California Style Manual* can be significantly different from the other two manuals for a variety of authorities.

Signal	*ALWD*	*CSM*
See	Authority supports proposition either implicitly or in dicta.	Citations to weaker support.
e.g.	Authority states proposition other, not cited, authorities do as well.	For example (from the original Latin to which citation refers).
See, e.g.	Several listed authorities for a proposition.	May be used for authorities that are examples of the stated proposition's application.
See also	Authority cited is additional support for the stated proposition (but less direct than that indicated by "*see*" or "*accord*").	Used to indicate additional authority indirectly supporting the stated proposition.
See generally	Authority presents useful background (often with added parenthetical explanations).	Introduces useful background authority.
Accord	Used following a citation when additional authorities support the cited proposition.	Used after a primary authority is cited and introduces decisions providing the same holding.
Compare … with	Compares authorities, usually with accompanying parenthetical explanations.	Used to contrast decisions from separate authorities.
But see	Authority clearly supports the contrary proposition to the one stated in the preceding text.	Used to indicate a holding somewhat contrary to the main authority just cited.
Contra	Authority directly states the contrary of the proposition just stated in the preceding authority.	Cites cases squarely contrary to the proposition stated.

Each citation manual designates a specific format for citing cases, statutes, and other sources such as publications and websites. Each manual also contains a list of general and court abbreviations that should be used for certain words. Each citation manual also contains a list of the various state and federal reporters in which cases are published, and each manual includes appendices with specific information on the primary sources for each jurisdiction, local court citation rules, and citation rules for taxation materials and administrative agencies.

Citation manuals all serve the purpose of ensuring consistency in the way authorities are identified in a legal document. The format requirements may differ from one manual to another, but they provide a method that allows a reader to easily identify the source of a rule. And the citation provided in the document will then allow the reader to find that source should the reader want to explore the basis for the rule or otherwise probe deeper into the reasoning behind the rule.

What follows is a general survey of the basic formats for each of the three primary manuals noted above for citing to cases, constitutions, statutes, rules, regulations, and secondary sources.

1. Cases

The components of an *ALWD* case citation are the names of the first listed plaintiff and defendant (last name or business entity name), the reporter(s) in which the case was published, the court that decided the case, and the year the opinion was issued. The following is an example of a basic *ALWD* case citation:[5]

International Shoe Co. v. Washington, 326 U.S. 310, 316 (1945).

In this example, the plaintiff is International Shoe and the defendant is the State of Washington. Only the first named plaintiff and defendant are included in the citation even if there are multiple parties. The cita-

---

5. The full citation rules covering various types of cases can be found in the *ALWD Manual.*

tion that follows the case name, "326 U.S. 310, 316," indicates the volume of the reporter in which the case was published and the page number on which the case begins, followed by the page where the specific reference appears.

In the above example, the court is not separately identified because "U.S." indicates that the citation is from a Supreme Court decision. (The United States Reporter, abbreviated U.S. is the official publisher of Supreme Court cases.) If the issuing court is clear from the citation, it does not have to be listed again. Consider the following example in which a case is published in a federal reporter and the issuing court is identified after the reporter information.

> *United States v. Anderson,* 56 F.4th 748, 756 (9th Cir. 2022).

In this example, the case was published in a federal reporter that contains published cases from the thirteen federal circuit courts. The reporter information does not identify which circuit court issued the opinion, so the issuing court is identified immediately after the reporter citation. Here we can see that the opinion was issued by the Ninth Circuit in 2022.

The *Bluebook* style of case citations is very similar to the *ALWD* style, with only minor differences. In both the *Bluebook* and *ALWD* citation styles, case names can be either italicized or underlined. That option is a matter of preference for the writer. The components, layout, and spacing of case citations are largely the same. Some abbreviations might vary between the two manuals. The correct abbreviation can be confirmed by checking the abbreviation appendix in each manual.

The *California Style Manual* (*CSM*) method of case citation differs significantly from the *Bluebook* and *ALWD* styles. For example, the *CSM* places the year immediately after the case name instead of at the end of the full cite, does not include a comma after the case name, and does not include spaces for reporters and court abbreviations. The *CSM* also places the citation in parentheses, which the *Bluebook* and *ALWD* manuals do not require. However, the writer has the option of not using parentheses. The following example illustrates the difference between a *Bluebook*/*ALWD* citation and a *CSM* citation.

Bluebook/ALWD

People v. Foranyic, 74 Cal. Rptr. 2d 804, 805 (Ct. App. 1998).

OR

People v. Foranyic, 74 Cal. Rptr. 2d 804, 805 (Ct. App. 1998).

California Style Manual

(*People v. Foranyic* (1998) 64 Cal.App.4th 186, 188.)

2. Constitutions

The *Bluebook* and *ALWD* manuals use the same format for citing constitutions. Constitutions are identified by the name of the constitution, the article number, the section number (with any subdivisions indicated in parentheses), and the clause number.

The *CSM* format for citing constitutions differs slightly from the *Bluebook* and *ALWD* format in that the citations are placed in parentheses and a comma is included before the Article number. In citations to the California Constitution, subdivisions are designated with the abbreviation "subd." and paragraphs are designated with the abbreviation "par." with commas in between each section.

Below are examples of constitution citations in the *Bluebook/ALWD* format and the *CSM* format.

Bluebook/ALWD

U.S. Const. art. I, § 9, cl. 2.

Cal. Const. art. XIII, § 28 (f)(3)

California Style Manual

(U.S. Const., art. I, § 9, cl. 2.)

(Cal. Const., art. XIII, § 28, subd. (f), par. (3).)

3. Statutes

The *Bluebook* and *ALWD* manuals use the same format for citing statutes. If the full statute is being cited, the name of the Act is listed first, followed by the title number, the abbreviated name of the code, the sections and subsections, and the year. If a state statute is being cited, the state abbreviation appears first, then the sections and subsections. In citations to state statutes, the publisher is also included before the year. If an individual provision of a code is being cited, the full name of the Act is not included.

The *CSM* format for citing statutes is similar to *Bluebook* and *ALWD* but with slight differences. In the *CSM* format, statute citations are placed in parentheses and the year is not included. In citations to the California Constitution, subdivisions are designated with the abbreviation "subd." and paragraphs are designated with the abbreviation "par." with commas in between each section.

Below are examples of statute citations in the *Bluebook/ALWD* format and the *CSM* format.

Bluebook/ALWD

Comprehensive Environmental Response, Compensation and Liability Act, 42 U.S.C. §§ 9601–9675 (2000).

42 U.S.C. § 1983 (2000).

Cal. Evid. Code § 451(b) (West 1995).

California Style Manual

Comprehensive Environmental Response, Compensation and Liability Act (42 U.S.C. §§ 9601–9675 (2000)).

(42 U.S.C. § 1983.)

(Evid. Code, § 451, subd. (b).)

4. Regulations

The format for citing regulations is the same in both the *Bluebook* and *ALWD* manuals. Federal regulations are identified by the title number, the abbreviation "C.F.R." (Code of Federal Regulations), the section number, and the date in parentheses. The writer also has the option of including the name of a regulation if it is commonly designated by its name or if referencing the name will assist the reader in the identification of the regulation.

The *CSM* format for citing federal regulations is almost the same as *Bluebook* and *ALWD* with the one difference being that the *CSM* citation is enclosed in parentheses. California regulations in the *CSM* differ in that a comma is included after the code name and the year is not included. Additionally, subdivisions are designated by the abbreviation "subd." and the citation is enclosed in parentheses.

Below are examples of regulation citations in the *Bluebook/ALWD* format and the *CSM* format.

Bluebook/ALWD

7 C.F.R. § 319.76 (2005).

Cal. Code Regs. tit. 15, § 3084.1(a) (2005).

California Style Manual

(7 C.F.R. § 319.76 (2005).)

(Cal. Code Regs., tit. 15, § 3084.1, subd. (a).)

5. Rules

The format for citing rules is the same in both the *Bluebook* and *ALWD* manuals. Rules are identified by the geographic reference to the jurisdiction, followed by the abbreviation for the code or rule compilation that contains the cited rule.[6]

The *CSM* format for citing rules differs in several important ways from the *Bluebook* and *ALWD* format. As with other citations, rule citations are enclosed in parentheses. Additionally, in the *CSM* the word "Rules" is spelled out in the citations, while in the *Bluebook* and *ALWD* format it is abbreviated as "R." "Procedure" is abbreviated as "Proc." in the *CSM*, while in the *Bluebook* and *ALWD* format it is abbreviated as "P." In the *CSM*, the word "rule" is also stated again after the identification of the rule compilation, which is not the case in the *Bluebook* and *ALWD* format.

Below are examples of rule citations in the *Bluebook/ALWD* format and the *CSM* format.

---

6. Williams, *ALWD Guide to Legal Citation*, p. 174.

Bluebook/ALWD

Fed. R. Civ. P. 12(b)(6).

Fed. R. Evid. 410.

California Style Manual

(Cal. Rules of Court, rule 224.)

(Fed. Rules Civ. Proc., rule 12(b)(6), 28 U.S.C.)

6. *Secondary Sources*

Secondary sources include books, journals, and other periodicals. *ALWD* and *Bluebook* use the same format for citations of periodical materials. Periodical works are designated by the author, title, volume number, periodical abbreviation, initial page, pinpoint page (or page range), and date.

For non-periodical works, *ALWD* format italicizes the title, while *Bluebook* does not. Non-periodical works are designated by the volume number if applicable, the author's full name, the title of the book, the page cited, the editor's full name, the publisher of the edition cited, the edition number, and the year of the edition cited. The *Bluebook* format also includes the original date of publication.

The *CSM* differs from both the *ALWD* and *Bluebook* formats in citing secondary sources. The *CSM* includes only the author's last name rather than the full name of the author. The edition information is placed after the title instead of at the end. The entire citation is enclosed in parentheses. Additionally, it is recommended that the chapter name is included in the citation.

Below are examples of citations in the *Bluebook*/*ALWD* format and the *CSM* format.

Bluebook

David Rudovsky, *Police Abuse: Can the Violence Be Contained?*, 27 Harv. C.R.-C.L. L. Rev. 465, 500 (1992).

6 Bernard E. Witkin, California Procedure § 90, at 491 (4 ed. 1997).

ALWD

David Rudovsky, *Police Abuse: Can the Violence Be Contained?*, 27 Harv. C.R.-C.L. L. Rev. 465, 500 (1992).

6 Bernard E. Witkin, *California Procedure* § 90, at 491 (4 ed. 1997).

California Style Manual

(Rudovsky, *Police Abuse: Can the Violence Be Contained?*, 27 Harv. C.R.-C.L. L. Rev. 465, 500 (1992)).

(6 Witkin, Cal. Procedure (4 ed. 1997) Procedure Without Trial, § 90, p. 491.)

Chapter Summary

Any legal document that addresses a legal issue must include citations to the authorities that support the analyses or arguments the writer presents in the document. Finding those authorities requires a systematized approach to legal research that formalizes the process of taking notes on the authorities found in the research.

Citations need to be included for any authority that is either expressly mentioned (or quoted from) or is implicitly referred to (by way of the rule it supplies) in the document. The format for the citations might be dictated by a national or regional manual (such as the *ALWD* and *Bluebook* manuals and the *California Style Manual*). Citations to cases should indicate the precise page (pinpoint cites) on which the rule or concept referred to can be found.

While citing to authorities in a legal document is a more mundane part of the writing process, it must not be taken lightly. A mistaken citation can be a source of extreme frustration for a reader, and multiple incorrect cites can even cause the reader to lose confidence in the substantive points the citations were intended to support. Or, in the worst of circumstances, they can lead to the document being put in the read-later pile.

Chapter Eight

The Ten Steps of the White-Glove Inspection

A. Introduction
B. Step One—Logical Consistency and Organizational Flow
C. Step Two—Paragraph Structure and Paragraph Length
D. Step Three—Logical Sentence Flow and Cohesiveness
E. Step Four—Sentence Accuracy, Simplicity, and Brevity
F. Step Five—Grammar and Punctuation
G. Step Six—Case and Party Names and Citations
H. Step Seven—Typos
I. Step Eight—Spell and Grammar Check
J. Step Nine—The Pleasure Read and One-Voicing
K. Step Ten—The Printed Version
L. A Final Point—The Value of Cleaning as You Go

A. Introduction

In Chapter One, we introduced the white-glove inspection as both a way to proofread a final draft and as a way to understand the various requirements that a writer must satisfy to create a legal document that will be read and understood.

In this chapter, we consider how each of the steps of the inspection should be accomplished and how the basic skills of writing can be incorporated into a full proof of the final draft of a legal document. Some of the specific information provided in the steps that are described have already been covered elsewhere in the book. In those instances, they are repeated here to ensure that they are fully grasped and completely incorporated into your view of how every assignment to write a legal document should be approached.

B. Step One—Logical Consistency and Organizational Flow

1. The Format and the Delineation of Substantive Points

Errors in the structure of your document can appear in a number of ways. A common error, one that even seasoned attorneys sometimes make, is to deviate from the accepted numeration of points covered in the brief or memo.

Assume, for example, that a brief addresses two separate issues and that two separate primary assertions are made for each issue. Assume further that those primary assertions are presented in a series of arguments, some of which have sub-arguments contained within them. The proper delineation of the brief, just in terms of the numeration used for each argument, would be as follows:

```
I.
    A.
        1.
        2.
            a.
            b.
                i.
                ii.
    B.
        1.
        2.
II.
(Repeat pattern)
```

Note the progression as the delineation of arguments proceeds: The first designation is with an upper-case Roman numeral. The first level of subordinate designations consists of capital letters. Succeeding levels of subordination (and more finitely identified arguments) are shown with Arabic numbers, lower-case letters, and then, if necessary, with lower-case Roman numerals.

Errors can occur in the numeration in a brief when the normal order noted above is not followed, as when a Roman numeral is immediately followed by a lower-case letter or when an upper-case letter is immediately followed by a lower-case Roman numeral (Romanettes).

Another error that can occur in the formatting of the brief is when a single sub-point is noted. The simple rule is "you can't have an A without a B; you can't have a 1 without a 2." Properly understood, sub-points are divisions of main points, and since you can't divide one into less than two parts, you can't have a main point with only one sub-point. In such an instance, one of two things needs to happen in your white-glove work. You either have to figure out what the second sub-point is and label and denominate it as such, or you have to eliminate the sub-point as a separate designation and subsume it into your main point.

Skilled attorneys and judges understand and follow this method of formatting the office memo or brief. These professional colleagues will expect your documents to conform to this method. Evaluate the organization of your document by making sure you have the proper order of numeration for your points (from the most broadly stated to the most finite) and that you always have at least two sub-points under each point if you are dividing broader points into more finite ones. Your table of contents serves as a good way to double-check that you have conformed to these rules.

2. Headings and Umbrellas

Once you have established the proper format for your document, you need to provide your reader with guideposts to help your reader appreciate the way the organization lays out. Headings and umbrellas serve as those guideposts.

Headings are signposts for the reader. They tell the reader what the reader is about to encounter in the reading of the document. Headings should be provided for each separate substantive point in the format of your document. Thus, every time you have a delineation of a separate point, whether it is designated with a capital Roman numeral, an upper-case letter, or any of the other format designations noted above, you should have a heading that identifies the topic or subject of the designated substantive point.

As indicated in earlier chapters in this text, in a persuasive document, like a law and motion brief (a memorandum of points and authorities), the headings should be stated persuasively. In a predictive memo, they should present the point to be discussed in more neutral terms, while still perhaps containing the prediction the writer will be explaining in the text that follows. They should state the argument to be made in a concisely written assertion. They should not include authorities or citations but should read as a simple statement of the assertion that will immediately follow with legal support.

Subordinate points should also be noted with headings, and they should also be stated persuasively in a brief, more neutrally in a predictive memo. In all instances, headings that serve as the opening conclusions in the CREAC or C-RAC paradigms should contain a "because" clause (that part of the heading that gives the basic reason for the assertion or prediction that is made in the text that follows).

Umbrellas serve as introductions to the substantive points that will follow. They should be short, normally a single paragraph, and should be used as roadmaps for what will follow. Thus, if a substantive point will be divided into two or more sub-points in the discussion or arguments that will follow, an umbrella will provide the reader with an understanding of that division and of what each sub-point will concern.

Umbrella paragraphs can also be used to cover basic points that are foundational for the sub-points that will follow. But if you use an umbrella for this purpose, the same basic points should then not be made in each of the sub-points, because doing so would be redundant, and redundancy is another error that a reader-friendly document should not contain.

Inspecting your headings and umbrella paragraphs to make sure they accurately and effectively state the points you then make in the following text will keep your document organized and ensure against redundancy.

3. Logical Flow and Leading with Your Best

Organizational errors can occur in at least two other ways, both of which can be more troubling in terms of how your reader receives and accepts your document.

The first of these possible errors can occur if you open with an argument or analytical point that isn't particularly compelling. Readers tend to focus the greatest amount of their attention on the beginning of a document. Thereafter, their attention will tend to drift over the succeeding sections, picking up at the end of the document. Therefore, all other things being equal, the best way to begin your document is with your strongest point, and the best way to end it is with your second strongest point.

But you also have to pay attention to the logical flow of the arguments or analytical points you present in your document. Leading with your strongest argument or analytical point won't work well if that particular point can only make sense if it is preceded by a foundational point that needs to be made first.

Thus, the first rule of the substantive organization of your document is that the points you make must be made in a logical sequence. That sequence might be adjustable, depending on the way you decide to make your case or present your analysis, but however you end up structuring your document, the substantive points contained in it must flow logically from one to the next.

So, in this first of the white-glove steps, you need to read the entire document with that perspective in mind. When specific points seem out of place, you need to move them, and, if possible, you want to place your strongest point in the first position.

A well-organized document, with proper numeration of points made, good headings that serve as signposts, umbrella paragraphs that serve as roadmaps and that establish necessary foundational points, and a logical flow that leads with the strongest of your points and closes with the second strongest, will be a well-received document. And with that organization, that document will allow your reader to better appreciate the hard work you invested in preparing it.

C. Step Two—Paragraph Structure and Paragraph Length

Paragraphs serve two important purposes. First, they develop a single idea that is part of the larger point that the entire section of the document addresses. Taken together, a series of paragraphs may constitute a minor thesis that, taken with other minor theses, makes up a complete argument or substantive analysis. For this reason, no paragraph should ever contain more than one substantive point.

Therefore, the first goal of the second white-glove step is to review each paragraph in the document to ensure that it does not violate this first rule. If a paragraph is found that addresses more than one substantive point, that paragraph needs to be divided into separate paragraphs, one for each point. Of course, paragraphs can also be faulty if they do not address any substantive point, and that kind of paragraph should be quickly identified and eliminated in this white-glove step.

The second purpose of paragraphs is to give the reader a chance to take a mental breath. Most readers subconsciously look for the breaks that come at the ends of paragraphs as an opportunity to stop for a brief moment to consider what they have just read and to let the thought thereby obtained register in their mind.

For this reason, overly long paragraphs are not reader-friendly. Think about it. Do you like the sight of an overly long paragraph? If you are like most readers, you do not. And the reason is, essentially, that they appear to require that we have to work too hard to consume the information contained in them.

So, the second possible error in paragraph construction that this step of the white-glove work seeks to correct is overly long paragraphs. Happily, most long paragraphs can be conveniently split into shorter ones.

The third paragraph check is to ensure that paragraphs are properly constructed. Proper paragraph construction is another aspect of your writing that will be appreciated by your reader.

Back when some of us were in grade school, we were taught that a paragraph should have a topic or thesis sentence, followed by several sentences (at least three in the popular construction rule) that develop the topic, followed by a sentence that summarizes the topic. That approach to paragraph construction was, in its time, most definitely the norm. But consider the effect on the reader of a succession of such "ideally constructed" paragraphs. All those topic and summary sentences are giving the reader a lot more to read and, potentially, are making some paragraphs overly long.

Another approach—one that can be more reader-friendly if it also reduces or eliminates a number of overly long paragraphs in your document—is to start a succession of paragraphs that deal with the same topic with a topic sentence, and then to conclude that succession of paragraphs with a summary sentence. Thus, a string of shorter paragraphs can replace what would otherwise be one overly long, extremely ponderous, and very reader-unfriendly paragraph.

Consider the following examples, the first being the traditional "ideally constructed" paragraph and the second being the same exact text in a succession of shorter paragraphs:

First example:

> Malice in support of a murder conviction can be found in a number of ways. It can be found when the defendant clearly and expressly intended to kill the victim and did so with an act that brought about that result. A defendant who aims a loaded gun at a victim and pulls the trigger, intending to thereby kill the victim, exhibits malice. Malice can also be found when a defendant intends to cause severe bodily harm to a victim and does so with death resulting. A defendant who intends to torture an individual by chopping off the victim's hand exhibits malice. And malice can be established when a defendant acts willfully and wantonly so as to create the likely result of death of an individual even when that death may not have been specifically intended. A defendant who fires a loaded gun into a crowded movie theater may exhibit this form of malice even if the

defendant claims not to have intended the death of anyone. And finally, malice can be established by law if a death occurs during the commission of a violent felony that the defendant was committing. Under this form of malice, a defendant will be guilty of murder if the defendant engaged in a robbery of a gas station and the attendant at the gas station died of a heart attack because of the robbery. Thus, at least four methods of finding malice exist: by specific intent to kill; by intent to cause serious bodily injury; through willful and wanton misconduct; and by virtue of the felony-murder rule.

Second example:

Malice in support of a murder conviction can be found in a number of ways. It can be found when the defendant clearly and expressly intended to kill the victim and did so with an act that brought about that result. A defendant who aims a loaded gun at a victim and pulls the trigger, intending to thereby kill the victim, exhibits malice.

Malice can also be found when a defendant intends to cause severe bodily harm to a victim and does so with death resulting. A defendant who intends to torture an individual by chopping off the victim's hand exhibits malice. And malice can be established when a defendant acts willfully and wantonly so as to create the likely result of death of an individual even when that death may not have been specifically intended. A defendant who fires a loaded gun into a crowded movie theater may exhibit this form of malice even if the defendant claims not to have intended the death of anyone.

And finally, malice can be established by law if a death occurs during the commission of a violent felony that the defendant was committing. Under this form of malice, a defendant will be guilty of murder if the defendant engaged in a robbery of a gas station and the attendant at the gas station died of a heart attack because of the robbery. Thus, at least four methods of finding malice exist: by specific intent to kill; by intent to cause serious bodily injury; through willful and wanton misconduct; and by virtue of the felony-murder rule.

Which of the two examples is more likely to be read willingly and will be more easily understood? Which of the two is reader-friendly? The answers suggest a good rule of thumb for all good legal writers: Never let a formalistic rule of construction become a roadblock to a reader-friendly presentation of substance.

The best legal writers understand the preferred rules of construction but are also able to depart from them when necessary to make their documents less burdensome for their readers. Thus, the second white-glove step should include careful consideration of the length as well as the content of every paragraph.

D. Step Three—Logical Sentence Flow and Cohesiveness

A reader-friendly legal document is one that effectively makes the reader feel as if the reader is on a smooth ride that gently goes through a succession of mental tour stops and ends with a sense of both specific highlights (strong arguments and analyses) and an appreciation for the entire trip (recognition of, if not agreement with, the document's principal thesis).

To create that feeling, the writer must be sensitive to how the brain digests information in the process of reading. Essentially, it involves a silent voice in the brain that hears the words from the document much as the brain hears words that are spoken in conversations. What is heard or written is then interpreted and, ultimately, understood.

Hiccups, as we have noted in Chapter One, interrupt this smooth ride. The smooth ride that a well-written document creates for a reader limits one source of these hiccups by allowing the reader to move easily from one paragraph to the next, indeed, from one sentence to the next.

So, a separate step in the white-glove inspection involves ensuring that each sentence flows logically from the one that precedes it and leads logically to the one that follows it. In part, this result can be attained by using transition words and phrases. Such words and phrases include "therefore," "in that regard," "however," "in furtherance of," "similarly," "on the other hand," and "in this respect."

Each of those words and phrases, and the many others that might be in your document, serve to tie one thought to the next, giving the flow of the document a cohesiveness that makes it easier for the reader to grasp the substance of the text. The best way to find points in your document that would benefit from transition words and phrases is to look for sudden jumps, either substantively or tonally, in the text of your document. The value of the transition word or phrase is that it links the prior sentence to the succeeding one.

In this regard, compare these two examples:

> As the mens rea requirement for murder, malice can be satisfied by less than a specific intent to kill the victim. Courts have held that extreme forms of wanton conduct can suffice.
>
> As the mens rea requirement for murder, malice can be satisfied by less than a specific intent to kill the victim. Thus, courts have held that extreme forms of wanton conduct can suffice.

Note how the mere addition of the word "thus" ties the second sentence to the first, thereby making it easier for the reader to comprehend immediately that the second sentence describes a form of malice that is not specific intent to kill.

But the flow of a document can also be affected by the substance of the text. So, this step of the white-glove work should also include a review of all of the potential bumps in the road for the reader that appear in the document.

One such bump can be quotations. Quoting to legal authorities is a common way to enhance the persuasiveness of an argument or an analytical point. But using quotes carries a risk that every writer should appreciate. That risk is that the quoted passage, assuming the reader actually reads it at all, introduces a new "voice" in the reader's brain, and, therefore, creates the potential for a break in the reader's concentration (*i.e.*, a hiccup).

Therefore, this step of the white-glove work should include careful consideration of each quote in the draft that is being inspected. First, you should ask yourself whether the quote is really necessary to make the point you want to make. If the substance of the quote is desirable, can you paraphrase it, thereby avoiding the break in the reader's internal voice a full quote will be likely to create? If you still deem the actual quote to be necessary, can you shorten it, perhaps with the use of ellipses, so as to make the intrusion on the reader's attention to the flow of the text minimal?

As risky as the use of quotes can be, the inclusion of block quotes in a legal document can be absolutely disastrous. Think about how you react to block quotes in material you read. Do you experience a sense of dread at the mere sight of them? Do you often think to skip them entirely, or if not, to just skim them to gain a quick sense of what information they contain?

Most readers would answer yes to those questions because block quotes are a severe intrusion on the brain as it works on the substance of your text. So, in this step of your white-glove work, you should seek, if at all possible, to remove those block quotes from your document. At least find a way to break up the quote to less than fifty words so that it does not need to be blocked.

Some quotes will survive this step of your white-glove work, but at least your reader will not be burdened with an excessive number of interruptions and possible hiccups that can result from an abundance of quotes. Remember, quotes don't substitute for your reasoning and analysis; at best, they only support them.

Another intrusion on your reader's brain in its attempt to receive and appreciate the information your document seeks to impart can be the placement of citations in mid-text. The importance of citing accurately is covered in a different step (#6) of the white-glove work, but in this step the task is to make the citations as unobtrusive as possible. Placing those cites at the end of sentences rather than in the middle of them is the best way to accomplish that goal.

Placed in mid-sentence, a cite, especially a lengthy one, is an invitation for a mental hiccup, primarily because your reader won't expect to see it there. The key is to construct the sentence requiring the cite so that the cite can appropriately be placed at the end of the sentence.

Consider these two examples, both imparting the same substantive information:

> The location of the warning sign in *Messa v. Sullivan*, 61 Ill.App.2d 386, 209 N.E.2d 872 (1st Dist. 1965), was held to be inadequate to constitute actual notice of the danger.
>
> In one case, the court held that the location of the warning sign was inadequate to constitute actual notice of the danger. *Messa v. Sullivan*, 61 Ill. App.2d 386, 209 N.E. 2d 872 (1st Dist. 1965).

Obviously, the second is far less likely to burden the reader since it does not intrude on the reader's attempt to read the sentence and can easily be skipped over by the reader if the reader is not interested in knowing the name of the case or the court that issued it or where it can be found in the two reporters that have printed versions of it.

An even less obtrusive way to present a citation is with a footnote, and some courts encourage (or at least do not object to) the use of footnotes to note citations (and the cases referred to in the text in some instances). Whether this alternative is acceptable in any particular document and for any particular reader may depend on the rules of the court or the dictates of the office where you work. Either way, removing case citations from the middle of sentences in this white-glove step will go a long way to making your document reader-friendly.

E. Step Four—Sentence Accuracy, Simplicity, and Brevity

Consider the beauty of a well-constructed sentence. Sentences are the basic unit of communication. They are where effective communication starts and where it can end. A well-constructed sentence says what the writer wants to say clearly, concisely, and accurately. A poorly constructed sentence can leave a reader confused and frustrated, even to the point that the document gets placed in that dreaded read-later pile, or even worse in that circular file to the side of the reader's desk.

Every sentence in your document should be constructed so as to say precisely what you want it to say in as few words as possible. It should be constructed in such a way as to impart the information you want to impart and to encourage, or at least to entice, your reader to read the sentence that follows it. We aren't talking about creating a page-turner novel here, but you should be trying to create in your reader an impetus to keep reading. And ensuring that each sentence in your document is a separate thing of beauty will accomplish that goal.

Consider the two sentences that follow, each of which is an attempt to say the same thing:

> Attorneys can draft wills, contracts, and partnership agreements, among other documents, in the states where they are licensed.
>
> Attorneys, being licensed by the state where they practice law, can draft, among other documents, wills, contracts, and partnership agreements.

Both sentences contain the critical components of the thought the writer is trying to convey. But the first sentence places those components—the subject, the verb, and the object—at the very start of the sentence, while the second spreads them out over the entire length of the sentence. The first sentence is preferable because it gives the reader all of the essential information right at the start of the sentence.

Readers look for these basics in every sentence: Who did what to whom. In essence, everything else is excess, some of it undoubtedly necessary, but none of it as important as the basic component parts of the sentence. If the rest is more important, the sentence should be structured with those items in the position of subject, verb, and object.

Thus, one of the first things to check, as to every sentence in your document, is whether you have succeeded in placing the subject, verb, and object of each sentence as close to the beginning of the sentence as possible.

A similar rule of sentence construction is to keep the who-did-what-to-whom parts of each sentence close to each other, even if an introductory phrase moves them away from the opening of the sentence.

Consider these examples:

> Even with the best of intentions, a lawyer, despite years of training and practice, might raise, due to the pressure of the moment, an inappropriate objection.
>
> Even with the best of intentions and despite years of training and practice, due to the pressure of the moment, a lawyer might raise an inappropriate objection.
>
> A lawyer might raise an inappropriate objection due to the pressure of the moment, even though the lawyer had the best of intentions and had years of training and practice.

The first of the examples is made unduly difficult to read because the subject, "lawyer," is separated from the verb, "might raise," which is further separated from the object, "an inappropriate objection." The second example cures that deficiency but violates the previous rule by putting all three elements at the end of the sentence. The third sentence keeps the three elements together and places them at the start of the sentence.

Now consider these two sentences:

> The witness wept while she recounted the details of the accident.
>
> The witness became overly emotional, even to the point of weeping, as she proceeded with her testimony, which provided the specific details of the incident that was the basis of her lawsuit.

Both of these sentences impart the information the writer wants to convey about the witness's testimony, but the first does it directly and simply, while the second does it in a laboriously long-winded flow of information that forces the reader to digest many more words than may be needed to convey the desired information. There will certainly be occasions when the longer sentence will be justified precisely because it does impart the information with more emotion or sentiment, but if all your reader needs to know is the basic information, keep it short.

The general lesson to be learned is that shorter sentences are better than longer sentences, primarily because they make the task of reading them easier for the reader. But there is another reason to keep your sentences short.

Consider this sentence:

> The attorney tried to conduct a probing cross-examination of the witness, being a skilled debater and an accomplished public speaker, but he couldn't overcome the resistance he encountered, which often seemed to be the result of her coaching by the opposing counsel.

What is wrong with this sentence? Well, for starters, it is certainly too long. Its length alone is enough to frustrate the reader (especially if the document is replete with sentences of similar length and construction). But look at what else has happened in the writer's attempt to squeeze everything possible into the single sentence: The writer has lost track of the subject and has concluded the sentence by shifting the focus from the attorney to the witness and opposing counsel.

Note, too, that the sentence is also imperiled by a misplaced modifier that suggests the witness is "a skilled debater and accomplished public speaker." Thus, short sentences are not only reader-friendly, but they are safer from the risk of containing a grammatical error that doubles down on the potential negative impact on the reader.

As important as all the sentences are in your document, perhaps none are more important than those that state the rules or legal principles on which your arguments or analyses are based. Thus, extra-special care should be given to those sentences. In many instances, they will also constitute the topic or thesis sentences for the paragraphs they start, making their significance even more paramount.

Consider these two rule statements that might be used in a brief opposing a motion to dismiss:

> A motion to dismiss must be denied if facts are alleged that establish a cause of action.
>
> Facts that suggest the existence of a cause of action can be sufficient to make a motion to dismiss inappropriate.

Both rule statements express a rule that would then form the basis for an argument that would presumably focus on the particular facts in the case at hand. But the first is crisply stated and is succinct to the point of the argument that will follow. The second, on the other hand, states the point of the rule far less directly and much less succinctly. It may even leave the reader in some doubt as to exactly what argument it is meant to introduce.

Of course, a longer, less crisply stated rule might be strategically desirable in a particular argument, as when the essence of the rule could be detrimental to your client's case. In such an instance, a less concise rule, one that perhaps suggests ambiguity or uncertainty, may be the more desirable approach. But if the rule you want to apply works in your client's favor, the best approach is to state it as directly and succinctly as you can.

Every sentence in your document should be an easy read for your reader. Even if the subject matter is dense, the sentences that describe and explain that subject matter should be constructed so as to be easy to digest. If your reader has to stop to consider what the sentence means, you risk losing your reader. Some readers may stop reading because they don't have the patience or the energy to deal with the subject matter, but no reader should stop because they can't figure out what you're saying.

Therefore, this step in your white-glove process should consider whether each sentence says exactly what you want to say in as few words, and with as little room for confusion or uncertainty, as possible. If your document consists of well-tailored sentences, it will be far less likely to end up unread, and far more likely to be appreciated for the writing talent that it represents.

F. Step Five—Grammar and Punctuation

Although writers of literary fiction frequently take license with the rules of grammar and punctuation, the legal profession has not followed suit. Grammar and punctuation rules are closely followed, as they must be in the drafting of rule-making documents, where a missing comma can sometimes make a difference between absolutely requiring something and merely permitting it.

Because they are trained to write with precision, lawyers and judges understand the importance of grammar and punctuation and expect what they read to also reflect that understanding. So, if for no other reason than to establish your bona fides as a member of the profession, you need to submit documents that are devoid of grammar and punctuation errors.

The fifth step of the inspection, then, is to review every sentence for possible grammar and punctuation errors. This is painstaking work, but it can be successfully accomplished if you know what you're looking for.

Without intending to cover all the rules of the mechanics of writing, the following are some of those most commonly violated in poorly written legal documents. To gain a complete understanding of the mechanical rules of good writing, study the many rules on grammar and punctuation that are provided in Chapter Six. (Your legal writing professor may also have a list of recommended texts or may even require one to supplement your assignments in your course.)

1. The Requisites of a Complete Sentence

A complete sentence requires a subject and a verb. That's it—just a noun or pronoun that is the subject of the sentence and a verb that attaches to the subject to indicate the action the subject took.

Hence, it should be easy to write complete sentences, and, in most instances, it is. In fact, it is hard to compose an incomplete short sentence because we almost always think in terms of someone doing something when we start to write a sentence.

It's when our sentences get longer that problems can arise. Consider this example:

> The attorney, never intending to create the grounds for objection, which the opposing counsel then raised, but instead hoping the question would pass unnoticed. Still, the attorney managed to utter a response before the judge ruled.

The first attempted sentence is, of course, incomplete, as it lacks a verb that would attach to the subject "attorney." What happened to cause this error?

Most probably, the writer had in mind to say that the attorney "hoped the question would pass unnoticed," but in the midst of making that point, the writer thought to add what happened next, which was the opposing attorney's objection. The incomplete sentence could have been written as three short complete sentences that would have told the whole story.

> The attorney never intended to create the grounds for an objection. Instead, he hoped it would pass unnoticed. But the opposing attorney did object as soon as the question was asked.

It could also have been written as one complete sentence, as in this alternative construction:

> The attorney never intended his question to create the grounds for an objection, hoping instead that it would pass unnoticed, but opposing counsel raised one anyway.

The single corrected sentence is long, which may make it less desirable in reader-friendly terms, but it is a correctly composed compound-complex sentence and thus is grammatically correct. Is it more reader-friendly than the three shorter sentences in the previous example? That decision might depend on what surrounds this passage in the entire paragraph or series of paragraphs. Good writing and good white-glove work require careful consideration of whether to construct grammatically correct longer sentences or simple shorter ones.

But you can't leave incomplete sentences in your document. They will inevitably cause a major mental hiccup for your reader and can, if too many of them appear in your document, lead the reader to place the document in the purgatory of the "read-later" pile.

2. Commas, Comma Splices, and Run-On Sentences

Commas serve a purpose, but that purpose is not just to indicate a pause, as some may believe. Rather, commas indicate to the reader how to comprehend the sentence the reader is in the midst of reading.

Perhaps one of the most common uses of commas is to denote the items in a series. Legal writers often have need for serial commas because legal documents often include lists of things. When a list of items is included in a sentence, a comma must precede each item in the list after the first item. In a short list, the comma can be omitted before the last item, but in longer lists, it should be included before the word (usually "and" or "or") that precedes the last item.

Consider these two examples:

> Crimes requiring malice include murder, mayhem, and arson.
>
> Malice can be satisfied by a specific intent to kill, by an intent to cause serious bodily injury, by willful misconduct, or by application of the felony-murder rule.

In the first sentence, the last comma can be omitted without risking any confusion for the reader. That said, many writers will include it anyway. (The current preference among folks who dwell on this kind of thing is to include it.) In the second sentence, leaving the last comma out would make it more difficult for the reader to understand that a fourth form of malice is the felony-murder rule. In both sentences, however, the commas delineate the different items in the series, which is the purpose of serial commas.

Commas are also used to identify for the reader that the reader is reading a compound or a complex sentence.

Compound sentences are sentences that contain two independent clauses—clauses that contain both a subject and a verb that attaches to the subject—that are joined by a conjunction (*e.g.*, and, but, or). Complex sentences contain one independent clause and one dependent clause—a clause that contains a subject and a verb but cannot stand alone as a complete sentence because it is "dependent" on the independent clause to which it is joined. Commas are used in complex sentences to note the break from one clause to the other but only when the dependent clause precedes the independent clause.

Consider, again, the example concerning the attorney who wanted to pose a question without getting an objection.

> Hoping to avoid an objection, the attorney asked the question of the witness, but opposing counsel did, indeed, object.

The sentence contains four properly placed commas. The first notes the end of the introductory participial phrase. The second notes the beginning of the independent clause, the conjunction "but" introducing the subject and verb "opposing counsel did." The third and fourth indicate the added modifier "indeed."

But as valuable as the commas are in that sentence, pulling together essentially three different thoughts in a cohesive single sentence, commas cannot be used to attempt to bring separate thoughts together indiscriminately. Consider this attempt:

> The attorney hoped the question would pass unnoticed, he didn't intend to create the grounds for an objection, but opposing counsel raised one anyway.

The second comma in that attempt at a sentence is fine. It marks the introduction of an independent clause that is preceded by the conjunction ("but"). But the first comma is an attempt to bring the two independent clauses ("attorney hoped" and "he didn't intend") together in a single sentence. But we can't join independent clauses without a conjunction if we are trying to join them with a comma.

This particular punctuation error creates what is called a comma splice, where the comma is being used incorrectly to try to "splice" together the two independent clauses. (Splicing is a word that was in vogue in the old days when reel-to-reel tapes—ask your grandparents—were the common recording devices. The tapes would often split, and small pieces of tape were used to "splice" them together.)

The intended joining of the two independent clauses can be accomplished in a single sentence (thereby avoiding a comma splice) in one of two ways. First, a conjunction can be added before the second independent clause, thereby creating a compound sentence. Or, the two independent clauses can be joined with a different punctuation mark: the semi-colon. Or, a third way to cure the comma splice would be to end the first clause with a period, thereby making them two separate sentences.

What we can't do in an attempt to correct a comma splice is just remove the comma. Doing so creates a different problem, one we call a run-on sentence.

> The attorney hoped the question would pass unnoticed he didn't intend to create the grounds for an objection, but opposing counsel raised one anyway.

Run-on sentences, such as the one above, are rarely caused by a lack of knowledge of punctuation rules. Most writers would recognize the need for some form of punctuation after "unnoticed" in the sentence above. That kind of error is more likely the result of hasty writing and poor editing—yet another reason this white-glove step is critical.

Commas have other useful functions, but, again, they must be used correctly. One such instance is to set off a parenthetical phrase that is contained within a complete sentence. Consider this example:

> The attorney asked the question, never intending in so doing to elicit an objection, but opposing counsel made one anyway.

In that sentence, the commas mark off the phrase that is the equivalent of a parenthetical insert. The sentence would be complete without the phrase, but the writer wants to include the added information. The addition is understood as such by the reader because the commas set it off. But it would be an error, one that might well cause a mental hiccup for the reader, if either comma were missing in the sentence.

Commas also serve to tell a reader that the heart of the sentence will follow, as when a lengthy introductory phrase precedes the subject and verb in the sentence.

> Disregarding the possibility of an objection from opposing counsel, the attorney asked the question.

The comma in the preceding sentence tells the reader that the essential part of the sentence will follow. Without the comma, the reader will hesitate, if for only an instant, to comprehend the structure of the sentence. The properly placed comma in that instance keeps the reader in the rhythm of the read, as all reader-friendly writing should.

3. *Colons and Semi-Colons*

For legal writers, these two punctuation marks serve critically important functions. They are used in a most common part of legal writing: the creation of lists.

Lists in the law are ubiquitous. Attorneys are always identifying factors or elements or some combination of the two, and almost as often listing series of events that compare favorably or unfavorably to some existing authority or that comprise the key facts in a case we are using in an argument.

Properly used, the colon introduces the list, and properly used, the semi-colon notes the separate items in the list. But there are rules for what constitutes "properly used" for each.

If you introduce the series of items with only a subject and a verb, a colon is not required and would be inappropriate. Thus, if your sentence begins with, "These factors include," you would not use a colon to introduce the series of factors that would follow. The colon introduces the items in the series only when you add an object to the subject and the verb that introduces the series, as in, "These factors include the following:"

Why the different rule depending on whether that third part (the non-essential part) of the sentence is included? The answer is that usually if the list is short or uncomplicated we don't need the object, as in the following example, "These colors include red, green, and yellow."

It would be excessive to say, "These colors include the following: red, green, and yellow."

But if the list is more complicated than a simple list of colors, the introduction to that list might well need to include the object ("the following") as a way to identify for the reader the nature of the list that will follow. In that regard, consider the following example:

> These are the factors that control the decision: whether the defendant knew the victim; whether the defendant had previously engaged in the same kind of conduct; whether the defendant was shown, through expert testimony, to have a mental disease or defect of reason; and, whether the defendant was intoxicated at the time of the act.

The colon in that sentence introduces the series properly. If the sentence had begun with only "These are the factors" we would still use the colon, because we'd still have the required subject, verb, and object introducing the list. But if the list were only preceded with "The factors are" a colon would be improper. But note that for such a long and complicated list, that introduction would not be helpful in terms of alerting the reader to what was about to follow. For reader-friendly purposes, if not out of grammatical necessity, the slightly longer introduction is necessary for longer, more complicated lists, and the colon is the punctuation that accompanies the longer introduction.

Semi-colons are also appropriate punctuation in listing a series of items. They are used to separate the items in a series in two instances: when the items in the series are long and when they include internal commas. In both instances, the purpose of the semi-colon is to identify for the reader where one item ends and another begins. In that regard, let's again look at the example we just used.

> These are the factors that control the decision: whether the defendant knew the victim; whether the defendant had previously engaged in the same kind of conduct; whether the defendant was shown, through expert testimony, to have a mental disease or defect of reason; and, whether the defendant was intoxicated at the time of the act.

Note the placement of the semi-colons in the series. The items in the series are long enough to justify the use of semi-colons, but the third of the items also contains internal commas, thereby justifying the use of semi-colons as well. The alternative would be to separate the items in the series with commas, but it isn't as helpful to the reader to use commas in lengthy and complicated series, and thus isn't as reader-friendly.

But if the list is simple, as in our color example above, commas work just fine. So, just as with the use of colons to introduce a list of items in a series, the use of semi-colons to separate those items should be limited to when the rules call for them.

Semi-colons are also useful as a way to avoid a comma splice, as noted above. But we need to clarify another form of comma splice that many writers are not cognizant of. These are sentences that separate two independent clauses with conjunctive adverbs: words like "therefore," "however," and "rather."

When you join two independent clauses with these words, as in the example below, you need a semi-colon before the joining word.

> Sentences that consist of two independent clauses can be joined by a comma and a conjunction; however, if they are joined instead by a conjunctive adverb, they must be joined by a semi-colon.

Obviously, to make correct use of the semi-colon in sentences of this type, we need to be able to distinguish between conjunctions and conjunctive adverbs. Fortunately, the distinction is fairly easy to identify. Conjunctions are short, single syllable words (all consisting of only two or three letters) that comprise a relatively short list. The acronym for the list is FANBOYS, as in **f**or, **a**nd, **n**or, **b**ut, **o**r, **y**et, **s**o.

All other joining words are conjunctive adverbs, and they all must be immediately preceded by a semi-colon and immediately followed by a comma (unless it is a single-syllable word like "thus," in which case the following comma is not required).

Admittedly, the rules for these two punctuation marks can seem irksome, but, in truth, they aren't all that complicated. Spending a little time learning the rules for their use will allow you to perform this part of your white-glove work with relative ease.

4. Parallelism in Series

When you have occasion in your document to set out items, they should be constructed in parallel form. Parallelism in series makes what might be a dense set of details easier to read and, therefore, makes it easier for your reader to grasp and appreciate the substantive information contained in the series.

Compare these two examples, both listing the same factors used to summarize the defendant's tortious conduct in a case:

> The commission of the tort in this case is established by these facts: defendant failed to exercise due care; injury of the plaintiff; the act causally related to the injury; absence of a recognized defense.

> The commission of the tort in this case is established by these facts: the defendant failed to exercise due care; the plaintiff suffered injury; the defendant's act was causally related to the injury; and, the defendant cannot assert a recognized defense.

Note that both summaries contain four items that the writer lists as the facts that establish the tort. In the first summary, the items are written without regard for the form of any of the others. Thus, the entire sentence is difficult to read and the specific facts may be difficult to relate to each other. In the second summary, each item is written in the same form: The subject is preceded by "the" and followed by the verb and the result or occurrence.

When items in a series are listed in random form, the reader is likely to struggle to get through it. When items in a series are written in the same basic form, the reader reads with a rhythm that facilitates understanding.

Writing in parallel form can be more difficult and can take more time than writing in random form, but the consequence for the reader, especially with respect to detailed and complicated lists, can be significant. Writing series in parallel form is reader-friendly and is one way to establish your bona fides as a good legal writer.

5. *Quotation Marks and Parentheses*

Quotes must be noted with quotation marks. That rule should be easy enough to employ, but it can be the source of a punctuation error if the end of the quote is not noted with the second closing quotation mark. This error can slip into a document because the writer will simply forget to mark the end of the quote.

It can get more complicated, however, when the quote is in a parenthetical, as in the following example:

> The court held that malice could be found by way of the felony-murder rule. (*People v. Smith*, 28 Utop.2d 346 (1946), holding that "in the action

> by the defendant of starting the fire that spread to the adjoining property ... even though the fire would not have consumed that property ... malice existed as a matter of law.)

Obviously, the closing quotation marks are missing in the parenthetical, and they were probably overlooked by the writer due to the greater concern of constructing the parenthetical correctly. A lot is involved in constructing this kind of parenthetical, including the proper citation for the case. But the closing quotation marks are not only necessary; they may be essential, especially if the quoted part of the case ended after the second ellipsis, with the writer adding "malice existed as a matter of law" to complete the intended point.

The other area of possible error with respect to quotation marks and parentheses is where the ending punctuation should appear. As to quotation marks, the American rule is that periods and commas must be placed inside the quotation marks, while all other punctuation marks (colons, semi-colons, question marks, and exclamation points) must appear outside of them, unless, of course, those punctuations are part of the original quote, as in these examples:

> She shouted, "Fire!"
>
> The attorney's next question was, "Did you know he hated you when you struck the fatal blow?"

Note that in both examples, the closing punctuation mark within the quote serves as the last punctuation mark in the sentence, even though, theoretically, a period would be expected to note the end of the sentence.

The rule for closing punctuation marks for parentheses is a little easier to understand. A period will always go inside the parentheses if the parenthetical consists entirely of a single sentence that is not within a larger sentence. Otherwise, the closing punctuation is placed after the closing parenthetical mark. Consider these two examples of those rules:

He concluded his argument by bowing his head. (Whether he was praying or just containing his emotions was not clear.)

He concluded his argument by bowing his head (not thereby revealing whether he was praying or just containing his emotions).

We make ample use of quotation marks and parentheses in legal documents (although the use of quotes should be carefully considered and limited, as noted in Step 3). The rules for when they should appear and how other punctuation marks appear relative to them are not difficult, but they can be tricky and, therefore, must be applied carefully in this white-glove step.

6. *Apostrophes*

Apostrophes are commonly used in two instances. The most common use in a legal document is to indicate a possessive. The other use, less likely in most legal documents, is to show a contraction of two words into one.

Contractions should not be used in most instances in a legal document. Using them is generally considered too casual for a document that may become part of an official transcript or court file. Even for internal file documents in a law office, the use of contractions will often be discouraged.

The only time a contraction problem in the use of an apostrophe is likely to be an error is with respect to the distinction between "its" and "it's." (Note, and please remember for all time, that *its'* is not a word, has never been a word, and never will be a word, unless we someday develop a different meaning for the word "it." Think about it; can an "it" ever be a plural? Wouldn't the "it" then become "they"?)

The distinction between *its* and *it's* is simple. "Its" is the possessive form of it. It does not include an apostrophe. "It's" is the contraction for "it is." It always includes the apostrophe. If you use "its," you must be referring to a possessive for the thing that "it" identifies in your document. If you use "it's," you are saying "it is" in the looser, less formal manner. (And, as already noted, that form is not preferred in legal documents.)

As for all other uses of apostrophes, the rules are relatively simple. If you are speaking of someone's or something's possession of something, place an apostrophe at the end of the noun and add the letter "s." If you are speaking of more than one person or thing that possesses something, add an "s" and then add the apostrophe. Consider these two examples:

> The co-conspirator's statements were incriminating.
>
> The co-conspirators' statements were incriminating.

The first example refers to a single individual's comments. The second refers to the statements of more than one individual. Obviously, placing the apostrophe in the wrong place can create the wrong understanding of whether the statements of one or more than one individual were incriminating.

Apostrophes that appear incorrectly in a legal document can create confusion for the reader, but more frequently they lessen the regard the reader will have for the writer's efforts. Incorrectly placed apostrophes, perhaps more than any other punctuation mark, are a sign of sloppy and unprofessional work, something no attorney would ever want as a reputation.

7. Misplaced Modifiers

A commonly encountered problem for readers occurs when a sentence includes a modifying word or phrase that is unclear with regard to what in the sentence it is supposed to modify. And, because we use modifiers frequently in legal documents, misplaced modifiers need to be found and removed from all legal documents.

Consider the following sentence:

> To determine if he was insane, the judge allowed expert testimony regarding the defendant's psychiatric evaluation.

The modifier in the sentence, "to determine if he was insane," is placed immediately before the subject in the sentence, the judge. A reasonable interpretation by the reader, therefore, would be that the judge wanted to determine the judge's own state of sanity. Obviously, we know from the rest of the sentence that it is the defendant whose sanity is in issue, but the misplaced modifier runs the risk of creating a mental hiccup (perhaps in the form of an unintended chuckle) by the reader.

The preceding sentence could be corrected in a number of ways, but the best way would be to place the modifier as close to the word it is intended to modify as possible, as in this alternative construction of the sentence:

> The judge allowed expert testimony regarding the psychiatric evaluation of the defendant to determine if the defendant was insane.

8. Pronouns

Pronouns will be used frequently in a legal document, and normally they will not be the source of an error. But there are two instances where pronouns can be used incorrectly. Consider these examples:

> Dogs, like the one Mr. Simpson owns, can be a danger to others, especially if it attacks friendly visitors.
>
> An attorney is at risk of sanctions if they violate the code of ethical conduct in court.

In the first example, the writer has lost track of the subject of the sentence to which the pronoun is intended to refer. If the subject, "dogs," is plural, the pronoun must be as well. Sentences that include modifiers ("like the one Mr. Simpson owns" in the example) are most at risk of this kind of error and thus must be reviewed with special care in this white-glove step.

The second example is similarly wrong but probably for a different reason. In the bad-old days, it was all too easy to assume that any attorney was a male; thus the pronoun would have defaulted in that sentence to "he." But in modern America, attorneys are just as likely to be women; thus, the question becomes what pronoun to use. This issue is not so much one of political correctness as pronoun consistency. In the example above, the writer is using the plural pronoun "they," where the singular pronouns "he" or "she" are grammatically required.

Many legal writing professors are struggling with this problem. Some choose to switch genders (from "he" to "she" and "him" to "her") without thereby intending to create confusion (or, presumably, make a political statement). Others just use the combinations of "he and she"/"him and her" whenever a neutral singular pronoun is called for. At some point, a single-word, gender-neutral pronoun may enter the lexicon to solve the problem. But until then, the plural pronoun in reference to the singular subject should be avoided. (A separate issue regarding pronouns arises when a person with a non-binary gender is the subject of the sentence. In that instance, some writers are using "they" as the pronoun representing the individual. That usage, however, is not universally accepted. The issue is, at present, unresolved, or at least is open to debate.)

Of course, an easy way to cure the error would be to make the subject plural, as in the following alternative construction:

> Attorneys are at risk of sanctions if they violate the code of ethical conduct in court.

Some grammatical errors, like this one, are easily fixed. Others require much more work. But they all command the attention of a writer of a professionally prepared, error-free, reader-friendly legal document.

One last pronoun usage merits attention, especially since it takes a while for law students to get comfortable with it. The rule is that when referring to a court, any court, the proper pronoun is "it," not "they." The same rule applies for a business.

Consider these examples:

> In the court's opinion resolving the issue, it referred to the long-standing rule on willful misconduct as a form of malice.
>
> The business noted its approval of the union contract in a press release it issued. ,

The point of using the singular pronoun in the first sentence is to indicate that a court, irrespective of the number of judges involved in the hearing of a case, is always identified as if it were a single individual or entity. The same rule applies for a business, as the second sentence reflects.

G. Step Six—Case and Party Names and Citations

Perhaps no errors in a legal document are more unacceptable than the misspelling of the names of the parties involved in the case you are analyzing. Obviously, misspelling the name of your own client would be beyond embarrassing, but any misspelled names in your document reflect poorly on your overall sense of professionalism and on your specific interest in the particular case you are writing about.

Case names must also be spelled correctly. Many cases consist of names that are easily misspelled. Is it, for example *Schneckloth v. Bustamonte* or *Shneckloth v. Bustomonte*? Spelling them correctly and consistently doing so can be a taxing task, but it is one that a writer committed to professionalism and to providing the reader an error-free document will attend to.

The citations you provide to support your legal arguments are of even greater concern. The purpose of a citation, as is explained in detail in the previous chapter, is to provide your reader with the source for the statement about the law that you include in your document. Citations represent the writer's professional integrity more, perhaps, than any other aspect of the written document. If your citations are inaccurate, you risk not only irritating your reader (should the reader seek to review the cited authority), but you also put your professional reputation (and, if the errors are egregious and numerous, your professional license) in jeopardy.

So, with that concern in mind, this step in the inspection process can be particularly intense because it requires that every cite in your document be checked. And the cites must be checked to ensure not just that they conform with the requirements of the citation manual you are required to use for the document, but that they are accurate as to the location of the source, should the reader decide to review it.

Cite checking, as anyone who has done staff work as a law review editor can tell you, is painstakingly time-consuming work. For pinpoint cites, the exact page of the case cited must be accurately noted, and finding that particular point in a case, especially if it was originally noted incorrectly, can be grueling work. But it must be done in this step of your white-glove work.

One way to approach this task that may make it somewhat easier would be to cite check all cites for the same case throughout the document. In this way, the spelling of the name of the case can also be verified for each cite. You may discover other ways to make this step of the inspection process a little less time consuming, but don't treat your goal lightly. Judges and their clerks, as well as senior associates and partners in your firm, will quickly ascertain your commitment to your craft and to your ethical obligations by the accuracy of your citations.

(The same concern on citations applies for cites to the record in the case your brief is written for. Record cites must be as accurate as case cites.)

H. Step Seven—Typos

Typographical errors are the bane of every writer's existence. How do they occur? Why do even the best writers let them occur? The answers to these questions are best left to psychologists. For our purposes, the task is not to determine why or how they happen, but to make sure they are found and corrected before the document leaves your office.

Can typos be the source of mental hiccups for your readers? Read this typo-laden paragraph and decide for yourself:

> The statue in question has been criticized in any number of treaties, some on which even go so far is to suggest political malfeasance if its passage. Form a review of several similar statues, one commentator has drawn the conclusion that the state's legislature wax lead by corrupt infusions of cash. Others report that now only are legislators subject to corruption, but that many candidates far office succumb to the attraction of the almighty dollar even before them are elected.

Did you get frustrated trying to work through the dozen typos in the paragraph? Now read the corrected version:

> The statute in question has been criticized in any number of treatises, some of which even go so far as to suggest political malfeasance in its passage. From a review of several similar statutes, one commentator has drawn the conclusion that the state's legislature was led by corrupt infusions of cash. Others report that not only are legislators subject to corruption, but that many candidates for office succumb to the attraction of the almighty dollar even before they are elected.

Obviously, typos are potential minefields in a document, creating continuous risks of losing your readers (either because of the constant case of mental hiccups they will be suffering with or because they finally give up and stop reading entirely). And yet, until technology develops a system that allows us to dictate our documents and not have to type them (and we may not be far from that point), this part of the entire inspection will remain among the most daunting of the ten white-glove steps.

Various methods might work to catch and correct all of the typos in your final draft. Reading the draft backwards, from last sentence to first, might make spotting the typos easier, since you won't be as likely to focus on the substance of the document by doing so. Reading sections, or even paragraphs, out of order might also help, as might reading the document aloud. Or you can just go line-by-line, word-by-word, studying each one for the otherwise innocuous typo that somehow slipped into your otherwise perfectly written document. No single method is guaranteed to catch them all, which is why many writers use a combination of them.

Of course, as you've probably appreciated by now, by the time you get to this step of the inspection, many of the typos that were in your original final draft should have already been corrected as a by-product of the earlier steps in the inspection. Many will also have been corrected if you have used the "clean-as-you-go" approach that is discussed more fully at the end of this chapter.

But whatever approach you use, and no matter how long it takes, you must catch and correct all of the irksome typos in your final draft before your document leaves your office. The goal of providing your reader with an error-free, reader-friendly document requires nothing less.

I. Step Eight—Spell and Grammar Check

This one is easy, certainly a lot easier than the steps that have preceded it. But with the gift that our modern technology has provided to check our spelling and our grammar, it would be foolish to ignore it. And even though your particular software application may default to indicate a spelling or grammar error where there is none, you should verify each red, green, and blue underlining to make sure you aren't dealing with one of those rare times when the computer is right and you are wrong.

And beware of the spell check programs that do not work on material that is typed in ALL CAPS, as is required by some courts for point headings in briefs. Other anomalies may exist with your particular software, so be careful not to over-rely on your spell- and grammar-check functions.

Of course, after completing the first seven inspection steps, the expectation would be that there would be few, if any, red, green, and blue underlines in the entire document, but on the chance that there may be at least a few spelling and grammar glitches that you haven't caught, this step will provide the opportunity to catch them and correct them.

J. Step Nine—The Pleasure Read and One-Voicing

At this point, the document should be completely clean. And so, this step is just that last chance to enjoy your work and to appreciate the effort you have expended to produce a quality legal document that represents your best work and that is error-free and reader-friendly.

So, sit back, relax, and read it one last time, just to enjoy the feeling that comes from striving for perfection. And as you read your document in its pristine state, if you should happen to find one last typo that you somehow didn't catch, or one errant apostrophe that somehow survived your earlier scrubbing, or one case that you misspelled, or one heading that doesn't accurately identify the argument that it introduces, then make the necessary correction and thank yourself for taking the time to read your now perfectly clean document this one last time.

And as you enjoy your work, take the opportunity to consider whether the entire document reads as if it had been written by one person. Look for changes in tone or style that suggest more than one author of the document. One-voicing a document is your last check for a writing glitch that could disrupt the flow of information you want your reader to receive.

K. Step Ten—The Printed Version

Now that you are fully satisfied that your document is as error-free as it can possibly be, you have only one more item to check, and that is what the document will look like to your intended reader. This step requires you to print out a final version of your document and to inspect it one last time, not for content or for typos or for grammatical errors, but for its appearance.

The look of your document can be as important as the substantive points it contains and the writing that communicates those points. And, even though our wonderful computers appear to show our document on our monitor in the exact form we expect to be duplicated in the printed version, sometimes, for whatever reason, the printed version will be slightly different.

Here are a few things to look for in the printed version of your document.

1. Pagination

Is each page of your document correctly paginated? Do the page numbers all appear in the same place (the place you want them to appear) on each page of your document? Are the pages numbered in proper sequence? If you have non-substantive pages (*e.g.*, a table of contents) that you wanted to have numbered with Romanettes, do those designations appear on those pages? And finally, do the page numbers on your table of contents match the page numbers in the text of your document?

2. Widows and Orphans

Widows are single lines that appear at the bottom of a page. Orphans are single lines that appear at the top of a page. Widows and orphans are commonplace in all printed materials, including legal documents. If they are merely the first (in the case of a widow) or last (in the case of an orphan) line of a paragraph, and if page limitation isn't an issue, the better approach is to avoid these single-line misfits.

One absolute no-no, however, is when a point heading or subheading is split into a widow and an orphan. Those instances should be avoided if at all possible, lest the reader suffer a mental hiccup, caused by having to switch back to the previous page to fully grasp the significance of the heading. Similarly, entire headings (widowed headings) that show at the bottom of a page can be disconcerting for the reader and potentially less impactful as well.

The preferred approach is to eliminate widowed headings and split headings, assuming that moving the full heading to the top of the next page does not put the entire document at risk of exceeding an imposed page limitation. (Happily, many courts and firms are moving from page limitations to word limitations, thereby removing this concern.)

3. Skipped or Blank Lines

Every so often, a different kind of typo will appear on the printed version of the document. The skipped line or blank page is an error that may not be evident until the printed version is carefully inspected. Once found, these errors can be corrected, but if they aren't seen, they most certainly won't be.

4. Italics and Underlines

Did you put all of your case names in italics or underline them? Are they all in italics or underlined in the printed version of your document? Were you consistent in your use of one or the other of those two alternatives?

Are your headings underlined (or in bold, if required) where you intended them to so be? If you intended to add emphasis to any quotes or textual material in your document, do they so appear in the printed version? And, finally, are there any random italics or underlined portions that you did not intend to appear in that form?

You may think you gave correct instructions to your computer, but this check will allow you to fix any miscommunication between you and your PC or Mac.

5. Margins

Similarly, the margins you intended may not be as you expected. This last check will give you the opportunity to correct to the court's (or your firm's) requirements. Also related to margins are the sizes of indents for paragraphs. These should always be the same throughout your document.

6. Hard Copy for Mailing

If you are submitting your document by mail (or personal delivery, as when it is just going upstairs to your senior partner), carefully inspect the copy your reader is going to receive. Is the print quality excellent? Nothing less than excellent print quality is acceptable in an error-free document. If your printer needs toner or some other adjustment, make your document the one that forces that matter to be taken care of.

And now look at every page of the document, just to make sure the pages are in proper order and that no page somehow came out cockeyed, another anomaly that can inexplicably occur even with the best of printers.

L. A Final Point—The Value of Cleaning as You Go

By now you are probably thinking that performing the ten-step inspection is more burdensome than the entire process you went through in researching and writing the document in the first place. At its worst, white-gloving your document can be, depending on its length, an extended task that consumes the better part of a work week (or most of a weekend).

But if you have been diligent and vigilant throughout the process of drafting your document, the ten white-glove steps needn't be as imposing. In the military boot camp scenario, the new recruits quickly learn the value of "cleaning as you go," and you should, too.

To clean as you go means that you make corrections (grammatical and otherwise) as you are composing each of the drafts that lead to your final draft. A document that has already been cleaned of its obvious errors before it gets to final-draft status is far less likely to need much polishing in the ten white-glove steps.

So, clean as you go. It's step zero in the "white-glove inspection."

Chapter Summary

And so now you are finally finished. The document is on its way to your intended reader. It reflects your best work, the result of your thorough research and your solid analysis of the issues. It is well-written and presents your thesis, prediction, or argument in compelling terms.

And you have subjected it to a thorough "white-glove inspection" that consisted of these ten, fully completed steps (with breaks, to allow your head to clear, after each step):

1. You reviewed the document's organization;
2. You considered the length and content of each paragraph;
3. You confirmed that each sentence followed logically from the one that preceded it;
4. You made sure that every sentence said exactly what you wanted it to say and in as few words as possible;
5. You checked every sentence for grammatical accuracy and correct punctuation;
6. You ensured that all party names and case names were spelled correctly and that all citations were accurate and correctly positioned;
7. You corrected all typos;
8. You re-checked all possible spelling and grammar errors with your computer's software application;
9. You read the final draft one more time, thereby catching any remaining glitches that you somehow hadn't previously caught; and
10. You carefully inspected the printed copy your reader will receive to make sure it was as perfect in appearance as you had intended it to be.

The result will be a legal document that effectively presents your well-researched and properly cited analyses or arguments and that will be appreciated for its clarity, accuracy, and brevity. Additionally, the reader of your document will respect you for your professional approach to your work and for your ability to present your thoughts in well-written, cogent prose that is both informative and, hopefully, persuasive. And it will, most importantly, be error-free and reader-friendly.

Index

A

A=B=C, 56, 79, 138
Accuracy, 13, 195, 206, 234
Adjectives, 44, 117, 130, 133, 175
Adverbs, 44, 117, 130, 175
Ambiguity, 70, 80
Analogical reasoning, 65
Analogies, 61, 64–66, 80, 98, 102, 120, 121
Appellate courts, 29, 31–36
Apostrophes, 134, 151, 160, 222, 223, 230
Articles, 8, 22, 23, 25, 72, 184
Authority, 46, 72, 79, 102, 161, 177, 180, 181, 185–188, 194, 198, 204

B

Because clauses, 93, 198
Block quotes, 161
Brackets, 151, 159
Brevity, 110, 195, 206, 234

C

Case briefs, 17, 31, 32, 34, 35, 39–41, 46, 56
Citations, 59, 64, 94, 97, 101–103, 111, 161, 174, 177–179, 184–189, 192–194, 206, 221, 226, 227
Citation manuals, 151, 186-194, 227
Citation triggers 185
Clauses, 116, 121–123, 145, 152, 154, 156, 159, 168, 169, 172, 214, 215
Cohesiveness, 195, 203, 204
Colons, 142, 143, 149, 155–158, 163, 164, 217, 218
Comma splices, 123, 152, 215, 218
Commas, 121, 122, 145, 149–153, 163–165, 167–171, 189, 190, 211, 213, 215, 216, 218, 219
Complex sentences, 116, 122, 137, 214
Composite rules, 52–55, 59, 61, 75
Compound sentences, 121, 122, 166, 167, 215
Conclusionary headings, 89, 90, 92, 140–142
Conclusions, 51, 60, 67, 73, 78, 81, 88–90, 92, 93, 105, 140, 141, 146
Conjunctions, 117, 121, 122, 136, 145, 146, 152, 166, 167, 214, 215, 219
Conjunctive adverbs, 154, 219
Contractions, 222
C-RAC, 45, 47, 48, 51, 52, 61, 74, 75, 77–79, 81, 83, 88, 89, 92, 93, 95, 97, 99, 111, 139–142, 198
CREAC, 45, 47, 48, 51, 52, 60–62, 73–75, 77–79, 81, 83, 88, 89, 92, 93, 95, 99, 111, 138–142, 198
CREAC conclusions, 73
Counter-analogical reasoning, 65, 66
Counter-analogies, 61, 64, 80

D

Dangling modifiers, 131
Dashes, 157, 158
Dependent clauses, 116, 122, 123, 145, 152, 154, 168, 169, 214
Determiners, 118, 133

Deductive reasoning, 67
Double negatives, 133
Double possessives, 134

E
Elements of a rule, 52
Elements of a sentence 115, 116
Ellipses, 162, 205
Error-free documents 5, 11-15, 225
Exclamation points, 155, 156, 221

F
Factors of a rule, 52
Facts, 17–19, 32–46, 50, 64–67, 70, 73, 76, 78–81, 89, 92, 99, 139, 140, 146, 182, 184
Footnotes, 94, 161, 174, 206
Formulated rules, 36–40, 46
Fragments, 164, 167

G
Grammar, 149, 150, 163–166, 176, 195, 211, 229, 230, 234

H
Headings, 51, 73, 84–90, 92–97, 111, 139–141, 198, 231
Holdings, 36–39, 46, 59, 69, 187
Hyphens, 158

I
Independent clauses, 121, 145, 154, 168, 169, 214, 215
Inductive reasoning, 64, 65, 67
Inherited rules, 36–40, 46
Interjections, 118
Introductory clauses, 169
Introductory phrases, 169, 207, 216
Irrelevancy, 84, 97, 108, 112
Issues, 18–20, 32-35, 38-39, 41-43, 45, 56, 76–81, 88–90, 92–93, 96, 120, 137–140, 175, 180–181, 194, 196
Italics, 232

J
Jigsaw puzzle of the Law, 17, 19, 40
Jigsaw puzzle pieces, 80
Jurisdiction, 22, 24–26, 28–32, 46, 179

L
Legal briefs, 88, 162
Legal document, 5, 7, 13–15, 18, 19, 41, 43, 46, 49–51, 58, 65, 67, 79, 83–85, 95, 105, 113, 114, 120, 123, 130, 134, 136, 145, 146, 155, 160, 165, 173–176, 180, 213, 222, 223
Legal memos, 68, 99, 185

M
Mandatory authority 24, 25, 31, 72
Mirror-image approach, 56, 60, 61, 63–65, 67, 74, 79, 80, 99
Misplaced modifiers, 119, 131, 209, 224
Mixed constructions, 126

N
Next case, 72, 80
Nominalizations, 129
Non-restrictive phrases 170
Non-sentences, 116, 167
Non sequiturs, 106, 107
Nouns, 115–117, 129, 130, 132, 133, 146, 160, 169, 211, 223

O
Objects, 116–119, 125, 143, 145, 156, 172, 207–208, 217
Orphans, 231
Outlines, 182
Overly long sentences 171

P
Pagination, 14, 231
Paragraph length, 47, 49, 96, 195, 200

Paragraphs, 4, 10, 47–51, 53, 54, 56, 64, 79, 109, 126, 141, 175, 200–201, 232
Parallel construction, 144
Parallelism, 219
Parentheses, 157–159, 172, 173, 189–193, 220–222
Parenthetical citations, 159
Parenthetical phrases, 158, 170, 215
Parentheticals, 59, 98–101, 159, 170, 172, 173, 220, 221
Participial phrases, 98, 116, 168–170, 214
Parts of sentences, 149, 167
Passive construction, 119, 124, 126, 131, 132, 145
Passive voice, 124, 125, 127, 141
Periods, 151, 153, 166, 168, 215, 221
Persuasive arguments, 51, 70
Persuasive authority 24, 25, 31
Persuasive brief, 41, 79
Persuasive paradigm, 74, 75
Phrases, 98, 104, 116, 135, 152, 154, 157, 158, 167–171, 204, 207
Pinpoint citations 185
Pleadings, 18
Point headings, 85–90, 93–96, 139, 140, 231
Policy-based reasoning, 71–73, 80
Precedence, 29–31
Precision, 45, 54, 64, 69, 131, 137, 178, 211
Predictive analyses, 51
Predictive memo, 41, 53, 54, 60, 73, 74, 77, 78, 81, 83, 107, 108, 198
Predictive paradigm, 52, 59, 60
Prepositional phrases, 116, 117, 170
Prepositions, 116, 117, 135, 136, 146, 170
Present participles, 98, 99, 111, 172
Primary authority 24, 25
Primary headings, 89, 90, 92, 140
Pronouns, 115–117, 121, 128, 129, 132, 211, 224–226
Proofread, 3–5, 10–14
Punctuation, 11–13, 123, 142–144, 149–153, 155, 156, 159, 161–163, 165, 167–169, 171, 176, 195, 211, 215, 216, 218–223, 234

Q

Question marks, 156, 221
Quotation marks, 160–162, 220–222
Quotations, 155–157, 159, 161, 162, 173, 204

R

RA paragraph, 48, 59–61, 63, 64, 68, 70, 71, 73, 77, 78
Rationale-based reasoning, 68, 70, 73, 80
Redundancy, 109, 112
RE paragraph, 48, 53, 54, 58–61, 63, 67, 68, 70, 71
Research outlines, 177, 182, 184
Restrictive phrases 170
Resulting rules, 37, 39, 40
Rifle research approach 180, 181
Rule application paragraphs 59
Rule-based reasoning, 67, 68, 73, 75, 80
Rule explanation paragraphs, 54
Rule of Law, 30, 31, 65
Rules, 18–20, 22–24, 30, 31, 35–40, 43–46, 48, 52–61, 63–72, 74-77, 79, 80, 142, 165, 192
Rule statement, 54, 55, 57, 59, 64, 79, 137, 138
Run-on sentence, 166, 215

S

Secondary authority, 22, 25
Semi-colons, 142, 143, 149, 153–155, 163–167, 215, 217–219
Sentence tails, 172
Shotgun research approach 181. 182
Signals, 84, 97, 101–103, 111, 177, 186

Simplicity, 195, 206
Socratic Method, 31
Split infinitives, 135
Squinting modifiers 131
Stare decisis, 29–31
Sub-headings, 85–87, 89, 90, 110, 139
Subjects, 115, 116, 118, 119, 121–123, 125, 127–129, 137, 138, 143, 145, 154, 156, 167–169, 207–209, 211, 212, 214, 217, 224, 225
Subject-pronoun disagreements 128
Subject-verb disagreements, 127
Synthesized rules, 52–55, 59, 68, 73, 75, 76, 80, 142

T
Transitional phrases 104, 105, 204
Transitions, 103–105, 121, 204
Trial courts, 26, 28, 29, 31–34
Typos, 160, 227-229, 232

U
Umbrella paragraphs, 86, 87, 89, 90, 92, 95–97, 139, 140
Underlines, 232

V
Verbs, 115–118, 121–123, 125, 127, 129, 130, 135, 138, 143, 145, 146, 154, 156, 168, 169, 172, 207, 208, 211, 212, 214, 216, 217, 220

W
White-glove inspection, 9, 10, 12–15, 17, 40, 112, 195, 203, 233, 234
Widows, 231